The Afghan Wars
1839–1919

THE SHADOW ON THE HILLS

THE AFGHAN WARS

1839–1919

'Tis all a Chequer-board of Nights and Days
Where Destiny with Men for Pieces plays:
Hither and thither moves, and mates, and slays,
And one by one back in the Closet lays.

Fitzgerald's *Omar Khayyam*

by

T.A. Heathcote

SPELLMOUNT

Frontispiece: *The Shadow on the Hills.* This cartoon by Charles Keene was published in *Punch* during the diplomatic tension prior to the outbreak of the Second Afghan War. The figure of armed India, flanked by the British lion, looks towards Afghanistan, where the shadow of the Russian bear lies upon the Khyber hills.

British Library Cataloguing in Publication Data:
A catalogue record for this book is available
from the British Library

ISBN: 978-1-86227-408-2

First published in the UK in 1980 by
Osprey Publishing Ltd
New edition, Spellmount, 2003

This paperback edition first published in 2007
by Spellmount Limited
Cirencester Road
Chalford, Stroud
Gloucestershire GL6 8PE

Tel: +44 (0)1285 760000
Website: www.spellmount.com

1 3 5 7 9 8 6 4 2

Printed in Great Britain by
Oaklands Book Services
Cirencester Road
Chalford, Stroud
Gloucestershire GL6 8PE

Contents

To Victoria's Grandparents

I

The Afghan Chequerboard
The country and the peoples of Afghanistan

Afghanistan, the land of the Afghans, has at different periods of history extended over various tracts of territory. But it has always been centred on the vast mountain ranges of the Hindu Kush, a western offshoot of the even mightier Himalayan chain. A further series of ranges runs south-wards from the Hindu Kush, forming the Suleiman Mountains and the Safed Koh, which block the north-western approaches to the Indian sub-continent. These hills have an elevation of from ten to fifteen thousand feet above sea-level, and include peaks that tower five or ten thousand feet above their surroundings, rocky, hostile, devoid of vegetation, snow-bound in winter, baking hot in summer.

North of the Hindu Kush (the 'Hindu-killer', so called because so many slaves brought from India died there on their way to Central Asia) the country forms part of the basin of the Oxus, which flows west and then north to the Aral Sea. South of it, the country belongs to the basin of the Indus, which drains southwards to join the Arabian Sea and the Indian Ocean. Thus Afghanistan, astride the watershed, is simultaneously the southernmost state of Central Asia and the northernmost state of South Asia.

West of the Hindu Kush the land is lower and flatter, turning in places to areas of level desert. This is drained by the River Helmand, which, after flowing alongside an area known as Registan, the place of sand, finally disappears in a vast swamp, the Hamun. This western region, with Herat in the north and Kandahar in the south, was until recent times the only all-weather route between South and Central Asia when the winter snows blocked the passes of the Hindu Kush.

The term Afghan, though in recent times applied to any citizen of the state of Afghanistan, generically refers to a people of Indo-Iranian stock. In the same way the term Englishman, though it may be applied to any citizen of England, normally means someone of Anglo-Saxon stock. Thus,

1

many Afghan citizens are not ethnic Afghans, and indeed many ethnic Afghans are not citizens of the Afghan state, but subjects of neighbouring countries. The area north of the Hindu Kush, known as Afghan Turkestan, comprising the ancient provinces of Balkh and Badakhshan, is populated mostly by Uzbeks, a people of Turkish stock. Many of the western areas around the Hindu Kush are peopled by Hazaras, descendants of Mongolian garrisons settled there by Genghis Khan. Around Kabul, the present capital of Afghanistan, live the Qizilbashes, descendants of Iranian garrisons, settled there by Nadir Shah to hold his conquests. These, like most Iranians, belong to the minority Shi'a sect of Islam, while the rest of the inhabitants of Afghanistan are more orthodox, Sunni, Muslims.

The ethnic Afghans are otherwise called Pathans, from a local word *Pasht*, the back of a mountain range. They are divided into two main branches, with certain linguistic distinctions. In very general terms, the western Pathans speak Pa*sh*tu, and inhabit the country from Herat to Kandahar, while the eastern Pathans speak Pa*kh*tu and live in the mountains and valleys around Peshawar. This, they would call Pe*kha*war, but the official title is that given in the days when the western Pathans, the Durranis, were politically dominant. Between the two great branches of the Pathan people, in the region south of the Hindu Kush from Kandahar to Kabul, live the Ghilzais. These are said not to be true Pathans but an amalgam with peoples of Turkish stock.

But all these Afghans have generally been regarded by their Indian and Iranian neighbours as wild savage hillmen, uncouth barbarians, ever ready to prey on each other, to rob travellers passing through their country or even to sweep down upon the more fortunate and richer countries outside their own borders. The 1908 *Imperial Gazetteer* of India summed up what writers had recorded of the Afghans since they first appeared in history:

> Their step is full of resolution, their bearing proud and apt to be rough. Inured to bloodshed from childhood, they are familiar with death, audacious in attack, but easily discouraged by failure. They are treacherous and passionate in revenge. ... They are much under the influence of their Mullas, especially for evil.

They were also generally agreed to be proud of their country, their tribe, their descent, their prowess in arms, and, above all, their independence. Other races were despised as effete, and among themselves each man considered himself as good as or better than his neighbour. In short, the Afghan has always been like other highlanders in the way in which he is regarded by his plains-dwelling neighbours with mingled apprehension and condescension, for his high regard for personal honour, for his clan loyalty, for his readiness to carry and use arms to settle disputes, for his lack of respect for other people's property, and for his religious intolerance.

The main wealth of Afghanistan has always been its flocks and herds of sheep and goats. Large numbers of camels and horses were necessary prior to the coming of modern automobiles, and were bred for export and for use in the carrying trade. Wool and hides still form an essential part of the economy. Traditionally, the government income on these commodities was levied in the form of customs transit dues, and a grazing tax of one animal in every forty.

The real money, in revenue terms, came from the land revenue, or government share of the crop – mostly wheat or barley, but also lucerne grown for fodder, and orchard fruits. This was assessed at rates varying from up to one-third, where land was irrigated from rivers, etc., to one-tenth, when it was dependent only on rainfall. Revenue was collected in kind, and taken to local treasuries. Whatever was not needed for the use of the government's own men and beasts as sold to merchants and then back by them to the local consumers. But if there was a better market elsewhere, such as, for instance, a well-financed army of occupation, then the local consumer and his animals might well find themselves going hungry, as inflation drove up the price of their food. Thus, as we shall see, even an army that paid for what it took was bound to be hated, and the government it supported unpopular, because in a poor season there simply was not enough local produce to go round.

The tribal system, which ordered the life of most people outside the city areas, was certainly as potent in political terms as the national-state system of Europe in 1914. Men felt a fierce loyalty to their own tribe, such that, if called upon, they would without hesitation assemble in arms under their own tribal chiefs and local clan leaders. In the same way, men throughout Europe flocked to the colours in 1914, forming up in regional divisions and battalions, under command of the local nobility and gentry. In theory, under Islamic law every believer is under obligation to bear arms at the ruler's call, but there was no more the need to enforce this than there was to introduce conscription to fill up the British Army in 1914. The Afghan shepherd or peasant, when called on, went to war for much the same mixture of reasons as the more 'civilized' European clerk or factory worker – a desire for adventure, a desire not to be left out, nor to lose esteem in the eyes of his fellows, a dislike or contempt of foreigners, perhaps even the chance of extra cash or enhanced personal prospects. The tribal system was not something particularly backward, or warlike. It was simply the best way of organizing large groups of people in a country that was geographically difficult, and in a society that had an uncomplicated way of life. Indeed, even at the present time, it is a force that governments disregard at their peril.

The administration of the country was conducted by a combination of this patriarchal tribal organization and the more sophisticated *jagirdari*, or quasi-feudal system. The relative importance of these two elements varied from area to area, according to the poverty or difficulty of the terrain. In areas that were remote or without much in the way of a crop, central government rarely had the power or desire to exert detailed control, and there tribalism predominated. In the plains and around the cities, which were accessible and worth having, central government asserted itself and the *jagirdari* system was the stronger.

The head of the tribe or great clan was the Sirdar, a title corresponding in importance to that of Earl or Count in medieval Europe. Sirdars were always from the same noble family of their tribe, though not necessarily succeeding through primogeniture. Their election (for life) was by the assembled elders of their tribe, ratified by the central government, usually as a matter of course.

The extent to which a tribal chief could enforce his authority depended on a number of variable factors. These included his own force of personality, the independence of spirit of his clansmen, and especially his success or failure in delivering financial rewards. The latter consideration, after all, weighs heavily with voters in any modern electoral system. In Afghanistan it was measured by the open-handedness of the chief in giving feasts, or presents to his followers, and in providing them with extra emoluments and employment as official retainers. (Nineteenth-century Afghans, demonstrably, have not had the monopoly of this attitude to government on the part of the governed.)

To fulfil his obligations to his supporters the Sirdar needed funds and patronage. The central government, on the other hand, needed troops, which it lacked the machinery to pay and maintain other than in limited numbers. The problem for both parties was resolved by a system of military tenure. Those able to provide fighting men (in practice the Sirdars, because of their claim on the loyalty of their tribesmen) were granted *jagirs*, commonly referred to as estates, but actually liens on the land revenue, the government's share of the crop.

To all intents and purposes the *jagirdar* became the government of the area whose revenue was assigned to him, partly because the prime concern of government was to collect the taxes, and partly because, as the local bigwig, the *jagirdar* was naturally looked to by people as the man who dealt with local problems or grievances, or who enforced legal judgements. The law itself was a combination of Muslim holy law and local custom, and interpreted by local religious leaders learned in the scriptures.

The power of the *jagirdar* was all the stronger when he was also the Sirdar or patriarch of the people in the area.

In return for the revenue the *jagirdar* retained the services of a specified number of fighting men whom he undertook to arm, equip and put into the field when required. After a limited period of mobilization, the cost of maintaining these troops fell to the government, a factor that tended to reduce the amount of time an army could be kept in being.

Any ruler who decided to resume *jagirs*, either because the military service for which they had been granted was no longer needed or had not been performed, was bound to provoke trouble. Without the revenue from *jagirs* the Sirdars would lack funds with which to avoid the charge of being a miser (a most damaging accusation among Afghans), and without the right to raise contingents for the army he lacked patronage with which to give his followers the chance of extra cash. And if the revenue from resumed *jagirs* were used by the ruler to employ regular troops, specifically mercenaries from outside the country, the Sirdars' own importance as the holders of military power would be diminished. So these factors too played their part in influencing the outcome of the Afghan wars.

One other factor in the culture of the Afghans played a part in influencing their minds about war. It was, curiously enough in view of their subordinate position, the place of women in Afghan society. As mentioned above, the teachings of the Holy Law were strictly enforced, and this was nowhere more the case than with respect to the female half of the population. No respectable woman appeared in public unveiled, and the normal outdoor garment was the voluminous *burkha*, a sort of black shroud which enveloped the wearer from head to toe, with only a small lattice for her to see through. Indoors women were rigidly secluded in their own rooms, the *zanana*. *Zan* (women), *zar* (gold) and *zamin* (land) are the three 'z's' from which Pathans say all quarrels derive. Girls were married in their early teens, and spent the rest of their lives shut away from all but their husbands and closest male relatives. Despite the clear prohibitions set out in the Holy Law, homosexual practices were not uncommon among the Afghans, and some neglected their wives in favour of the company of young men. Even in normal times one result of this was that adultery was said to be a common offence among Afghan ladies.

It is difficult to assess the truth of this. By the nature of things, extra-marital affairs would not be likely to produce the sort of documents that an historian, or a husband, might discover. And much the same sort of story was told about the virtue of English ladies in the Indian hill-stations, though generally speaking these were neglected by their husbands for the service of the government of India rather than for the sake of any more personable rival. But on the other hand there *were* cases of adultery among the English ladies, though their own life was restricted by the social conventions of the time, and though the punishment – divorce, disgrace, and possible penury – was severe. In Afghanistan the punishment could be even more severe – mutilation or death – but nevertheless, numerous cases of adultery were reported. Whether, either in Afghanistan or British India, the incidence of marital infidelity really was as high as it was believed to be by the disapproving or the envious is difficult to say. But certainly the effect of bringing any foreign army (with the customary licentious predilections of professional soldiers) into Afghanistan (where men regarded the seduction of any of their wives, sisters, or daughters as an insult to be avenged in blood), was bound to be explosive, and so, as we shall see, it was.

It was through this land that invaders had passed since before the dawn of history, from the steppes of Central Asia to the rich and fertile plains of India. Some, like the ancient Aryans, came to settle; some, like Alexander the Great, only to round off an empire; some, like the Mongols, to loot and murder. Wave after wave of conquerors came through over the centuries, establishing dynasties within India and gradually losing control of their Central Asian homeland to new invaders after them. Inevitably, Afghans became involved with the passing armies, sometimes as enemies, but frequently as allies. An Afghan prince of Turkish stock, Mahmud of Ghazni, known as the Iconoclast, made extensive raids into India during the eleventh century AD. After him came other Afghans, Turks and Pathans, who established the Sultanate of Delhi, which ruled over the whole of northern India until eventually it was replaced by the Mughals, another dynasty of Central Asian origin, in the early sixteenth century.

During the rise and fall of these various Iranian, Indian and Central Asian empires, the country of the Afghans was occupied by each in turn, according to its strength and weakness, and was at times divided between two or three at once.

It was not until the middle of the eighteenth century that the beginnings of the present Afghan state emerged. It was founded by one Ahmad, a chief of the Sadozai clan of the western branch of the Pathan people, then called the Abdalis. He commanded the Afghan bodyguard of the Iranian conqueror, Nadir Shah, who in 1737 humbled the Mughal Empire, sacked Delhi and slaughtered the citizens. This monarch added a new word to the Hindustani language – a *Nadirshahi*, or holocaust. On his departure from Delhi, after a stay of two months, he took with him all the Mughal imperial gold plate and jewels (including the fabulous Koh-i-Nur diamond), horses, silks, elephants and even the famous Peacock Throne itself, which was to become synonymous with the throne of the Iranian Empire. All the remaining Mughal provinces east of the Indus were ceded to Nadir Shah's rule.

In 1747 he led his army to deal with a revolt of the Kurdish tribes in the central Iranian highlands. When in camp at Kashan he ordered his Afghan officers to arrest on the morrow a number of Iranian commanders whom he suspected of plotting against him. Events proved his suspicions well founded, but his timing less so. A spy in his tent warned the conspirators, who, on the principle that 'thrice armed is he who hath his quarrel just, but four times he who gets his blow in first', resolved to act at once. Three of them entered the Shah's tent in the night and murdered him there. As the tumult spread through the camp, the Afghan commander, Ahmad Shah Abdali, and some of his men fought their way to the royal tent to try and rescue Nadir, only to find his headless corpse lying in a pool of blood. Ahmad Shah had now to prevent himself and the other Afghans sharing their late employer's fate, for they were surrounded by much larger numbers of Iranian soldiers, the Qizilbash or 'red-tops', so-called from the colour of their uniform head-dress. The Qizilbash disliked the Afghans because they had been the favourites of Nadir Shah, and had helped keep him in power; because they were foreigners, and rather barbaric ones at that; and because they were Sunni, not Shi'a, Muslims.

Swiftly the Afghan division mounted and made its way out of camp. After a journey comparable with that of Xenophon and the 10,000 Greek mercenaries who long ago had themselves had to cut their way out after the overthrow of another Persian emperor, Ahmad Shah and his men reached Kandahar.

On the way out of Iran they met a large caravan bringing up much of the treasure that had been looted from Delhi eight years before, the Koh-i-Nur diamond included, all of which Ahmad appropriated to his own use. Finding himself not only in command of a force of experienced and battle-hardened soldiers, but also with the money to pay them and others who supported him, he soon made himself master of Afghanistan. Iranian government of the country had died with Nadir Shah, and the Afghan nobles elected Ahmad Shah to be their king. Ahmad Shah took the title Durr-i-Durran, or Pearl of Pearls, from a pearl earring it was his custom to wear, and from this time his tribe, the Abdalis, became known as the Durranis.

Ahmad Shah seized Kabul from the Qizilbash garrison left behind by Nadir Shah, and in 1748 followed the historic route down into India. His first attempt was repulsed by the defenders of the existing empire, but he returned the following year, and in 1749 the Mughal Emperor Shah Alam only saved Delhi by agreeing to cede to Ahmad Shah all the trans-Indus territory previously ceded to Nadir, plus the province of Sind.

He then turned to the north of Afghanistan, and after a siege of fourteen months captured the city of Herat. He went on to bring the city of Nishapur and the surrounding province of Khorasan, in north-east Iran, under his sway. Next he marched east from Herat and occupied Maimena, Balkh and Badakshan, thus by 1750 establishing his rule over the territory lying between the Hindu Kush and the Oxus. In 1752 he again marched into India, annexed Lahore and incorporated the West Punjab into his empire, and in the same year wrested control of Kashmir from the now helpless Mughals. In 1756 he raided Delhi, and carried off all the loot he could find there.

The kingdom which he had created, stretching from the Indus to the Oxus, and from Kashmir to Khorasan, he handed over to his son Timur. Afflicted now with a cruel illness, thought to be a cancer of the face, Ahmad Shah retired to a fortress in the Suleiman Mountains, where he died in 1773, aged fifty, in the twenty-sixth year of his reign.

Timur Shah was Ahmad's second son, though his father's chosen successor. His brother, Suleiman Mirza, proclaimed himself king in Kandahar, but was soon forced to flee. Timur transferred the capital of his kingdom from Kandahar to Kabul in summer and Peshawar in winter, moving from the plains to the hills at the onset of the hot weather as the Mughals had done and as the British would do in time to come. Timur's reign was a long and generally stable one. It lasted for twenty years, and although during this time Sind became virtually independent, as did Balkh and the Oxus valley (aided by the Amir of Bokhara), the Afghan kingdom was still a large and potentially important state.

'Shah Shuja ul Mulk', the Sadozai Durrani king of Afghanistan. He deposed and succeeded his brother Mahmud Shah in 1802, but was in turn deposed by Mahmud Shah in 1809. Restored by Anglo-Lahore forces in 1839, he was assassinated in April 1842. (Lithograph after Vincent Eyre.)

Timur left twenty-three sons, from various mothers, but had not nominated an heir at the time of his death (possibly from poison) in 1793. There followed a period of anarchy, bloodshed and civil wars. Zaman Shah, fifth son of Timur Shah by his first wife, was in control of the Kabul garrison, and when his brothers assembled there to choose the new king, he imprisoned them until they were obliged by starvation to agree that Zaman had the best claim to the succession. One of the two brothers who had not gone to Kabul, Mahmud, escaped to Iran, and eventually established himself at Herat.

Zaman Shah followed his father's policy of building up the central government to make himself less dependent on the great tribal Sirdars. Thus he appointed as his Wazir or Treasury Minister (and thus, since the business of most governments is concerned with the levying and disposal of the revenue, his chief adviser) one Wafadar Khan. But Wafadar Khan was held in little esteem by the Afghan nobles, who regarded him as a creature of Zaman's, and accused him of misappropriating revenue to his own use. A party plotted together to get rid of Wazir Wafadar, and if Zaman Shah would not agree, to depose him and replace him by his brother Shuja-ul-Mulk. They were arrested and beheaded in Zaman Shah's presence. Among those executed was Painda Khan, head of the second great division of the Durranis, the Barakzai clan, though his part in any actual conspiracy was by no means certain.

Painda's eldest son, Fateh Khan, escaped to join Mahmud Shah at Herat, and urged that prince to place himself at the head of the Barakzais against Zaman Shah. Mahmud responded to the call, the Barakzais flocked to his banner, and with their help he captured Kandahar. Zaman Shah's army deserted him. He himself was betrayed and handed over to Mahmud, who had him blinded and imprisoned in the Bala Hissar, the great fortress-palace of Kabul.

The real power behind Mahmud's throne was Fateh Khan, the Barakzai Sirdar. It was he who had obtained the surrender of Kandahar, he who had arranged the desertion of Zaman Shah's army, and he who suppressed a rising of the Ghilzais. In 1801 he encountered and defeated an army under Shuja-ul-Mulk, and followed up the victory by occupying Peshawar on Mahmud's behalf.

But while Fateh Khan was fighting to win the Indian provinces, Mahmud had become indolent, and back at Kabul a new conspiracy was formed to overthrow Mahmud and place Shuja on the throne. Shuja, in 1802, was at Quetta, in northern Baluchistan, where he levied a forced loan on a rich caravan passing through the Bolan Pass, and with the proceeds made his way to Kabul. There he found the city in an uproar and Mahmud besieged in the Bala Hissar by the city mob. Fateh Khan, returning from the Khyber with an army of 10,000 men, found that Mahmud's cause was lost, and even his own levies refused to fight against Shuja.

Mahmud, deserted by all, was deposed. Shah Shuja took the vacant throne and released his blinded brother, Zaman, whose blindness, by Islamic law, disqualified him from ruling over a Muslim land. Mahmud was imprisoned, but later released and allowed to go to his own estates at Herat. The merchants of the Bolan caravan were given their money back, an act of unexpected generosity. Only Mulla Ashik, the man who had arrested Zaman Shah, his king and guest, and given him to Mahmud, suffered the death penalty in an otherwise remarkably bloodless change of rule.

Despite Shah Shuja's generosity, neither Mahmud nor Fateh Khan relaxed their enmity towards him, nor their determination to seize power once more for themselves. Despite a serious defeat in 1808, they renewed their hostilities against Shah Shuja in 1809, at a time when he himself was in Peshawar, but many of his best troops were trying, unsuccessfully, to restore Durrani rule over rebellious subjects in Kashmir. News came almost simultaneously that Mahmud had captured Kabul and that the army in Kashmir had been cut to pieces in the narrow mountain passes. Shah Shuja moved to meet Mahmud with what troops he could muster, but was defeated. Mahmud Shah resumed his throne in 1809, but his second reign was to prove even more disastrous than the first.

9

At first all went well. Shuja was driven out of Peshawar in 1810. In 1811, Mahmud Shah came down from Kabul to look at his new conquest. He went on to a meeting at Rawalpindi with the Maharaja Ranjit Singh, once the viceroy of the western Punjab under the Durranis, now ruler of a powerful and growing Sikh kingdom based on Lahore. Fateh Khan occupied Kashmir in the spring of 1813, one move ahead of Ranjit Singh, who (having conquered the neighbouring province of Jammu) had hoped to add it to his own domains. But, on the other hand, Ranjit did obtain control of the city and fort of Attock, the best crossing place on the Indus, where the Durrani governor had defied both Mahmud's and Shuja's authority. This governor, Jahandad Khan, fearing Fateh Khan's approach, gave up his keys to Ranjit Singh. Fateh Khan then brought his army into action against that of Ranjit Singh, but, his fortune beginning to turn, was defeated at the battle of Attock (July 1813).

Shah Shuja-ul-Mulk was at this time in Ranjit Singh's camp. The Maharaja used his considerable powers of guile and persistence to persuade Shuja to present to him, in exchange for a promise of Sikh aid in recovering Kabul when an opportunity arose, the famous Koh-i-Nur diamond. Shuja had little real choice, for he was virtually now a prisoner of state. In 1814 he was allowed by Ranjit Singh to cross into British India. The British authorities granted him a state pension to enable him to keep up his household and family in a reasonable standard of dignity.

In Afghanistan, Mahmud Shah had relapsed into sadistic gloom, and was more and more influenced by his vicious son Kamran. In 1818 Fateh Khan was in Herat, at the head of an army with which he had driven back an attempt by the Iranians to capture the city. Kamran, who was the local governor, refused to open the provincial treasury to enable Fateh Khan to pay the troops. Fateh Khan, as Wazir, had every right to control the government's money, and was not prepared to tolerate opposition from Kamran, nor to conceal the fact that he was himself the power behind the throne, an Afghan 'Warwick the King-Maker'. Accordingly, he sent his young brother, Dost Muhammad, accompanied by his Sikh lieutenant, to seize the money that they needed. Dost Muhammad had already gained something of a reputation for wild behaviour (his nickname at this time was 'Little Wolf') and the two of them broke into Kamran's palace, where they laid violent hands not only on the treasure but also on Kamran's sister. This princess, a young woman who seems to have inherited all the spirit of her Durrani ancestors, was wearing about her person a famous jewelled girdle, which after a struggle they succeeded in removing.

Kamran used this incident as an opportunity for disposing of Fateh Khan, whom he regarded as an over-mighty subject who should be put down. The Wazir, returning to Kabul expecting to be rewarded for saving Herat, was suddenly accused of conniving at the rape of a Muslim lady by an idolatrous Sikh. He was blinded, and subsequently put to death in the presence of Mahmud and Kamran in circumstances of revolting cruelty.

'Muhammad Akbar Khan, Barakzai', son of the Amir Dost Muhammad. This imaginative representation, from the Illustrated London News *of June 1842, shows the way the British public saw the man who drove them from Kabul, a doughty opponent with overtones of Saladin and the wars of the Crusades.*

The twenty-one brothers of the murdered Wazir swore to avenge his death. At the head of their Barakzai clansmen they rose in rebellion, and within a few months swept Mahmud Shah and Kamran out of Kabul, Ghazni and Kandahar, driving them to Herat, where sporadic fighting between the two parties continued for some years. Eventually, on his father's death, Kamran set up an independent state of Herat, and a renewed attempt by the Shah of Iran to absorb this into his own domains was one of the many events leading up to the First Afghan War. Not until 1863 was Herat reunited with the main Afghan state.

After the revolution of 1818 there followed a period of instability and feuding among the Barakzai brothers. During this period Afghan control over the outlying provinces steadily diminished.

In 1826 Dost Muhammad Barakzai came to power, partly through his own powers of leadership, partly because he was even more successful at intrigue and treachery than his surviving brothers, partly because he had been Fateh Khan's favourite, and partly because he was supported by the Qizilbash palace guard, his mother having belonged to one of the noble Qizilbash families which lived around Kabul. But with a sense of reality as to the extent of his kingdom, which was virtually restricted by now to Kabul and Ghazni, he styled himself Khan rather than Shah. His brother Kohen Dil Khan ruled independently over Kandahar, while another brother, Sultan Muhammad Khan, governed Peshawar and the neighbouring areas as a tributary of Ranjit Singh.

Shah Shuja never accepted the Barakzais' control over his country. In the confusion following the flight of Mahmud Shah he had attempted to re-establish himself in Upper Sind and the Derajat, at the foot of the Suleimans. He actually held Peshawar for a few days, but by 1821 was back in his residence at Ludhiana under British protection. In 1832 the Amirs of Sind, apprehensive of being swallowed up by the expanding British Indian Empire, offered to recognize Shah Shuja as their nominal sovereign and give him free passage through Sind to Kandahar, from where he could advance on Kabul. Ranjit Singh offered him the men and money for this plan in return for the formal cession of Peshawar to the state of Lahore. Shah Shuja, not being in possession of Peshawar, agreed to this diminution of the kingdom he hoped to regain, and so marched, via Sind and the Bolan Pass, to occupy Kandahar for a few months in 1834. Dost Muhammad advanced to meet him, and Shah Shuja was defeated in battle. His mercenaries lost heart, and Shuja was forced to flee to Herat, where Kamran repaid the generosity once shown to his father, and allowed Shuja to return to Ludhiana in 1835. Dost Muhammad, to celebrate his victory, gave himself the title of Amir.

The real beneficiary of this episode was Ranjit Singh. Now claiming to be the lawful ruler of Peshawar he sent a large army, which drove out Sultan Muhammad and annexed the province to his own domains. Sultan Muhammad at first took refuge with his brother Dost Muhammad, even though he resented the latter's claim to be Amir. The governorship of Peshawar was entrusted to a Sikh general, Hari Singh.

Whereas the rest of the Punjab had never really been colonized by the Afghans, the Peshawar area was peopled predominantly by Muslims of Afghan descent and had, since the decline of the Mughals nearly a century before, been an Afghan province. Dost Muhammad decided to contest Ranjit's title by force. He therefore sent his best troops, under his eldest son Muhammad Akbar Khan, down the Khyber in April 1837. At the end of the month Akbar attacked the fort of Jamrud, guarding the southern end of the pass. The Sikh army in the field was defeated, and the gallant Hari Singh slain. But the fort held out, and after a few days' plundering, Akbar Khan led his army back through the Khyber Pass to Jalalabad.

It was over the question of who was to rule the province to Peshawar, Sikh or Afghan, that British attempts to establish friendly influence over both of these states were to fail. The British had to come down on the side either of Ranjit Singh or of Dost Muhammad, or else replace one of them by someone who, for the sake of British friendship, would resign himself to the loss of the province.

II

The Beginning of the Great Game
British strategy and the North-West
of India, 1800-38

The British became involved with Afghanistan in order to secure the overland route to India. It was not that they wished to use this route them-selves, but rather that they wished to control, even if necessary to deny, the use of this route by others. To the British, supreme at sea, the favoured route to India lay on the water, where their merchantmen sailed under the serene protection of the all-powerful Royal Navy, and where enemy warships or troop transports had little chance of reaching Indian shores. But the route through Afghanistan was one which no line-of-battleship could block. As other European powers, first Napoleonic France, and then Imperial Russia, began to show interest in this fact, the minds of British statesmen grew uneasy. They began to take measures to bar the inland gateway to their Indian Empire.

There are some curious resemblances between the courses of the Napoleonic Wars and the Second World War. In both of them, a powerful dictator sought to impose a New Order on Europe. In both of them, there were times when Britain, seeing herself as the last bastion of freedom, stood alone against an embattled continent. In both of them, Russia at one time became an ally of the tyrant, only to be invaded by him, and then to form an alliance with the British. In both cases, when the tyrant was defeated, the Russian rulers were for a short time the darlings of Western liberals. And in both cases, too, disillusion soon set in and the defeated nation came to be regarded as a potential ally against the expansion of Russian despotism.

During the Napoleonic period proposals were made for Iranian troops with French support, or Russian troops with Iranian co-operation, to march from the territory of the Shah to threaten British India. But British diplomatic counter-measures, and the ending of the Franco-Russian alli-ance, brought these to naught. In the post-war period, British policy was to contain Russian expansion by propping up the Sultan of Turkey and by trying to forestall Russian influence at the court of the Shah of Iran. But by 1830 there seemed an increasing likelihood that both these potentates would eventually fall under Russian domination, and in January that year instructions were sent to the British Governor-General in India to inaugurate a new diplomatic initiative towards the independent states of north-west India and Central Asia.

It was feared by the British that, if the Russians, or Russian influence, became established within striking distance of India, this by itself would be enough to unsettle any Indian princes discontented under British rule. Thus the British would have to spend considerable sums on defence not only against the remote threat of a Russian invasion, but also the real possibility of internal disorder, inspired by the hope of Russian aid, if not by the actual appearance of Russian agents and Russian money. The Russians must therefore be kept at a distance. In particular, Bokhara and Khiva should be the targets of British commercial penetration, and although no military aid was to be promised to these states, the Government of India was authorized to offer liberal financial aid in order to secure their friendship. To make the passage of British goods into Central Asia quicker and cheaper than was possible by using the only route then open to them (sea to Calcutta, then up the Ganges and overland across the Punjab to Peshawar), a more direct route was to be opened. This was to be by sea to Karachi on the coast of Sind and then up the Indus, either to Sukkur and overland to Kandahar via the Bolan Pass, or on to the Punjab and overland to Kabul via Peshawar. These routes would give the British lower transport costs than their Russian competitors, and British piece-goods, with their textile industry in the full flood of industrialized production, would then undersell the Russians with ease.

It was decided to make a gift of six dapple-grey English dray-horses to Maharaja Ranjit Singh of Lahore, who delighted in filling his stables with good horses presented in the cause of diplomacy. The horses were to travel, not overland from the British frontier with the eastern Punjab, but up the Indus to the western Punjab, thus giving the British an excuse for obliging the Amirs of Sind to allow British vessels on that river. The Amirs gave in to British pressure, and in March 1831 the river boats duly went up the Indus, with British officers charting the river bed and surveying the adjacent lands as they went along, which was in fact one of the objects of the whole operation.

The officer responsible for actually presenting the horses to Ranjit Singh was Alexander Burnes, then aged twenty-five, a lieutenant in the East India Company's Bombay Army who had already made his mark as an promising young member of the political service. After making the presentation he went from Lahore overland to Simla, the summer capital of British India. On the way, in August 1831, he paid a visit of courtesy to the Afghan Shah Shuja-ul-Mulk, then resident at Ludhiana as a pensioner

14

'*Sir Alexander Burnes,*
1806–1841'. Bombay
Political Service. The Elchi
or diplomatic representative
of the British at Kabul,
where his womanizing
caused great offence to
the Afghans. He, together
with a number of male and
female companions were
murdered by the Kabul
mob, 2 November 1841.
(Lithograph after Vincent
Eyre.)

of the British, who remarked that were he back on his throne he would be only too glad to open to the British the road through his domains to Central Asia.

Iran, since her defeat by the Russians in 1828, had almost become a Russian satellite, and thus any extension of Iranian territory was seen by the British as an increase in the area under Russian influence. The British special envoy at Teheran, Hugh Ellis, had the difficult task of trying to persuade the Shah that his best interests lay in friendship with the British, as a defence against further Russian pressure, while at the same time warning that Iranian expansion in the direction of India would not be acceptable to the British. The Russian Ambassador, Count Simonich, had the easier task of encouraging the Shah in what he wanted to do, which was to return to the scene of his previous military successes on Iran's eastern border. He had actually been besieging Herat in November 1834 when the news of his grandfather's death had come, and obliged him to break off the siege in order to claim his throne. The Russians, by encouraging him to renew this venture and reclaim Herat for the Iranian Empire to which it had historically belonged, not only made themselves congenial to the Shah but also diverted his attention from any thoughts of regaining the northern provinces his grandfather had been obliged to cede to them. Ellis, in vain, represented to the Shah that the military adventures to which the Russians urged him could only have the effect of weakening his army and his treasury, and thus of impairing his independence still further.

Lord Palmerston, the British Foreign Secretary, lodged a protest at Simonich's proceedings. The reply, from the Russian Foreign Secretary, Count Nesselrode, was that the British must surely have been misinformed. Count Simonich, said Nesselrode, had no instruction to urge the Shah to attack Herat, and had indeed tried to dissuade him from so doing. Certainly, he added, the Czar's government did not believe that the Shah's own best interests would be served by prosecuting a military campaign against Herat.

Thus, when the Shah again marched against Herat, in July 1837, the British and Russian ministers at his court both declined to accompany his court, and remained with their suites at Teheran as a mark of diplomatic disapproval.

The Shah, nevertheless, was determined to finish the task he had begun three years before. Kamran Shah, the Afghan ruler of Herat, was more than just the last symbol of the dynasty of Abmad Shah Durrani, who had humiliated the Iranians in the previous century. He was, as ever, faithless and treacherous, and had openly broken the truce made with the Shah in 1834 by raiding and taking slaves from the Iranian districts of Sistan.

A lengthy march of four months' duration brought Shah Muhammad and his army under the walls of Herat at the beginning of December 1837. Kamran's garrison, secure behind their defences, defied the Iranians, but no-one could tell which side would exhaust its supplies first. The siege dragged on, and in March 1838 the British Ambassador, John McNeill, joined the Shah's camp, persuaded him to put off a planned assault, and at a meeting with Kamran's able though unscrupulous Wazir, Yar Muhammad, secured terms which seemed to meet all the Shah's demands. On returning to the Iranian camp he discovered that Count Simonich had followed him from Teheran and, during his own absence inside Herat, had persuaded the Shah to proceed with the siege.

Tension between McNeill and the Iranian court steadily worsened. At the beginning of June 1838 he decided to break off diplomatic relations and departed from the Shah's camp, stating that he would leave Iranian territory and cross into Turkey. At the end of June a desperate assault by the Iranian troops, spearheaded by a battalion of Russian mercenaries under General Berowski, a Polish adventurer in the Shah's service, was thrown back by the defenders of Herat and Berowski himself was killed. Russian military prestige began to diminish in the Iranian camp. British military prestige began to increase when it became known that a leading part in the defence was being played by Lieutenant Eldred Pottinger, of the East India Company's Bombay Artillery.

McNeill, in early July, heard of the failure of the Russian-led assault at Herat, and also of the landing of a small British force on the Iranian island of Kharak in the Persian Gulf. This had been sent in response to his previous requests for a military demonstration to show that the British really meant what they said about keeping the Shah out of Herat. At the same time he received clear authority from Palmerston to warn the Shah that he must withdraw from Herat or face the consequences, which would be war with the British. The Shah, disappointed in the achievements of his Russian friends, yielded before the ultimatum and abandoned the siege. Count Nesselrode declared that Simonich had far exceeded his instructions and that he was being recalled.

But no-one had been sure that Herat would hold out, nor that, faced with a British ultimatum, the Shah would turn back from his march to the east. So policies had been put in train to ensure that the three countries between Iran and British India (Sind, the Punjab and Afghanistan) were either friendly to, or dominated by, the British Government.

The Punjab was simple enough. Some of the small Sikh states were already directly under British protection. The rest of the country was ruled by Maharaja Ranjit Singh of Lahore, who had been on terms, if not of friendship, at least of agreement, with the British since the treaty of Amritsar, 1809. Lahore, with its large army of regular troops, trained and equipped on the European model, had become a powerful buffer state. Indeed the only anxiety was lest it become too powerful and be not a buffer against external invaders, but a threat to the British themselves.

Thus, in August 1836, the British Governor-General, Lord Auckland, warned Ranjit Singh that his apparent inclination to follow his annexation of Peshawar, by expanding down the Indus to take over control of Shikarpur and Upper Sind, would not be welcomed by his British friends. After a few months' negotiation, the Maharaja accepted that Sind was, at least for the time being, outside his sphere of influence.

Ranjit Singh's claim to Shikarpur, once part of the Durrani Empire, but since 1824 held by the Amirs of Sind, was that Shah Shuja had ceded it to him in return for supporting Shuja's attempt to regain the Afghan throne in 1833–4. The fact that Shuja, despite his pretensions, had not actually held Shikarpur either before or after the failure of his expedition, seems to have embarrassed neither side, any more than it did in the similar case of Peshawar. But Peshawar did not control the Indus, nor the route to southern Afghanistan via the Bolan Pass. Expansion by Lahore in the area of Peshawar affected the route to Kabul via the Khyber Pass, but the Sikh state already controlled access to this route from the Indian side, and there was no special reason for the British to object to Ranjit Singh implementing this part of his treaty with Shuja.

The Amirs of Sind were glad enough to have British friendship when Ranjit Singh pressed his own claims to Shikarpur. But they were reluctant to pay the price the British then asked in return. With the Shah of Iran under Russian influence and openly speaking of his intention to take Herat, the British wanted nothing less than paramountcy over Sind to build up their tier of friendly buffer states. Reluctantly, and under the implied threat of being abandoned to fight their own battle against Ranjit Singh, the Amirs accepted British terms. But even then it took the British Envoy, Colonel Henry Pottinger, more than twelve months to overcome the Amirs' constant evasion and procrastination before, in April 1838, the new treaty was sealed. A British Resident or permanent Ambassador was to be accepted in Sind, and any future disputes which might arise with the Maharaja of Lahore would be decided by the mediation of the Government of India. Thus the British effectively secured control over the foreign policy of Sind to complement its existing right of access to the country for British trade and navigation.

In May 1838 a diplomatic envoy was sent by the British to Kabul, none other than Alexander Burnes. He had travelled there, though without official credentials, five years before. Despite Burnes's own friendship with the Afghans, and his support of Dost Muhammad's cause, his mission was bound to fail. Dost Muhammad was certainly prepared to ally himself with the British against the Shah of Iran and the Russians, but his price – British support in recovering Peshawar from Ranjit Singh – was one the British were not prepared to pay. Indeed, even the lower price, of a British guarantee against further advances into Afghan territory by Ranjit Singh, was not one which the British would pay either. What was the point of alienating their powerful and well-armed Sikh neighbour in favour of the distant and shadowy regime of Dost Muhammad? Ranjit Singh, if provoked, could prevent British aid reaching Kabul through his own dominions, and might even himself go over to the anti-British camp.

To the Afghan chiefs there seemed more chance of doing a deal with the Iranian Shah and his powerful Russian friends. In February 1836 Hugh Ellis, in Teheran, reported that envoys from Dost Muhammad had arrived offering to support the Shah against Herat in return for help against Ranjit Singh. Ellis persuaded these envoys to return to Kabul and urge their master to seek the mediation of the Government of India in his quarrel with the Maharaja of Lahore. Indeed, following the battle of Jamrud in April 1836, Dost Muhammad did write to Lord Auckland, taking the occasion of offering formal congratulations on his assumption of office to raise this very question of mediation between Kabul and Lahore. But the only advice Auckland could offer, when he replied in the following August, was that Dost Muhammad should try to live in peace with Ranjit Singh, as there was no way in which the British could exert their influence on his behalf.

'Amir Dost Muhammad Khan, "The Great Amir"'. The first of the Barakzai dynasty to sit upon the throne of Kabul, he reigned from 1834 to 1863, with a period of exile during the First Afghan War 1839–42.

But Ellis was not the only European diplomat at Teheran. Count Simonich also made contact with the Afghans, and letters of courtesy were exchanged which represented the opening of diplomatic relations between the Amir of Kabul and the Czar of Russia.

Alexander Burnes reached Kabul on 20 September, 1837. From the beginning, Dost Muhammad and his brother and Wazir, Nawab Jubbar Khan, made it clear that Peshawar was the critical issue. One possible compromise suggested was that Ranjit Singh might re-appoint Sultan Muhammad Khan Barakzai to be his viceroy in Peshawar in place of the brutal Italian adventurer General Avitabile (who had succeeded the gallant Hari Singh after the battle of Jamrud). This idea collapsed when Dost Muhammad said he would prefer to have the Sikhs there, as his open enemies, rather than risk the plots that his brother would hatch against him if restored to Peshawar. Dost Muhammad offered to hold Peshawar himself as a tributary of Ranjit Singh, but as there was no reason for the Maharaja to agree to this arrangement except in response to pressure the British were not prepared to exert, nothing came of the idea.

But if the British would not help, what of the Iranians and their Russian friends? In November a letter reached Dost Muhammad from Count Simonich announcing that a Russian officer was on his way to deliver the Czar's reply to their previous correspondence. In the same month the Shah of Iran approached within striking distance of Herat and promised the Kandahar Sirdars that, after he had captured the city, he would grant it to them in return for assistance against any internal enemies should the need arise.

On 19 December, 1838, Lieutenant Vitkeivich, an officer in the Russian Cossacks, rode into Kabul bearing a letter to the Amir from the Czar. The letter, in itself, was unexceptionable. The Russian Emperor spoke of his friendship for the Amir and people of Kabul, and of his happiness to assist its traders entering his dominions, and indicated that the Russians would be happy to continue the diplomatic contact now made. Dost Muhammad, to show goodwill to the British, passed a copy of the Czar's letter over to Burnes, who in turn forwarded it to Auckland with the strongest possible recommendation that Dost Muhammad's handsome gesture should be recognized, and that something should be done to meet him over Peshawar. The Wazir, Nawab Jubbar Khan, told Burnes that Vitkeivich had offered the Amir an annual cash subsidy which could be used for defence against the Sikhs, in exchange for Afghan goodwill.

Back in India, Auckland was beginning to lose patience with Dost Muhammad. There was, after all, an Iranian army with a battalion of Russian mercenaries sitting down before Herat, and for the Amir of Kabul to entertain a Russian envoy at his court was scarcely an act of friendship to the British. At the beginning of January 1838, Auckland's envoy at the court of Lahore, Captain Claude Wade, suggested that in view of Dost Muhammad's unreasonableness in continuing to ask for Peshawar, British interests might be better served by supporting the restoration of Shah Shuja, who was well disposed towards his British paymasters. Moreover, having himself caused the present dispute over Peshawar by ceding it to Ranjit Singh, he would scarcely be in a position to claim its return as a condition of friendship to the British. Auckland, though not yet ready to think about overthrowing Dost Muhammad, began to take a harsher line. Unless the Amir accepted that Ranjit Singh was the ruler of Peshawar, and unless he agreed to have no relations with foreign powers except with British approval, the Burnes Mission would be withdrawn and British goodwill would come to an end.

Dost Muhammad and Burnes continued to negotiate throughout February and March 1838, each seeking to gain time. At the beginning of March the Amir seemed to accept all the British demands, but almost immediately afterwards re-opened the Peshawar question. He had, on reflection, decided that he would rather have his brother than the Sikhs in Peshawar, not least because Kabul was full of Afghan refugees from that province, whom he had to maintain and who were an unstable element inside his own state. Vitkeivich, for his part, remained at Kabul and was even rumoured to be preparing to contact Ranjit Singh about Peshawar on behalf of Dost Muhammad. Burnes, carrying out Auckland's policy, insisted that Vitkeivich be sent away and that Dost Muhammad write a letter to Ranjit Singh abandoning his claim to Peshawar. The Amir refused. He asked if the British would promise to protect Kandahar and Kabul against the Iranians. This Burnes refused, again acting on Auckland's instructions. Kamran Shah of Herat had British protection, but he had no quarrel with Lahore. Nothing could be done to help Dost Muhammad until he had made his peace with Britain's most powerful ally, Ranjit Singh, and this he resolutely refused to do. On 21 April, he received the Russian envoy in state with every mark of friendship and respect. On 26 April, Burnes ended his mission and left Kabul, with a secret note from the Wazir Nawab Jubbar Khan regretting his brother's decision and offering to help the British remove him from the throne if desired.

The decision by Auckland to offer support to Shah Shuja followed within a month. His policy, subsequently endorsed by his superiors in London, was clear enough. British interests required that the Shah of Iran should be kept out of Afghanistan, because if Afghanistan came under Iranian influence it would *ipso facto* come under Russian influence, and thereby the British position in India would be weakened. This, indeed, had been British policy for the past thirty years or more. But the rulers of Kabul and Kandahar were now offering friendship to the Shah, partly to protect their future interests if Herat fell (and he was still battering at its walls), partly (in the case of the Kandahar Sirdars at least) to secure his support in their own feuds within Afghanistan, and partly to gain support against Ranjit Singh. The British could not give arms to the Barakzais to enable them to stand up to the Shah if Herat fell, because it was more than likely that they would use them against each other, or even worse, against Ranjit Singh. Auckland needed Ranjit Singh's friendship more than that of the Afghans, especially since during the spring of 1838 he had received disturbing reports from his political agents of uneasiness within India. There was nothing tangible, but there was talk of possible war with Burma, or with Nepal, or even of intrigues by agents of Lahore. Faced with this uncertainty, Auckland determined to make the maintenance of the alliance with Ranjit Singh the cornerstone of his policy. In order to placate that monarch, he decided that the best course would be to place on the throne of Kabul a prince who would be friendly to both Lahore and the British. This condition was fitted perfectly by Shah Shuja-ul-Mulk.

Negotiations with Ranjit Singh on the Afghan question continued throughout June 1838. Ranjit was still aggrieved over being warned off Shikarpur, and it was important that he should not see British support for Shah Shuja as prejudicial to his own ambitions. Without the Maharaja's approval, the chance of installing Shah Shuja in a country 600 miles away from the nearest area of British India was not a good one. Ranjit Singh might even regard it as an attempt by the British to encircle him, and could easily be annoyed if the British, having denied Shikarpur to Lahore, were themselves to occupy it as a base from which to support Shah Shuja. But in the event, Ranjit Singh was more than agreeable to the idea of the British supporting his friend and ally Shah Shuja. As he put it, when asked by MacNaghten, the Secretary to the Government of India in the Foreign Department, what he thought of the British becoming a party to his agreement of 1833 with Shah Shuja, 'this would be like adding sugar to milk'.

Their first plan was for Shah Shuja to lead one army to Kandahar via Sind and the Bolan, while another army, of Ranjit's troops, would advance on Kabul from Peshawar. But this was altered when Burnes and others pointed out that the British must be directly involved for two reasons. Shah Shuja had gained the reputation of being unlucky. People in Afghanistan would not believe that any better fortune would attend his stars this time, unless he were accompanied by the supposedly invincible troops of the British Indian Army. Equally, no Afghan would support him if he appeared as a stooge of the Sikhs, to whom he had already given the Afghan province of Peshawar.

From the idea of including a token British force with Shah Shuja's expedition it was a short step to increasing the planned size and proportion of that force. Once the principle of actually employing any British troops at all was accepted, then they might as well go in strength. They would be more effective, because better trained, than the units Shah Shuja would have to raise from scratch, and whatever number of the Government of India's own troops were used would allow a compensating reduction in the number of Shah Shuja's proposed contingent. If the British were going to have to pay Shah Shuja's troops, at least until he was settled back on his throne and in receipt of his own revenues, they might as well save some of the money by employing their own troops whom they were paying already. Another argument in favour of sending a strong British contingent was that if there was to be a war with Iran over Herat, then British troops would be already in Afghanistan, and thus that much nearer should they have to march to Kamran's relief.

But as the enthusiasm of the British to march into Afghanistan increased, that of Ranjit Singh cooled. He did not want a British army operating in his own country, even as an ally. Nor was he prepared to launch his army into the narrow mountain passes, knowing what price in blood the Pathan tribesmen would exact from his soldiers, without some guarantee of reward at the other end, such as the cession of Jalalabad and the far side of the Khyber. But although earlier Auckland had indeed contemplated the possibility that Ranjit Singh might be encouraged to extend his power

'The residence outside Kabul of Nawab Jubbar Khan, Barakzai', brother of the Amir Dost Muhammad, and his chief minister or Wazir during the first part of his reign. The city was surrounded by such fortified houses, which in times of crisis proved difficult to subdue. (Lithograph after W.L. Walton.)

even to Kabul itself, by the end of June it was clear that Shah Shuja was no longer to be a puppet of the Sikhs, but a protégé of the British.

Thus on 25 June, 1838, was signed the Treaty of Simla, between Shah Shuja and Ranjit Singh, with the approval and agreement of the British Government. The friends and enemies of each of the three contracting parties were to be the friends and enemies of all. Ranjit Singh was confirmed in his possession of Peshawar and all the district he held across the Indus. He agreed, in return for an annual subsidy of two *lakhs* of rupees (paid on behalf of Shah Shuja by the British), to station 5,000 troops of his army, under a Muslim general, at Peshawar to assist Shah Shuja if required. Shah Shuja would accept British control of his foreign policy. He would not attack his nephew Kamran, the ruler of Herat. He would give up his claim to sovereignty over Sind in return for financial compensation of an amount to be fixed by the British Government. Ranjit Singh would leave his claim to Shikarpur to be settled by British mediation.

To save the British money the last two terms neatly cancelled each other out, at the expense only of the Amirs of Sind. They were made to pay to Shah Shuja Rs 2,500,000 as a once-for-all quittance for the thirty years' arrears of tribute claimed by him. Of this, Rs 1,500,000 would be paid to Ranjit Singh as compensation for not taking Shikarpur (promised him by Shah Shuja in 1833) from the Amirs, in deference to British wishes. The Amirs' protest that they had themselves paid Shah Shuja these arrears in 1833 was disregarded.

The decision to invade Afghanistan on Shah Shuja's behalf was made public in the Simla Manifesto, issued by Auckland on 1 October, 1838, in which the British case against Dost Muhammad was clearly set out. Dost Muhammad was an enemy of Ranjit Singh, Britain's ally. He was prepared to become the ally of Shah Muhammad of Iran, who, by attacking Herat, had become Britain's enemy. The British were thus driven to support Dost Muhammad's enemy, Shah Shuja, the legitimate monarch. Shah Shuja would enter his own country, at the head of his own army, and be restored by his own supporters (at this time all the British experts on Afghanistan really believed that Shah Shuja would be welcomed by the Afghans, if only as an alternative to Barakzai misrule). He would be supported by a British army against foreign intervention and the opposition of internal factions. The British army would be withdrawn as soon as Shah Shuja was firmly established, and British influence would be used to try and settle the feuds that had disturbed the peace and prosperity of Afghanistan for years past.

No mention was made of Russia. This was just as well from the point of view of European diplomacy, for at that very time the Russian Ambassador in London, now Count Posso di Borgo, was offering fresh assurances of the Czar's opposition to Iranian aggression against Herat. Simonich was being recalled, and his proceedings were disavowed. Vitkeivich journeyed back all the way to St Petersburg, arriving there in early May 1839. Shortly afterwards, he was found dead in his hotel room.

Despite the Shah of Iran's retirement from Herat, Auckland decided to continue the plan of placing a pro-British ruler on the throne of Kabul. Two divisions of British Indian troops were to be used, one from the Bengal Army, one from Bombay. The Commander-in-Chief Bombay, who was nominated to lead the expedition, went by sea from Bombay to Sind with his own division, while the Bengal division, followed by Shah Shuja's contingent and preceded by Alexander Burnes, marched down the Indus through British-controlled territory to Upper Sind. Protests by the Amirs of Sind at these unwelcome arrivals were met with threats of British reprisals, and by the end of February 1839 all was ready. The British 'Army of the Indus' crossed into Baluchistan and the territory of the Khan of Kalat. India was left behind. Central Asia lay ahead. The first military card had been played in the Great Game.

III

Over the Hills and Far Away
The first Afghan campaign 1839

In all, the combined forces thrown against Amir Dost Muhammad totalled more than 39,000 men. From the Bengal Army came the British 16th Light Dragoons (Lancers), complete with their pack of fox hounds, and the 13th Foot (Light Infantry), with one regiment of the Bengal European Infantry, two of Light Cavalry, two of Local Horse, and seven of Native Infantry. These were supported by one troop of horse artillery and two companies of foot artillery (all European) and two companies of sappers and miners (all Indian). The Bombay Army supplied the 4th Light Dragoons and the 4th and 17th Regiments of Foot (all from the British service), one regiment of Light Cavalry and one of Local Horse, two troops of horse, two companies of foot artillery (all European), four regiments of native infantry and one company of sappers and miners.

Shah Shuja's own contingent, two regiments of cavalry, four regiments of infantry (another two were raised later) and a troop of horse artillery, totalled 6,000 men. Although the British were anxious that Shah Shuja should be seen to enter his country surrounded by his own troops, it should be noted that his army was composed neither of his own subjects nor even his own countrymen. They were recruited and organized in the same way as the East India Company's own sepoy regiments, and indeed all their officers and many of the men had transferred from Company regiments in return for prospects of greater promotion. One regiment was even composed of Gurkhas from Nepal, and many other Hindus from traditional Indian martial communities filled up the ranks of the Shah's 'own troops' with which he was returning to take the throne of a fiercely Muslim country. Another army (6,000 Sikhs and 4,000 of Shah Shuja's men under Prince Timur, Shah Shuja's son and heir) was assembled at Peshawar, with the British represented by Lieutenant-Colonel Claude Wade and two companies of Bengal infantry.

The Afghan forces opposed to this army's advance were of variable quality. Amir Dost Muhammad's troops were composed mostly of cavalry levies, the men and horses hardy, self-reliant and as light cavalry the equal of any in the world. In individual combat the Afghan trooper, fighting with sword or lance, defended by metal helmet and chain mail,was a formidable opponent. But in a set-piece battle, lacking close-order training and with no incentive, as an individual, to risk his own horse and property if the tide of battle seemed to be flowing against him, he was less so. Against a demoralized or retreating army, on the other hand, he could be relied upon to press his attack closely and exact a heavy toll of life and booty. The standard firearm of horse and foot alike was the *jezail*, a long-barrelled arquebus or matchlock. The long barrel gave it greater accuracy than the British flintlock musket, and it fired a slightly heavier bullet, but its slow rate of fire – one round every two or three minutes, compared to two or three rounds per minute of the musket – meant that at battlefield ranges it would be overwhelmed by disciplined volleys of musketry. It was an ideal weapon for long-range sniping at stationary targets such as camps or formed bodies of men, and it was very useful in defence against troops advancing in the open. For offensive use, the *jezailchi* commonly carried two or three loaded weapons with him, discharged them rapidly at the enemy and then either withdrew or closed on him to fight with sword and shield. The foot soldier was generally armed with a small round shield and a short sword, the so-called 'Khyber knife'. Basically someone who had not been able to find a horse, his function in battle was to hold ground from which the cavalry would sally out to engage the enemy. But over broken ground, or in hilly terrain, he was able to advance or retreat with great rapidity as the situation changed. Many men, when fighting against Sikh, Hindu, or the *feringhi* (this word, the Arabic version of Franks, had been used for all western Christians since at least the time of the Crusaders), took the vows of a *Ghazi* or religious warrior, eager for death in battle against unbelievers. In the mass, *Ghazi* corresponded to suicide battalions or shock troops, anxious to close with the enemy and destroy him regardless of casualties, and their attitude to the invaders of their country remained like that advocated to English citizens in 1940 – 'take one with you'.

The difficulty of the country over which it was to march became clear to the invading army within a few days of leaving Shikarpur. All transport was animal transport, and nearly all of it was pack transport, roads for wheeled vehicles being unknown in this part of the world. Pack transport is less efficient than draught and thus increases the number of beasts required to move a given weight of stores. Animals, like men, need to be fed. But the amount of grazing in an arid country proved quite inadequate for the numbers of animals needed to carry the army's stores, not to mention those of the vast quantities of camp followers, servants, sutlers, grooms and bazaar merchants accompanying the troops, without which no Indian army was capable of taking the field. Because of the shortage of grazing, many camels had to be employed carrying fodder for the camels carrying munitions of war, and even the fodder-carrying camels had to eat a proportion of what they carried. The grand total of camels used by the Army of the Indus was in excess of thirty thousand, each beast occupying fifteen feet of road, travelling at a speed of approximately two miles an hour, with ten beasts a minute, if in single file, passing any given point.

The ordinary resources of the carrying trade proved quite inadequate for this task and, under British pressure, many animals and drivers from the camel-breeding districts of Sind and the surrounding areas were impressed or hired to support the expedition. Many of these beasts were from the breeding farms, unused to working as caravan animals, and scores died before even reaching Shikarpur. Even the 30,000 were insufficient to move the whole army, and there was a violent quarrel between William MacNaghten, now the British Envoy with Shah Shuja, who wanted priority of carriage given to the Shah's Contingent for political reasons, and Sir Willoughby Cotton, commanding the Bengal Division, who needed all the camels there were to move his own stores.

The route to Afghanistan lay through the deserts of Upper Sind, across the arid plain of Kacchi and so to Dadur, at the lower end of the Bolan Pass. Lack of water and forage steadily eroded the camel herd, the gun bullocks and the cavalry horses. Animals kept together went hungry. Animals turned out to forage for themselves were stolen by the predatory Baluchi tribes, who had long experience of preying on passing travellers.

The Bengal Division, moving a week ahead of the rest of the army, reached Dadur, at the mouth of the Bolan, on 10 March, sixteen days and 146 miles after leaving Shikarpur. After a halt of ten days, with only twenty days' supplies left, and no sign of any more being collected locally, Cotton decided to push on up the Bolan. Slowly but steadily the gradient increased. Day after day more animals collapsed. Luxuries, even necessities, were abandoned by the wayside, to be carried off by the ever watchful plunderers who dogged the column's foot steps. After ten days and sixty miles of constant climbing, the army came out of the gigantic, boulder-strewn gorge and reached the town of Quetta, standing in the fertile and well-watered plain of Shal. But the arrival of this large and hungry army soon exhausted the available food, and on 28 March, two days after his arrival at Quetta, Cotton put his army on half rations, and the followers on quarter rations. The Shah's Contingent and the Bombay Division were still in Kacchi at this date, because of the difficulty of feeding and moving the whole army as a single body. They marched up the Bolan a week after the Bengal troops, experiencing the unpleasantness of passing through the decomposing bodies of innumerable dead camels and the other detritus left by the Bengal troops, and suffering from the depredations of the Baluchi robbers, the want of supplies and the difficulty of the road, in much the same way as had the vanguard.

*'Shah Shuja's Contingent: The Horse Artillery'. The Shah's Horse Artillery
followed the pattern of the Bengal Horse Artillery. Note that some gunners ride the
lead horses, while others are carried on the gun carriage. The practice was different
from that of the Royal Horse Artillery, in which the gun detachment rode their own
horses, and only the three drivers rode on the gun team. The central group shows
one gun with its own limber, and two more ammunition limbers behind to complete
the sub-division. (After Capt. Cooper, Bengal Artillery.)*

On 4 April, ten miles from Quetta, Sir Willoughby Cotton met Sir John
Keane (the Commander-in-Chief) and announced that his own men were
down to quarter rations, with twelve days' supplies left and nothing to be
had locally.

British reaction to the dearth of supplies and to the generally unfriendly
attitude of the local people was to blame the local ruler, Mehrab Khan,
the Khan of Kalat. Kalat, the dominant state in Baluchistan, had in
earlier times paid tribute to the Durranis, but had long been *de facto*
independent.

At the end of March 1839 Alexander Burnes arrived at Kalat with the
draft of a treaty for the Khan's seal. Mehrab Khan was to acknowledge
Shah Shuja's supremacy and signify this by paying him a state visit in his
camp as he passed through the country. The Khan was also to use his best
endeavours to procure supplies and carriage for the army as it moved
from Sind to Quetta and to protect the supply convoys from attack by his
subjects. In return he would be paid an annual subsidy of a lakh and a
half of rupees.

While at Kalat, Burnes heard a few home truths from Mehrab Khan, who was a proud man and who resented the treatment he was now being given by Shah Shuja, to whom he had, in the days of Shah Shuja's earlier misfortunes and failures, given shelter and friendship. The British forces marching to restore the Shah had destroyed the crops, which even in plentiful years were poor enough and this year were especially scarce because of drought. They had helped themselves to water, which was needed to irrigate the crops and was doubly valuable in this year of drought. Despite this, he had seen the British safely through the Bolan to the best of his ability, but now, when he might instead have made an alliance with the Iranians (his western neighbours) or even with the Russians, he was asked to accept the supremacy of Shah Shuja. He warned the British of their folly in selecting as their protégés the worst possible candidates. First it had been the infamous Kamran Shah at Herat, and now it was the unpopular Shah Shuja at Kabul and Kandahar.

None of this was welcome to the ears of British officials, even though Burnes also reported that what little grain there was in the country was being placed at the disposal of the British and that where the Khan was able to help, by the provision of some 15,000 sheep, the real staple food of the country, he was doing so. When Burnes's camp was attacked as he travelled back to join MacNaghten in the Shah's camp, and the treaty (which the Khan had reluctantly accepted) stolen from his tent, it was at once assumed that the Khan was to blame. The Khan's failure to present himself at Shah Shuja's court was taken as further evidence of guilt, and MacNaghten, writing from Quetta on 6 April, recommended to Lord Auckland that Shal, Kacchi and Mastang (the three most profitable provinces of Kalat in terms of their revenue potential) should be annexed to Shah Shuja's personal dominions.

In fact, both the attack on Burnes's camp and the Khan's absence from Shah Shuja's court were the responsibility of the Khan's Wazir, or chief minister, Mulla Muhammad Hasan. Mulla Muhammad's father had been murdered on Mehrab Khan's orders, in 1833, and Mulla Muhammad himself now took the opportunity for revenge. He secured his own nomination as the Khan's envoy to meet the British and waited upon MacNaghten as the army passed through Kacchi. There he made out that though he himself was pro-British and a loyal supporter of Shah Shuja's pretensions, the Khan was hostile to them, which indeed was not too far from the truth. Returning to Kalat, he told his master that Shah Shuja and the British were out to ruin him, and in view of the depredations of the army on the country's supplies of food and water, and the claims made on the Khan's independence, this was not too difficult for Mehrab Khan to believe. The Khan's seal was affixed by Mulla Muhammad to letters sent to the Baluchi tribesmen exhorting them to harass and annoy the British army as it passed. Some of these letters fell into British hands and made them even

more convinced of the Khan's enmity. But it was Mulla Muhammad's men who plundered Burnes's camp and stole the treaty, and it was Mulla Muhammad who persuaded the Khan that if he went to Shah Shuja to pay his respects he would be arrested by the British and made a state prisoner. Necessity dictated that the columns should press on into Afghanistan, but the attitude of the British boded ill for Mehrab Khan when they should have leisure to deal with him.

The British marched out of Quetta on 7 April, 1839, and by early on 14 April the plain of Kandahar lay spread out below them. The mood began to change. Supplies began to come in, expensive but welcome, as the local people reached the conclusion that Shah Shuja and his allies had come to stay. Morale improved as the soldiers began to eat better, and there was less talk of there being an enemy behind every bush. In fact there seemed no enemy at all apart from the local bandits, who hung around the outskirts of the slow-moving, heavily laden columns.

On 21 April the army resumed its advance. Two days later, as it neared the outskirts of Kandahar, the Barakzai Sirdar Kohen Dil Khan and his supporters rode out of their city and made off towards the north-west. They eventually took refuge in Iranian territory. On 25 April Shah Shuja, surrounded by his troops and attended by the British officials and generals who had brought him, formally entered Kandahar and took possession of his ancestor's capital amid scenes of general rejoicing and popular enthusiasm.

There was a pause of another two months at Kandahar, where the Bombay Division had at last caught up with the main body. Shah Shuja, encouraged by MacNaghten, set about taking over the reigns of government of this part of his newly regained kingdom, though it soon became clear that he had no intention of being a mere cypher and that he would accept no interference from his British paymasters in the way he ruled his people. Much play was made with the fact that he retained in their posts the notoriously rapacious revenue officials whose activities had played a large part in undermining the popularity of the previous regime. But in this respect he was little different from the leaders of other incoming administrations, then or indeed now.

The lack of opposition to the army's advance against Kandahar was because Dost Muhammad had mistakenly assumed that the immediate threat came from his old opponents, the Sikhs, and that the allies would use the shortest route to Kabul, via the Khyber Pass and Jalalabad. Accordingly he stationed his best troops and his best commanders, including his son Muhammad Akbar Khan, the hero of Jamrud, to block that route, expecting that the British would leave Shah Shuja to establish himself at Kandahar while they themselves marched to Herat to prevent any renewal of the Iranian threat there.

Therefore, when, on 27 June, 1839, Keane led his army out of Kandahar on the road to Ghazni and Kabul, his Afghan opponents were caught

32

'The Kabul gate, Ghazni, after the battle'. This water-colour is by Henry Durand, the engineer officer in command of the party which blew in the gates prior to the infantry assault. It gives a good idea of the strength of the defences of what was one of the most famous fortresses in Central Asia, once the home of the great Sultan Mahmud who first brought Muslim rule to northern India.

completely off balance. Nevertheless, Dost Muhammad had not neglected his southern flank altogether, for one of his sons, Muhammad Haydar Khan, held Ghazni (one of the most famous fortresses in the whole of Central Asia) with a strong garrison. The Amir's eldest son, Afzul Khan, was in the field with 5,000 Ghilzai horsemen, ready to hang upon the flanks and harass the rear of the trailing British columns and to pour down upon them the moment they lost formation or relaxed their guard.

But Keane did not relax his guard, and on 20 July, with his army closed up behind him, his scouts sighted the minarets of Ghazni. The next day the advancing British reached the outskirts of the town and exchanged shots with the garrison. Then they withdrew out of range while their chief engineer rode around the fortress and made his report. The walls were impenetrable to anything but a properly equipped siege train, but the four siege guns which, with such labour, had been brought with the army from India were still lying in the ordnance depot at Kandahar. Keane therefore had to choose between besieging Ghazni with sap and mine until the arrival of the siege guns (a practice which had generally been followed by the Duke of Wellington in the Peninsular War thirty years before); or masking the fortress, leaving a strong detachment to deter its garrison from taking the field while he marched on to Kabul; or attempting to take it by a *coup de main*. He chose the third solution, having been informed by

33

an Afghan deserter from the garrison, one Abdul Rashid Khan, a nephew of the Amir, that while nearly all the gates had been bricked up, one had been merely barricaded to allow the entry of reinforcements expected to arrive from Kabul.

During the early hours of 23 July the troops took up their positions. There was no moon, and a howling gale drowned the noise of their approach. Lieutenant Henry Durand led a party of sappers and miners to lay 300 pounds of gunpowder at the Kabul Gate. They were challenged about 750 yards short of their destination, but rushed on to it, while the horse artillery and field guns opened fire at the ramparts from a range of 250 yards. A demonstration against another wall by three companies of the 35th Bengal Native Infantry distracted some of the defenders and Durand was able to blow in the gate successfully.

The forlorn hope, or advance storming party, under Colonel Dennie of the 13th Light Infantry, consisting of four companies from the European battalions, rushed the tunnel-like entrance. The main storming party, under Brigadier 'Fighting Bob' Sale, followed on, though stoutly resisted by a number of Afghans who had re-occupied the gateway after the forlorn hope had gone through. The reserve battalions poured in after them, and steadily the columns converged on the city's central square. Some of the defenders, disheartened at the success of the surprise attack, abandoned their posts and fled. Others, firing from roof-tops and behind walls, put up a stiffer resistance, but were gradually mopped up in desperate street fighting. By first light the British flag was seen to be flying over the citadel of Ghazni. After recovering from their astonishment, Afzul Khan and his horsemen abandoned their camp and fell back to Kabul. Thus, in the space of a single night Dost Muhammad lost one of his strongest fortresses, with 600 of its garrison killed and 1,600 captured, at a cost to the British of eighteen dead and 173 wounded.

Dost Muhammad sent his Wazir and brother, Nawab Jubbar Khan, to offer terms to Shah Shuja and the British. He would peacefully hand over rule at Kabul if he could be Wazir in the same way that his father had been hereditary Wazir to the previous Afghan monarchs. But as Dost Muhammad's brother, Fateh Khan, had as Wazir become virtually the ruler of the country, this proposal was not one which either the Shah or the British relished, and Jubbar Khan returned to Kabul with nothing more than the offer of honourable asylum for the Amir in British India. Before leaving he warned MacNaghten that the game was not yet over, and added: 'If Shah Shuja really is a King and come to the kingdom of his ancestors, what is the use of your army and name? You have brought him, by your money and arms, into Afghanistan. Leave him now with us Afghans, and let him rule us if he can.'

On 30 July the invading army marched out of Ghazni and headed towards Kabul, where Dost Muhammad was gathering his forces for a

'The storming of Kalat, 13 Novermber 1839', by T. Wingate. A contemporary lithograph showing the attempt by the British to follow up the retreating Brahuis and take the town by a coup de main. *The buildings on the right are a group of old tombs in which the assaulting infantry were driven to take shelter and regroup while their supporting artillery came into action.*

last stand. But his forces began to melt away even as he assembled them. It seemed that nothing was going to stop the invincible British, and many of those in the Amir's camp were more concerned to safeguard their own interests under the imminent new regime than to prejudice them by too determined a resistance in support of the collapsing one. An appeal by the Amir, riding among his army with a Koran in his hand, that all good Muslims should join him in at least one charge against the Frankish unbelievers, in which he would give his own life and so free them to make their own subsequent peace with Shah Shuja, fell upon deaf ears. Disheartened by the defection of men who had eaten his salt for the last thirteen years, and by the faithlessness and treachery of those on whom he should have most been able to depend, Dost Muhammad abandoned the hope of a last defiant gesture and on the evening of 2 August, accompanied by such of his army as remained loyal, rode off towards the Hindu Kush.

On 7 August Shah Shuja formally re-entered Kabul, the city which he had last seen thirty years before. After the usual parades and displays of pomp and ceremony, he began the task of establishing his new government. The Shahzada Timur arrived with Colonel Wade and the Sikhs via the Khyber and Jalalabad at the beginning of September, and another state entry was organized for the prince, even more splendid than that arranged for his father. Shah Shuja instituted an Order of the Durrani Empire, and bestowed decorations upon the officers of the allied forces. After six weeks of reviews, race-meetings, and general relaxation the army, which had carried out the British policy of installing a friendly monarch on the Afghan throne, began to prepare for its homeward journey.

It had started its march ten months before and had travelled over 12,000 miles, passing through some of the most difficult terrain that British troops had ever experienced. It had crossed rivers, deserts and mountain ranges. It had penetrated to the heart of a wild and warlike country, and swept away all opposition. It had needed to fight only one major engagement, at Ghazni, and resistance had collapsed in a night. Its battle casualties had been minimal. Its casualties from sickness, hunger or exhaustion had been significant, but not unacceptable. The only really important losses had been among the camel herd, which had lost 20,000 beasts along the route, some strayed or stolen, but most killed through overwork and lack of proper food or water. Nevertheless, the expedition had succeeded in its aim and was a very creditable achievement. But for subsequent events, it would have been recorded as one of the British Indian Army's most successful campaigns.

The Bombay Division left Kabul on 18 September to return to India. On its way home it detached a strong brigade under Major-General Sir Thomas Willshire to settle accounts with Mehrab Khan of Kalat. Mehrab Khan awaited their arrival with grim determination. The powerful leaders of the Brahui tribes over whom he ruled rallied to his support. Willshire reached Kalat on 13 November, 1839. He found before him a formidable fortress, protected by a number of rocky bills occupied by five guns, with large numbers of matchlockmen and swordsmen. He first attacked these hills, hoping that the Brahuis would be driven down into the fortress and that his own men would be able to rush the gates before they were closed. The first part of the plan succeeded, as the Brahuis could not stand against the shrapnel bursts that searched their positions. The tribesmen streamed down from the hills and made for the fortress gates. The British infantry followed close on their heels, but not closely enough. The gates were shut in their faces, and under heavy fire from the matchlocks on the walls they were forced to fall back to the shelter of some old tombs and enclosures on the approaches of the town.

The fatal weakness of the fortress, like so many in this region, was its main gate, quite unprotected against artillery fire. In what was by now a fairly standard tactic, the Indian gunners brought their cannon into action against the gates at a range of 200 yards. Some of the artillerymen went down under the fire of the *jezailchis* but a rapid bombardment was maintained until the gates were shot away. The infantry were ordered to advance, and after entering the gate drove the defenders, still fighting with great tenacity, back to the citadel. There Mehrab Khan, his ministers and chieftains around him, died sword in hand, receiving with the loss of his life and his poor capital the reward for having shown kindness and hospitality to Shah Shuja in his days of adversity five years previously.

'The Death of Mehrab Khan, ruler of Kalat'. A contemporary lithograph showing the final resistance of Mehrab Khan and his courtiers when British troops reached the Miri, or palace, during the storming of Kalat, 13 November 1839.

One of the few notables to survive the battle was the treacherous Wazir, Mulla Muhammad Hasan. Whatever hopes he had entertained of benefiting from his master's death, except for the enjoyment of a personal revenge, collapsed when the state apartments were searched and the extent of his double-dealing became known. But rather than admit that any redress was due to Mehrab Khan or his heirs, the British installed on the throne a rival claimant, Shah Nawaz Khan, whose ancestors had been deposed by Ahmad Shah Durrani. In return for his installation on the throne of Kalat, Shah Nawaz assented to the transfer to Shah Shuja's own dominions of all the most fertile provinces in his state, Shal (Quetta), Mastang and Kacchi. Mehrab's son, the young Nasir Khan, who had escaped from Kalat in the care of a faithful minister, the Daroga Gul Muhammad, took refuge with Sirdar Azad Khan, chief of Kharan, a desert region to the west of Kalat.

Although it appeared that Baluchistan was now settled, in Afghanistan proper things were not as simple as had been hoped. Amir Dost Muhammad was rumoured to be raising a horde of Uzbek horsemen from the provinces beyond the Hindu Kush, and so Shah Shuja's Gurkha Regiment, with a troop of horse artillery, was sent to garrison the northern frontier post of Bamiyan. It was, moreover, already clear that Shah Shuja himself was not being hailed by his subjects as a deliverer, but on the contrary would need the support of his British allies for some time to come before he could establish himself.

Nor were the problems in Shah Shuja's own domains the only consideration. At Herat, where the debauched and barbaric Kamran Shah had handed over government almost entirely to his unscrupulous and cunning Wazir Yar Muhammad, the British position was an extremely embarrassing one. Eldred Pottinger, who had been rewarded for his services during the siege with the appointment of political officer at Kamran's court, failed to stop the slave raids which gave the Iranians a good reason for attacking the city, and which at the same time made it difficult for public opinion in Britain to support the idea of a war in Herat's defence. But the possibility still remained that hostilities might recur with the Iranians and that British troops might yet be needed in that quarter.

So in October 1839, instead of the whole Bengal Division returning to India by way of the Khyber Pass, leaving only a few units in Afghanistan to see Shah Shuja safely settled, the reverse took place. The Sikh contingent returned to the Punjab, and Sir John Keane followed with his cavalry, a few companies of native infantry, a troop of horse artillery and most of the sappers and miners. On 1 January, 1840 they reached British territory at Ferozpur, where the Army of the Indus was formally broken up.

IV

The Failure of the Grand Design
British disasters 1840–41

Outwardly it appeared that the British had achieved the aim of their Central Asian policy; Russian influence had been prevented from approaching any nearer India and British influence had been extended far beyond. But then came news of the very thing which the British feared, namely the advance into Central Asia not merely of Russian influence but of a Russian military expedition. This was led by General Perovski and had orders to punish the man-stealing Turkman tribes for their continual raids into Russian territory, in which many of the Czar's subjects had been murdered or abducted for sale in the slave markets of Khiva.

Four times since 1609 Russian or Cossack expeditions had penetrated to the Khivan heartland. Four times they had been destroyed, the survivors cut down or sold into life-long captivity. But if they were to succeed this time they could be expected to press on to Bokhara and then the whole Oxus basin would be open to Russian steam boats, bringing them to the northern side of the Hindu Kush. Lord Palmerston, at the British Foreign Office, advocated the establishment of alliances with the rulers of Balkh or even Bokhara. 'It seems pretty clear,' he wrote on 14 February, 1842, 'that sooner or later the Cossack and the Sepoy, the Man from the Baltic and He from the British Isles will meet in the Centre of Asia. It should be our Business to take Care that the Meeting should be as far off from our Indian Possessions as may be convenient and advantageous to us. But the Meeting will not be avoided by our staying at Home to receive the visit.'

But events in the Khivan desert had already decided that the visit would be at least postponed. Two weeks before Palmerston coined his telling phrase about the sepoy and the Cossack, General Perovski and his frozen, half-starved troops had turned back towards Orenburg, having reached less than halfway towards their objective. Perovski, a general with experience in campaigning on this wild frontier, had deliberately chosen to march in the winter, in order to avoid the heat and drought associated with the Central Asian desert during the summer months. But he encountered weather of unexpected severity, and while the Russian troops trudged on through the ice storms, their supply lines were cut time and again by bands of Khivan warriors. As the Russians began to fall back, they were harried mercilessly by their foes; stragglers were picked off, stores and camps were raided.

The news of this, while comforting to British politicians, might have given British generals in Afghanistan food for thought. Two years later a similar scene would be enacted with their troops playing the part of the Russians, the Afghans that of the Khivans. But for now the British position seemed a strong one. Perovski, with the prestige of the Russian army at stake, urged that a fresh expedition be sent against Khiva, but at St Petersburg more moderate counsels prevailed.

Russian objection to Khivan slavers was not that they practised the institution of slavery as such. Indeed it was only since 1833 that this institution had been abolished even in the enlightened British Empire, while in Russia the lot of the serfs was such that frequently those captured by the Turkmans could hope for a rather more comfort able existence than that which they had previously enjoyed. The major objections were to the actual economic loss caused by the abduction of workers and their families, and the insult to the authority of the Czar that his subjects could be taken from him in this way. There were also religious and racial objections, to the thought of East European Christians being the slaves of Central Asian Muslims. A British officer from Herat, James Abbott, was sent to Khiva to try to secure the release of Russian captives and eventually arrived at Perovski's headquarters in Orenburg in May 1840, carrying letters and presents from the Khan of Khiva to the Russian Emperor. He was sent on to St Petersburg, but the Czar declined to receive him.

Despite this, the new British Ambassador at St Petersburg, John Bloomfield, was able to report a little later that the Czar had offered to open negotiations with the Khan of Khiva. Another officer from the British Mission in Herat, Lieutenant Richmond Shakespear, was sent to Khiva, and during the summer of 1840 he arranged with the Khivans to send an envoy, and a party of freed Russian captives, to the Russian frontier base at Orenburg. On 1 October he delivered the whole party in person. Going on to St Petersburg he was cordially received by the Czar. He then accompanied the despatches to London, where he was knighted for his efforts. Baron Brunnow officially informed Palmerston on 29 September, 1840, that the idea of another campaign against Khiva had been abandoned.

But though by the end of 1840 the Russian menace seemed to have subsided, the chances of the British garrison in Afghanistan being withdrawn to India grew steadily more remote. This was because Shah Shuja, so far from establishing his own authority over his subjects, was everywhere faced with outbreaks of rebellion. Even by early May 1840 Hobhouse had come to the view that if the attitude towards Shah Shuja of his most powerful subjects was as unreliable as MacNaghten's reports were suggesting, there was no way in which he could be kept on the throne without a British force being stationed in Afghanistan virtually indefinitely.

In Baluchistan a serious reverse was suffered by men of the Bombay Army. The British garrison at Kahan, the chief town of the Marri tribe of Baluchis, was attacked in April 1840, its supply train of several hundred camels was carried off and their escort, whose commander had made the fatal mistake of dividing his forces, was ambushed and massacred. An attempt to relieve Kahan was driven back with severe losses of men, stores and guns at the end of August.

At the end of September Captain Lewis Brown, the garrison commander, having exhausted his supplies and munitions and being without hope of relief accepted the terms offered by Dodar Khan, the Marri chief, that he should be allowed to march away unmolested if he gave up the fort. The Marris observed these conditions to the letter, as a mark of respect to the handful of brave men who had stood a five-month siege deep in enemy territory. On 3 October, 1840, Brown and his sepoys reached the British outpost of Pulaji, bringing with them their sick, their gun and their honour.

At Kalat, the reign of the new Khan, Shah Nawaz, had proved disastrous. The support of the powerful Brahui Sirdars, essential if the country was to be governed effectively, was not forthcoming. Too many had lost kinsmen at the storming of Kalat, for whose blood compensation had not been paid. Too many of them regarded Shah Nawaz as a quisling who had made common cause with the invader and had consented to the loss of all the country's richest provinces in order to improve his own prospects. Too many of them had held *jagirs* in those provinces which had now been resumed by Shah Shuja on the grounds that he required the revenue rather than the military service notionally rendered by the Brahui Sirdars, as *jagirdars*, and their retainers.

Accordingly, most of them joined the young Nasir Khan when in August 1840, accompanied by his father's faithful old minister, the Daroga Gul Muhammad, and by Sirdar Azad Khan of Kharan, he marched to reclaim the town and throne of Kalat. Lieutenant Loveday, the political officer at Kalat, with an escort of forty of Shah Shuja's sepoys, held out for a day and a night, but this force, weakened by treachery and divided counsels, was hopelessly inadequate to defend the citadel. Some of Shah Nawaz's courtiers made terms with the Brahuis, Shah Nawaz (a youth of fourteen) abdicated and Loveday was arrested. He was put into chains and treated with every form of degradation until November 1840. Then, as Nasir Khan's men prepared to abandon Kalat at the approach of a British army under Major General William Nott, someone found time to cut Loveday's throat before he could be rescued. A war of outposts and desert skirmishes continued until October 1841, when after months of patient diplomacy in Nasir Khan's camp by Loveday's successor, Colonel Stacey, an agreement was finally reached.

Signed by James Outram on behalf of the British Government, and sealed by Nasir Khan on 6 October, 1841, it was a masterpiece of compromise.

The preamble declared, rather baldly, that 'Whereas Meer Nusseer Khan, son of Mehrab Khan, deceased, having tendered his allegiance and submission', the British and Shah Shuja would recognize him as 'Chief of the principality of Khelat-i-Nusseer, on the following terms'. The first term was that Nasir Khan acknowledged himself the vassal of 'the King of Cabool, in like manner as his ancestors were formerly the vassals of His Majesty's ancestors'. The treaty did not specify any particular sets of ancestors, and thus left the precise degree of subordination carefully unspecified. The second article, another concession to the Brahuis, said that Kacchi and Mastang would be restored to Nasir Khan 'through the kindness of His Majesty Shah Shuja-ul-Mulk'. Quetta remained in Shah Shuja's dominions for a little longer.

The Amir Dost Muhammad, after being driven from his capital when the British arrived with Shah Shuja, had taken refuge first in Balkh and then, crossing the Oxus, with the Amir of Bokhara. This unamiable monarch, together with his Rais, or chief minister, had a gloomy reputation for oppression, slave-dealing, torture and general depravity surpassing even that of his neighbour Kamran Shah and *his* chief minister at Herat. The British had already tried to open negotiations with Bokhara at the end of 1838, when Simonich, the Russian Ambassador in Iran, anticipating General Perovski's expedition, declared that a Russian army was already on its way to Khiva and Bokhara. This diplomatic initiative failed disastrously. The first Envoy, Captain Arthur Connolly, was thrown into a filthy dungeon and similar treatment was accorded to the next, Colonel Charles Stoddart, who arrived a year later to try and rescue him. Eventually both were publicly beheaded in the Bokhara market place in June 1842.

Dost Muhammad soon found that his host was just as likely to become his gaoler. There were constant and pressing invitations to bring his household into Bokharan territory, where it could be assured of the ruler's protection. Dost Muhammad sent it in the opposite direction, southwards over the Hindu Kush to take refuge with his British enemies. The party, headed by Nawab Jubbar Khan, reached the British outpost at Bamiyan in July 1840 and was given safe conduct to India. Dost Muhammad, with two of his sons, Muhammad Afzal Khan and Muhammad Akbar Khan, continued for a time as guests of the Bokharan ruler, but then succeeded in evading surveillance long enough to slip back to Afghanistan, the fifty-year-old Amir having dyed his beard red, the more easily to avoid recognition.

During July and August Dost Muhammad gathered strength beyond the Hindu Kush. In early September 1840, together with his ally the Wali of Kulum, he led a force of 6,000 Uzbek lances over the Hindu Kush. A series of encounters followed and finally, on 2 November, 1840, the British trapped Dost Muhammad at Parwandara, about fifty miles north of Kabul. Two squadrons of the 2nd Bengal Light Cavalry were sent from the British advance guard and drawn up across the Amir's line of retreat. They were charged by about 200 Afghan troopers. For cavalry to stand still to receive a charge was fatal, so the British officers ordered a counter-charge and rode forward to meet the Afghans. Their soldiers, instead of following them, were so appalled at the sight of the oncoming Afghan horsemen that they turned and fled. Of the officers, three were killed and two severely wounded. Among the dead was Assistant Surgeon Percival Lord, the local Political Officer, whose restless spirit and thirst for adventure had put him in the forefront of a cavalry battle where neither his medical profession nor diplomatic calling required him to be.

The next day, his honour satisfied, Dost Muhammad rode with a single attendant to the outskirts of Kabul, where he met Sir William MacNaghten out for a ride alone. The Amir surrendered his sword to the British Envoy, who, not to be outdone in courtesy, at once returned it to him. Despite Shah Shuja's promise that if Dost Muhammad ever came into his power he would 'hang the dog', the former Amir was treated with every mark of respect by the British and sent under escort to Ludhiana, in British India, where he was accorded much the same privileges and honours that Shah Shuja had enjoyed there.

But despite the removal from the scene of his rival, Shah Shuja's regime did not prosper. The Shah himself like the restored Bourbons, had learned nothing and forgotten nothing during his exile. Whereas the parvenu Amir had gone out of his way to conciliate the chiefs of the country, being well aware that he was, so to speak, no better than they were (especially true as so many of them were his own brothers), Shah Shuja was very conscious of being the legitimate monarch, and though generally speaking a just and merciful ruler, he was quite unable to show the common touch which would have done much to endear him to his proud and independent-minded subjects. The great tribal Sirdars, to whom Dost Muhammad had perforce given a voice in the government, now found themselves virtually excluded from the privileges and perquisites of office, in favour of the Shah's own creatures and his British friends. The Shah's chief minister, previously master of the royal household in exile, was an elderly incompetent who exasperated Englishman and Afghan alike by being unable (or claiming to be unable) to remember in the afternoon decisions discussed in the morning. The fact that at an earlier period his ears had been cut off on Shah Shuja's orders as a punishment for some offence made his hearing as uncertain as his memory.

Another problem was that Dost Muhammad, like many other self-made rulers (such as Napoleon, Mussolini, Hitler, the Ayatollah Khomeini),

'Warriors from Kohistan' ('the country of the mountains') north of Kabul, 1840.
Typical Afghan fighting men of the period, they are well armed with the long-
barrelled jezail and carry a Khyber knife for hand-to-hand fighting. They wear
poshteens (leather coats with the fur inside) as a protection against the harsh
climate of their country in winter. (Painting by James Rattray.)

was strongly in favour of respectable family life, and had rigidly enforced
the laws pertaining to chastity and marital fidelity. Shah Shuja took a
more relaxed and sophisticated attitude towards these matters, possibly
the result of his long sojourn in India, possibly because, as the legitimate
ruler, he had no need to prove himself by so scrupulously applying every
detail of the Koranic teachings. But such laxity was unpopular. It was
still more unpopular when tales spread that Afghan girls were being
seduced, even abducted, into the households of members of the British
occupation forces. Such stories always abound when some thousands of
healthy young men are stationed in a country far from their own, whether
as allies or enemies, but in this case some of the alliances seem to have
been more than political ones. In particular, the recently knighted dash-
ing young assistant Envoy, Sir Alexander Burnes, was said to be a great
lady-killer. There were tales of carousing and music at the house of this

British *elchi*, of nocturnal visits by dark-eyed Afghan damsels, and indeed of flagrant immorality involving British officers and the wives of Afghan gentlemen.

The British garrison began to settle down to life in its spacious cantonments. There were dog-shows, horse-races, various entertainments for the ladies, who had come up from India to join their husbands and fathers, band concerts, parties, and in general all the social engagements, in miniature, of an army stationed in British India, or a friendly native state, which was what Afghanistan had, at least in theory, now become. On 20 August, 1841, after troops from Kandahar had put down a revolt among the local Durranis (which Yar Muhammad of Herat was thought to have financed with the subsidy paid to his master Kamran Shah by the British), Sir William MacNaghten wrote that the whole country was 'quiet from Dan to Beersheba'.

Seven days later, far away in London, a new House of Commons, meeting after the recent general election, voted out the Whig government headed by Lord Melbourne and voted in a Tory one headed by Sir Robert Peel. Auckland had sent home his resignation on hearing the result of the election and his successor was the Tory minister for Indian affairs, Lord Ellenborough. The new Tory government, anxious to cut government expenditure, saw the Afghan adventure as a drain on the revenues of India. So far from contemplating an expensive advance to Herat, such as the Whig ministers had at last begun to plan in their final weeks in office, the Tories decided to pull the Indian troops out of Afghanistan altogether. Peel spoke of the folly of the advance beyond the Indus and the ruinous consequences to the finances of British India. Even without the cost of keeping troops in Afghanistan, and of diplomatic expenses incurred on Shah Shuja's behalf, such as paying bribes to Afghan chiefs to support him, the East India Company's revenues were a quarter of a million pounds in deficit. The Afghan adventure, including the expense of keeping up a flotilla of steamboats on the Indus, was costing another one and a quarter crores of rupees per annum, or a million pounds at the then exchange rate.

Rather than squeeze the unhappy Indian taxpayer still more to pay for military campaigns in a distant land, Ellenborough decided to Afghanize the conflict. Shah Shuja's Contingent was to be doubled in size and the Indian Army's share of the garrison reduced. The British financial aid to Shah Shuja was to be cut back.

Under Ellenborough's orders, Sir William MacNaghten (consoled by the news that he had been nominated to be the next Governor of Bombay, a very highly prized appointment) began to wind down the British presence in Afghanistan. At the end of September he cut by half the allowances paid to the eastern Ghilzais, who held the passes between Kabul and Jalalabad. Another economy decided on was to send Sir Robert Sale's brigade, due to go back to India on the completion of its tour in Afghanistan, back down the Khyber while its relief waited for it at Peshawar.

The Ghilzais, feeling cheated by the reduction in their subsidy, rose in arms along his route. Sale had to fight his way up through the passes all the way to Gandamak and lost five officers and more than 100 soldiers killed or wounded on the way.

At the same time, late October 1841, there was a rising in Kohistan, north of Kabul. Lieutenant Rattray, the assistant political agent for the area, was killed by local chiefs after he had gone to a conference with them. Charikar, held by Shah Shuja's 4th (Gurkha) Infantry, then came under constant attack. On 13 November, the water supply having failed, the 200 men of the regiment still fit to bear arms broke out to try and fight their way to Kabul. Only two British officers, the indefatigable political, Major Eldred Pottinger (the former defender of Herat), and the battalion adjutant, Lieutenant J.C. Haughton, reached Kabul, with one sepoy. The wounded, together with the women and children left behind at Charikar, were massacred by the victorious tribesmen.

But neither of these episodes compared with what was to come. On 2 November a mob gathered outside the house of Alexander Burnes, including among them a number of irate fathers and cuckolded husbands. Burnes harangued them from his balcony with vituperative wit, but the situation got out of control and the house was attacked and set on fire. Following a desperate defence, Burnes, together with his brother, Lieutenant Charles Burnes, 17th Bombay Infantry, and Lieutenant W. Broadfoot of the 1st Bengal Europeans, were all murdered as they tried to escape in disguise.

In this crisis the British were handicapped by the individual weaknesses of their military commanders at Kabul. Sir Willoughby Cotton, who had assumed command of the troops after Sir John Keane's departure, had himself returned to India on medical grounds in December 1840, and had been replaced by Major-General William Elphinstone. Elphinstone had been a good soldier in his day and had fought at Waterloo in command of the 33rd Foot, part of the brigade which repulsed the Imperial Guard's last attack. His was a classic case of the disastrous consequences, to themselves and the army, of retaining in employment men who, however good their record, have grown too old for war. His own health was poor and although his powers might have been up to the peaceful life of the commander of a garrison based in friendly surroundings, he was certainly not fit enough to take part in operations. Indeed, he himself was well aware of this and had planned to go back to India when the next column of troops left. Major General Nott, the ill-tempered but efficient East India Company General at Kandahar, had already been nominated to succeed him.

Elphinstone's second-in-command, taking over when Sir Robert Sale marched out, was the one-armed veteran Brigadier John Shelton. Shelton was also from the British service and had seen service in the Peninsular War. His own regiment, the 44 Foot, was at Kabul with him, having arrived there after having previously been in the jungles of Arakan. Of Shelton's personal courage there is little doubt, though he was of rather a gloomy disposition – commonly called 'a croaker' in the slang of the period – making no effort to disguise his view of the strength of the enemy and weakness of his own troops. But the most un-officer-like quality in his make-up was that of personal disloyalty. He cordially despised his own commander, but though not the first, nor last, officer to be in this position, he made no attempt to correct his superior's deficiencies nor to ease his burden in any way. Rather he stood aloof; making no attempt to disguise his contempt, even rolling himself up in his sleeping bag and dozing off, or pretending to, during vital councils of war.

When the news spread of Alexander Burnes's death, the citizens of Kabul might well have held their breath to see what terrible revenge the British would take. This was not a part of the world where conquerors were expected to take the murder of their officers lightly. Had not Nadir Shah laid waste half of Delhi and slaughtered thousands of its inhabitants because they had killed in a riot a handful of his Afghan soldiers?

But the British, with uncertain leadership and low morale, did not see themselves as conquerors, but merely as allies of the Afghan state. Shah Shuja was responsible for restoring order in his own capital, and indeed tried to do so though without success. Elphinstone ordered Brigadier Shelton to take a column into the city, then countermanded him, then ordered him in again, then countermanded him a second time. Finally MacNaghten sent him to Shah Shuja's fortress-palace, the Bala Hissar, where Shah Shuja demanded to know by whose authority he and his troops had come. Thus Burnes and his comrades went unavenged.

Elphinstone had a strong force under command, seven regiments of horse and foot, with guns and sappers, English and Indian. He could either have tried to march to India or confiscated enough supplies to stay where he was. In fact he did neither. He remained in his cantonments and sent orders to Sale recalling him to Kabul, and to Nott ordering him to send up a brigade from Kandahar. Sale was still at Gandamak when the orders reached him. His wife and daughter were in Kabul, as well as the families of his officers and men. They had every reason to want to go back. But after a council of war Sale and his officers decided that they could not. Their appreciation was that they had neither the strength nor the supplies nor carriage to move back into the hills, with their sick and wounded, and fight their way through the gloomy defiles through which they had just come. As it was, they decided to push on to the summer capital, Jalalabad, three days' march away. Once there, they set about restoring the defences, with a view to holding it, midway between Kabul and Peshawar, as a base for troop movements in either direction.

'Kabul, November 1841'. In the background are the city of Kabul and the Bala Hissar. In the foreground is the crest of Bemaru ridge, with a group of Afghans hauling into position one of the guns with which the British cantonment, lying immediately below them, was bombarded. (After Rattray.)

From Kandahar, General Nott sent a brigade under Colonel McLaren towards Kabul, but the beginning of the Afghan winter blocked the roads with snow. With insufficient supplies, inadequate cold-weather clothing and no way of obtaining either on the line of march, this force returned to Kandahar on 8 December, leaving three companies of the 43rd Bengal Native Infantry as reinforcements for the garrison of Kalat-i-Ghilzai.

But at Kabul the rebel position seemed to grow stronger by the day. Reinforced by those who had massacred the Charikar garrison, and emboldened alike by the news that neither from Kandahar nor Jalalabad was there any sign of assistance to the garrison at Kabul and by the ineffective behaviour of that garrison itself, they pressed ever more closely around the cantonment perimeter.

On 23 November Shelton was sent to take nearly half the garrison to surprise the Afghans on the ridge of Bemaru, from which the British cantonment was being bombarded. The fatal mistake was to send only one gun, despite the standing orders that never less than a pair were to be used on any service. The reason for this regulation became clear when the surprise turned into a pitched battle. The gun, through repeated firing, became too hot for the gunners to 'serve the vent' – which was done by placing the thumb over the touch-hole when ramming. If the vent was not served, the forced draught ignited particles in the bore and caused a premature discharge. As the unsafe gun ceased firing the troops lost heart. The infantry, formed into squares by Shelton at the sight of large numbers of Afghan cavalry, were exposed to long-range fire from the *jezailchis*, who were able to shoot at an easy target while remaining out of range of the British muskets. When a body of Afghan foot soldiers did approach within battle range, the infantry declined to go forward. The cavalry behaved equally badly; only the men of the Bengal Horse Artillery, remaining by their silent gun until cut down by the exultant Afghans, were beyond reproach.

At last the infantry were induced to advance. A leading Afghan chieftain, Abdulla Khan, was mortally wounded, shot in the back by one of his own men bribed by Mohun Lal, the late Alexander Burnes's Indian assistant. The gun was recaptured and the position saved for a time. But large numbers of Afghan reinforcements appeared from Kabul and the surrounding villages, and the troops again gave way. The gun was abandoned. The wounded were left to their deaths and the whole force, horse and foot together, scrambled back into the cantonments.

On 25 November MacNaghten opened negotiations with the dissident Sirdars, who had now been joined by Muhammad Akbar Khan, the Amir's son. The Sirdars demanded that Shah Shuja and his household be handed over, that Sale evacuate Jalalabad and march to Peshawar and that the Kabul garrison surrender all its arms and ammunition and give up the European officers and families as hostages before being allowed to depart to India. These terms were rejected, although the cards which MacNaghten had been dealt by the military commanders left him a poor hand to play. Elphinstone warned that with 700 sick there was now no chance of fighting a way across two miles of fields and ditches to the Bala Hissar, even if there had been sufficient supplies to stand a siege, which he thought there were not. Shelton, who from the first had urged that the only course open was to abandon Kabul and withdraw to India, consistently opposed any other plan. When on 5 December the Afghans blew up the bridge over the Kabul River, which separated the Bala Hissar from the cantonments, the question became purely academic.

On 11 December, MacNaghten and his aides again met the Sirdars. He declared that he would not accept dishonourable terms, and that rather than do so the British would all die in the last ditch. But as all parties knew that now time and weather were both on the Afghan side, his only real choice was not between disgrace or defiance but between surrender or starvation. He therefore produced a treaty, the preamble to which stated that, as the sole purpose of the British in entering Afghanistan had been to promote the happiness of the Afghan people (which was not true), and as it was now clear that their presence was not welcomed by the Afghans (which was true), they had now no wish but to return whence they had come, and to allow Dost Muhammad to return to his own people.

The original plan was for the evacuation to begin on 15 December, but various delays occurred. Insufficient transport animals could be found. Muhammad Akbar Khan had difficulty in persuading the Ghilzai Sirdars to guarantee the safe conduct. The Sirdars were considerably incensed to discover that the resourceful Mohun Lal had put a price on their heads and that two of their number had since died in suspicious circumstances. MacNaghten, who was using Mohun Lal as a go-between in his dealings with the Sirdars, inevitably, though erroneously, was accused by them of being the author of this scheme, which eventually came to nothing when Mohun Lal refused to pay those who claimed the bounty he had offered, on the grounds that the actual heads had not been produced by the claimants.

But MacNaghten certainly still hoped that he could divide his Afghan opponents and so yet restore the situation. All his experience was that, given time, Asiatic princes would in the end place their own personal interests before any national feeling. It therefore came as no surprise to him when on 22 December, the second date set for the British departure, Muhammad Akbar Khan offered another treaty. In return for becoming Wazir, as his uncle had been before him, he would support Shah Shuja's remaining on the throne, arrange for the British to move into the Bala Hissar with enough supplies to last the winter and (as proof of his good-will) would seize Amanulla Khan, one of the Sirdars who had first started the rebellion, and hand him over to the British.

MacNaghten put his signature to these terms and arranged to meet Akbar the next morning. One of his political assistants, Captain Collin Mackenzie, warned him that it was a trap, but the envoy determined to stake all on this last card. But Muhammad Akbar Khan had already marked the pack. He showed MacNaghten's signature to the Ghilzais, and at the 'secret' conference, the chiefs gradually formed a circle around the British party. MacNaghten said something about the need for secrecy. 'It does not matter,' said Akbar with grim humour, 'for they are all in the secret.' MacNaghten was then seized and shot with the very pistol he had previously presented to Muhammad Akbar as a token of esteem. His body was dismembered and dragged about the streets of Kabul, and the mangled remains were then set up at the gates of the main bazaar.

The Sirdars then demanded that the British, whose good faith could no longer be taken for granted in view of MacNaghten's attempt to break the treaty, give up all their artillery and equipment except for six guns, all their treasury and all the married officers and families as previously agreed. Diplomatic control now devolved upon Eldred Pottinger, the senior surviving political officer. At a council of war, held on Boxing Day 1841, he stated plainly that the Afghans could not be trusted to keep their side of any bargain. He saw only two courses open. Fight their way into the Bala Hissar with what stores they could, or abandon the whole camp and break out towards Jalalabad.

But the military commanders would not accept either plan. The army relied upon local purchase and supplies from existing civilian sources in order to maintain itself. In the crisis these had disappeared, as they always tend to. Now there was nothing but to retreat to India, and no reason to fight their way there if an unopposed passage could be obtained by negotiation. The idea of the British garrison of Kabul, with its families and camp followers, fighting its way to India through the Afghan winter can be compared, in modern terms, with the British garrison in Berlin, with its dependents and locally employed civilians, fighting its way to West Germany through the Prussian winter. Elphinstone and Shelton, too, belonged to the generation that had seen the retreat to Corruna and the retreat from Moscow, and knew what could happen to an army making an opposed withdrawal through the winter snows. As long as there was the slightest chance of a peaceful settlement, this was what they preferred.

But the departure was postponed from day to day for one reason after another. The chiefs wanted more money in order to pay their retainers to escort the British through any hostile areas, an unpopular task, especially as there was now heavy snow on the ground and fresh falls daily. They demanded that the European families be handed over to them as hostages. Pottinger opposed this, but volunteers were called for and were offered lavish allowances. No-one was prepared to take the risk. One officer, Captain Anderson of Shah Shuja's Contingent, said he would rather put a pistol to his wife's head and shoot her.

Elphinstone issued and countermanded orders, demoralizing and confusing his men. Finally his commands degenerated into mere suggestions, or invitations to use their own judgement. Florentia, Lady Sale, whose husband, 'Fighting Bob' Sale, had left her at Kabul when he marched to Jalalabad before the outbreak, considered the army might yet, by forced marches, get through the snow and outdo the story of Xenophon and his 10,000 warriors. But all the while the precious stores of fuel, food and forage were going down. The troops were on half rations, the camp-followers on quarter, the transport herd starving.

At last, on January, 1842, no longer able to wait for the promised escort, Elphinstone ordered the army to move the next morning. About 4,500 soldiers, with nine guns, accompanied by 12,000 camp followers, struggled out of the cantonments leaving behind those too sick and badly wounded to march, whom the Sirdars promised to care for. As the troops moved out, Afghan marauders moved in, looting, burning and firing on the rearguard. The camp followers, jostling to get over a bridge to avoid fording the icy Kabul River, panicked and stampeded. Bearers and drivers abandoned their loads and ran. Most of the baggage was lost within a mile of the cantonments.

The first camp, in a freezing bivouac five miles from the starting point, was a nightmare. No areas were allotted, no supplies issued, no attempt made to provide for the rearguard which struggled in after dark. Elphinstone's headquarters, with enough staff officers for two divisions, had already simply ceased to function.

At dawn, it was found that many had died during the night from exposure and many more had suffered frostbite. The column moved on, no orders being issued, no bugle sounded, the troops continually finding the road blocked by refugee camp followers. The cold numbed the minds and limbs of the troops, and Afghan horsemen rode in and out of the column almost unopposed, cutting down stragglers, seizing baggage animals and snatching captives. After another five miles Elphinstone ordered the army to halt and camp.

The next morning was a repeat of the previous one. No orders were given, the road was choked with refugees, stores were left behind and everyone virtually paralysed with cold. But still the troops responded when given leadership. A menacing crowd of Afghans was driven off by local counter-attack. The Afghans fell back and took to long-range fire with their *jezails*. After some hours stationary under fire, during which

'The retreat from Kabul. The Third Day' (7 January 1842). Lithograph by Villain, after Loeillet, of incidents in the Khurd Kabul Pass. The central group depicts Lady Sale, who was wounded in the arm on this day; her son-in-law, Lieutenant Sturt, receiving his fatal wound; and Major-General Elphinstone, recognizable by his general officer's pattern mameluke sword. The incident in the left foreground represents the abduction of Captain and Mrs Anderson's small daughter, Mary. In the background, men of the 44th Foot vainly try to drive back the Ghilzai marauders.

'The Last Stand of the 44th Foot of Jagdalak'. Retreat from Kabul, 13 January 1842.
This late Victorian oil painting by W.B. Wollen was specially commissioned for
the regiment. The figure of Captain Soulter can be seen, with the regimental colour
wrapped under his poshteen.

time the horse artillerymen, fortified with abandoned rum, mounted and
offered to charge the enemy without orders, the column moved on to the
Khurd Kabul Pass. This was lined with enemy sharpshooters. Lady Sale,
galloping through with the irregular cavalry (she and her twenty-year-old
daughter Alexandrina had donned turbans and poshteens like the troopers to avoid attracting attention), was wounded in the arm. Her son-in-law,
Captain Sturt, who had married Alexandrina Sale at Kabul, was mortally
wounded. Captain Anderson's small daughter Mary was carried off in the
confusion, as were the wives and children of some of the 44th Foot.

That night Lady Sale heard that about 500 regulars and 2,500 camp
followers had perished at the pass. She had more immediate anguish too:
'Dr Bryce, Horse Artillery, came and examined Sturt's wound: he dressed
it; but I saw by the expression on his countenance that there was no hope.
He afterwards kindly cut the ball out of my wrist and dressed both my
wounds.' This all was in the freezing cold, the snow falling, with no anaes-
thetic, no antisepsis, no shelter, no warmth, no bedding. The next day she
attended to the funeral of her son-in-law, the only man in the entire retreat
to be given a decent burial.

The third morning began in the same way as those before. Half the force seemed to have frostbite or snow blindness, or be otherwise out of action. Some companies could put less than twenty men in the ranks. At this point Muhammad Akbar Khan sent in a messenger to the British camp to say that he had not yet been able to obtain agreement from the Ghilzais in the passes ahead to let the British through.

The attacks on the British had not been by any men of his, he told Pottinger, but by thieves, or by *Ghazis* over whom he had no powers. He knew there were English ladies and children with the army and it was clearly no place for them to be now. He offered them, and their husbands, honourable protection and safe conduct if they would come to his camp. The message was passed to Elphinstone, who accepted the offer. Muhammad Akbar was as good as his word, and in the days that followed treated his 'guests' with some chivalry, giving up his own and his officers' tents to the Englishwomen, and making available whatever simple luxuries were to be had in a poor country, in time of war, during a bitter winter. One of the English women, the wife of Sergeant Wade, actually deserted her husband during their captivity and went to live with an Afghan official. 'So incorrect a personage' was Lady Sale's description of Mrs Wade, following this conduct. Elphinstone waited a day at Khurd Kabul and then pushed on. At Tangi Tariki pass the Ghilzais were waiting. They blocked the narrow defile at each end, then rained down rocks and *jezail* fire from the cliffs before closing in with their Khyber knives. The sepoys of the rearguard were annihilated. Only Elphinstone and his staff together with 100 cavalrymen, the 44th Foot (down to under half strength) and sixteen horse artillerymen with one gun actually reached Tezin, on 10 January.

Akbar protested his innocence, and said that the Ghilzai tribesmen would not even obey their own chiefs and he had not enough men of his own to coerce them. He invited Elphinstone and Shelton to a conference. Once they had reached his camp he gave them food and shelter, but refused to let them return to their men.

Brigadier Anquetil, the Commandant of Shah Shuja's Contingent, now became the senior ranking officer. After nightfall on 12 January, he led the survivors of the army in an attempt to slip past the Ghilzais in the dark, leaving behind the sick and wounded. Any hope of surprise was destroyed by camp followers still hanging on to the troops. At dawn it became clear that the road was barricaded ahead of them and there was no retreat through the tribesmen massing behind.

Anquetil was killed looking after the rearguard. The infantry made a last stand near Gandamak. Captain Dodgin of the 44th alone killed five Afghans before going down. His men, ammunition pouches empty, fought on with the bayonet before being overwhelmed. Captain Soulter, also of the 44th, wrapped the regimental Colour, thirty-six square feet of embroidered yellow silk, around himself under his coat. Wounded, his life was spared by his captors, who imagined that the wearer of this rich garment was a great chief who might be worth ransom. Captain Nicholl led his European gunners, the élite of the Bengal Army, in one last mounted charge into the midst of their enemy. 'Had all the British fought like the Red Men,' said Akbar Khan, in allusion to the scarlet manes of the horse artillery helmets, 'they would never have been driven from Kabul.'

A few staff officers escaped, but one by one they were overtaken or ambushed. Three were killed within a few miles of Jalalabad. Only one of them, Assistant Surgeon Brydon, Shah Shuja's Contingent, wounded, unarmed, on a dying pony, survived to reach the British garrison at Jalalabad. Thus was fulfilled Muhammad Akbar Khan's promise to his followers, that he would destroy the whole army and leave one man alive to tell the tale.

In Jalalabad safety was not assured. Already there had been skirmishes on the outskirts with local tribesmen, such as the one at Piper's Hill shortly after Sale's arrival in mid-November. Now, hard on the heels of the few sepoy stragglers who made their way in after Brydon, came 6,000 Ghilzais led by Muhammad Akbar Khan, who had abandoned any appearance of neutrality.

At first, rather than try to rush the defence works which Captain George Broadfoot, Madras Engineers, commandant of Shah Shuja's sappers and miners, had organized, the Afghans tried diplomacy. Shah Shuja, in an attempt to retrieve his own position, ordered his former allies to leave Jalalabad and go to Peshawar, which had been part of the agreements the Sirdars had made with MacNaghten and Pottinger. Sale and his senior political officer, Captain G.H. MacGregor, supported by a council of war, and believing themselves without hope of relief agreed, subject to conditions. Broadfoot argued vehemently that his works would withstand any attacks by the Afghans and, supported by Captain Oldfield commanding the cavalry and Captain Backhouse of the artillery, eventually persuaded Sale to abandon the idea of a retreat and of giving more hostages to the Afghans. 'I am surprised,' said Oldfield 'that anyone should suggest such a thing, or regard an Afghan's word as worth anything.'

During the month that these negotiations lasted, Broadfoot laboured on his walls, constructing his defences with all the mathematical precision evolved over a century of scientific European siegecraft. On 19 February an earthquake flattened most of them. Lady Sale and the others in her party were about forty miles away at Badiabad, and saw the tremor approaching, throwing up dust like an exploding mine, as she knowledgeably described it. Amazingly, none of the hostages were hurt, even Lady MacNaghten's pet cat being dug out of her ruined quarters unscathed. Back at Jalalabad, Broadfoot drove on his working parties with demonic energy, making good the damage so well that when, at the end of the

'The remnants of an Army'. This famous late Victorian oil painting by Elizabeth, Lady Butler, depicts the arrival at Jalalabad of Dr William Brydon, Shah Shuja's Medical Service. Popularly known as 'The last survivor from Kabul', this painting with its fine draughtsmanship and vivid detail has done much to fix in British folk-memory the magnitude of the disaster that befell Elphinstone's army.

month, Muhammad Akbar Khan began a close siege, everything was in readiness for his reception.

On 7 April, their provisions nearly exhausted and believing that the relieving force had been unable to force the Khyber, the men of Jalalabad, the 'illustrious garrison' as Lord Ellenborough called them, sallied forth in one last desperate effort, 1,500 against 6,000. Colonel Dennie, leader of the forlorn hope at Ghazni, fell at the head of the 13th Light Infantry. Broadfoot's sappers and miners, their commandant lying badly wounded inside his defences, formed a square as Akbar's horsemen charged down on them. But at last the gunners and infantry were able to use their weapons and techniques in the open conditions for which they were designed. Their rapid fire overwhelmed that of the Afghans. Their steady, well-drilled manoeuvres unnerved their individualist opponents. The whole of the Afghan camp was taken. Four of the guns lost by Elphinstone's army were regained. Five hundred sheep were found and distributed among the troops for food, though the 35th Bengal Infantry insisted that their share went to the light infantrymen, saying that the white soldiers needed the meat diet more than they themselves did. Akbar Khan's army was dispersed and the Sirdar himself moved up into the surrounding hills, taking the British hostages with him. Showing his customary chivalry, he insisted that Ladies MacNaghten and Sale travel in his own equipage, though he had himself been wounded earlier in the fighting.

Following the destruction of the Kabul garrison, there was a general rising against all the red-coat posts throughout Afghanistan. Ghazni, garrisoned by the 27th Bengal Native Infantry, endured a siege until 6 March, 1842, when they accepted an offer to be allowed to march out with the honours of war in return for surrendering the place. But as soon as they left the citadel they were attacked by *Ghazis*. Most of the sepoys were massacred and their British officers were made prisoners with a view to ransom.

Kalat-i-Ghilzai, containing the 3rd Shah Shuja's Infantry, forty European artillery and the 43rd Bengal Native Infantry, was harassed throughout the winter, and suffered greatly from cold and privation as its supplies were intercepted. With the advent of spring, the Ghilzais mounted a close siege, but after several weeks were driven off by a determined sortie on 21 May, 1842. Seven days later they were at last relieved by a strong column from Kandahar.

Kandahar itself saw hard fighting. Nott pursued an aggressive defence, moving out in strength to attack any insurgent forces that approached. On to March, 1842, this policy nearly proved disastrous. As he marched farther and farther away from Kandahar, searching for the elusive Durrani main force, it was actually hammering on the city gates, in an attack that went on far into the night. One gate was set on fire and gave way, but a hastily built obstacle inside it, covered by well-sited artillery, held back the assailants. The defenders, men of the 2nd Bengal Native Infantry, managed to hold out until, on the approach of Nott's returning troops, the Durranis abandoned the attack. But not until 10 May, 1842, were reinforcements, ordered up from Sind through the Bolan Pass, able to reach the city and restore British supremacy in southern Afghanistan. In these encounters around Kandahar one of Shah Shuja's sons, Saftar Jang, led the insurgents; the eldest, Timur, remained in alliance with the British.

V

Retribution, Rescue and Recall
The British withdrawal 1842

The departure of the British from Kabul at the beginning of 1842 left Shah
Shuja's regime with an uncertain future. But it was by no means inevitable that it must collapse. He was, after all, still the legitimate ruler not a
usurper, and that counted for something among the people of his country.
An astute ruler could actually benefit from the withdrawal of the foreign
soldiers whose presence had been one of the most important reasons for
his unpopularity.

Indeed, some of the British at Kabul felt that Shah Shuja, if he had not
actually instigated a nationalist revolt as a way of getting rid of them, had
at least joined in it, to ensure his own survival once the nature and extent
of the rising became clear. Even so, this would have been little different
from the policy of the British themselves, who, so far from refusing to have
any truck with men in arms against their king, actually negotiated treaties
with them, even after these same men had set up Nawab Zaman Khan
Barakzai, the son of an elder brother of Amir Dost Muhammad, as a rival
king while Shah Shuja still reigned.

Shah Shuja remained secure inside the walls of the Bala Hissar. From
there, as a way of proving his support for the national cause, he sent messages to Jalalabad ordering Sale to quit Afghanistan in accordance with
the terms of the treaties made at Kabul. To keep what loyalty he could,
he agreed, at the beginning of April, to go out and review reinforcements
being sent to join the fight against the unbelievers at Jalalabad. Nawab
Zaman Khan guaranteed Shah Shuja's safe conduct, but as Shah Shuja
approached the review he was assassinated by Suraj-ul-Daulat, Nawab
Zaman Khan's son. The outraged father forbade the assassin ever again to
enter his presence, but this did nothing to settle the question of the succession to the throne of Kabul.

Fighting between the various chiefs at Kabul broke out at the end
of April and continued during the following weeks. Eventually, in the

middle of June, a compromise was reached and Fateh Jang, one of Shah Shuja's younger sons, was recognized as Shah, with Akbar Khan as Wazir.

When the new Governor-General, Lord Ellenborough, arrived in India at the end of February 1842, intent on withdrawing the British garrisons from Afghanistan, he discovered that Muhammad Akbar Khan and his confederates were in the process of doing this for him. Kabul had fallen, Ghazni was falling, Kalat-i-Ghilzai, Kandahar and Jalalabad were all under attack. Troops which had tried to get up the Khyber Pass to help Sale had been driven back at the end of January by the hill tribes. Now, at Peshawar, they waited for the arrival of a new commander, the men defeated and demoralized, some units on the verge of mutiny and 1,800 patients in hospital from frostbite, exposure, fevers and wounds.

The new commander was Major-General George Pollock, of the East India Company's Bengal Artillery. An experienced officer, his first task after he arrived on 5 February, 1842, was to restore the shattered morale of his troops. Tactful, firm and courteous, he gradually built up their stamina and self-confidence. He ruthlessly pruned the number of camp followers. He reduced his own personal baggage to as much as could be carried on one camel and two mules, and made the other officers follow his example.

Ellenborough had come out to India with the firm intention of withdrawing from Afghanistan. He still maintained that policy, but made it subject to the re-establishment of British military prestige. The British had to maintain their record of always winning the last battle. Therefore he planned that Pollock should march to relieve Jalalabad, England should march to relieve Kandahar and the Afghans should be brought to battle in a decisive encounter. The troops, having gained their victory and shown the world that they were not being driven out by the Afghans, would then return to India. The widespread nature of the revolt, and the depth of religious and national feeling against them, had convinced the British, even before his death, that the whole policy of trying to exert influence over Afghanistan by means of the alliance with Shah Shuja was now an irretrievable failure.

The winter passed, the snows melted and as the temperature rose so did the spirits of the English soldiers and Indian sepoys at Peshawar. The final reinforcements rode in at the end of March and Pollock made the first move of his long-awaited offensive. He now had under command a strong force consisting of the 3rd Light Dragoons, the 1st and 10th Bengal Light Cavalry and a squadron of the 3rd Bengal Irregular Cavalry; the 9th Foot, six battalions of Bengal Native Infantry and a corps of Afghan *Jezailchis*. In support he had a troop of horse artillery, two batteries of 9-pdr field guns, a pair of 18-pdr siege guns, and a company of the Bengal sappers and miners.

They found the entrance to the Khyber Pass blocked by a stone redoubt or sangar. They halted. Their Sikh allies made a diversion to draw off some of the tribal forces and the diplomats opened negotiations to obtain an unopposed passage up the pass. The negotiations failed.

'The Return through the Khyber Pass 5 April 1842'. Lithograph by Villain
after Loeillet. Here the French artist's impression draws heavily on the Algerian
campaigns. The East India Company's sepoys looked more like French Zouaves,

complete with vivandiere *giving water to a fallen soldier. In India, men known as* bhistis *or* pakhalis *were employed as water carriers in battle or on the line of march.*

Before dawn on April Pollock attacked, taking the Pathans by surprise. The surprise was not merely one of timing but of tactics, and Pollock entered Pathan folklore as the first plains-dwelling general to use their own technique of seizing the high ground or 'crowning the heights'. Flanking columns clambered up the hills on either side of the road, each party with its buglers warned to sound the 'advance' or 'halt' if it got too far ahead or behind its neighbours. Now it was the turn of the Pathans to be shot down by fire from above. After desperate fighting they were driven from crag to crag, and eventually the Khyber Pass was forced with a loss of 14 killed, 104 wounded, 17 missing.

Pollock pushed on to Jalalabad, which he reached on 16 April. There the garrison's successful sortie, made when they thought he had actually been beaten in the pass, had already defeated Akbar Khan, and the relieving column was played in to the strains of 'Oh but ye've been long in coming', selected with that sense of appropriateness for the occasion which military bandmasters love to demonstrate at the slightest opportunity.

Ellenborough was still anxious to cut British losses and withdraw from Afghanistan at the earliest opportunity. On 19 April, as yet unaware that Pollock had joined forces with Sale at Jalalabad three days previously, he instructed the Commander-in-Chief India, General Sir Jasper Nicolls, to order Nott to abandon Kandahar and fall back first to Quetta at the top of the Bolan Pass and then all the way back to Sukkur on the Indus. Sale and Pollock, he said, should also draw back to a position within easy reach of India. The position he had in mind was Peshawar, where the troops would still be separated from British India by the notionally allied, but decreasingly reliable, Sikh kingdom of Lahore. When he did hear of Sale's victory at Jalalabad, he expressed the view, in a letter to Sir Robert Peel, the Prime Minister, that this success had re-established the reputation of British arms and that therefore there was now nothing to prevent the withdrawal which he had ordered.

At Jalalabad, Pollock played for time. Reinforced by the arrival of the 31st Foot and the 6th Bengal Infantry, he now had at his disposal a strong cavalry brigade and four brigades of infantry supported by horse, field, mountain and siege artillery. Replying to Ellenborough's instructions, he wrote on 13 May, 1842, that a withdrawal at that time, with the hostages surrendered by the Kabul garrison still in Afghan hands, would be fatal to the maintenance of British prestige and that 'our character as a powerful nation would be entirely lost in this part of the world'. A few marches forward from Kabul would, he said, bring his troops to a more favourable climate and at the same time put pressure on Muhammad Akbar Khan and the other chiefs fighting among themselves at Kabul. But until he had sufficient camels to re-mobilize Sale's brigade, there was no question of a move in any direction. While he waited, he sent out columns to lay waste the surrounding villages, whose men had joined in the attacks on Sale.

At Kandahar, Nott was equally slow to comply with instructions to retreat. He had never had much faith in the way the war had been waged. He had described the late Shah Shuja as 'most certainly as great a scoundrel as ever lived'. He had refused to serve under Major-General Sir Thomas Willshire in the campaign against Mehrab Khan of Kalat over the question of their relative seniority. He certainly had no confidence in the diplomats, whom he considered were men selected by intrigue and patronage. 'The conduct of the one thousand and one politicals has ruined our cause,' he had written privately to his family as early as September 1840 '... and unless several regiments be quickly sent, not a man will be left to note the fall of his comrades.' He now said plainly that he saw no chance of being able to evacuate the various remaining garrisons in southern Afghanistan until October. The temperature was already beginning to soar, the necessary baggage camels had not yet reached him from Quetta and there were still large numbers of Durranis in the field against him.

Ellenborough had to accept this prevarication, though his main aim still was to bring the troops back. On 17 May, 1842, writing to Sir Henry Hardinge, the British Commander-in-Chief in London, he referred to the enormous cost of maintaining the troops in Afghanistan and to the continuing danger he considered they were in, separated from British India by the mountains and by the intervening independent territories of Sind and the Punjab. He complained to the Duke of Wellington that he was under great pressure to order the armies to retake Ghazni and Kabul, even though there were neither the supplies or carriage available, and referred to 'irrational schemes of extending our dominions to the westward'.

But the Duke of Wellington, himself an old sepoy general, although opposed to keeping the army too far from its supplies, was among those exerting pressure for some form of vigorous action against the Afghans. 'It is impossible to impress upon you too strongly the Notion of the importance of the Restoration of Reputation in the East,' he had written to the Governor-General on 31 March. He described the loss of the Kabul garrison as the result either of the grossest treachery or of the most inconceivable imbecility and very likely a mixture of both as, he said, they often went together. The defeat of British troops, armed with modern artillery, by scarcely more than twice their number of ill-armed irregulars, when in the past the British had generally been able to defeat ten times their number of native tribesmen, was especially deplorable. As for the surrender of hostages, he told Ellenborough in no uncertain terms:

There is not a Moslem heart from Pekin to Constantinople which will not vibrate when reflecting upon the fact that the European ladies and other females attached to the troops at Cabul were made over to the tender mercies of the Moslem chief who had with his own hand murdered Sir William MacNaghten, the representative of the British Government at the Court of the Sovereign of Afghanistan.

Ellenborough felt more and more isolated. In a letter to the Prime Minister dated 7 June, 1842, he complained of the difficulty in bringing back the troops to India. He felt that Nott's success had altogether re-established the reputation for fighting spirit of the British Indian troops, but there was now no chance of evacuating Afghanistan until the cold weather arrived, and the cost would be enormous. As for the two commanders who had successfully evaded complying with the instructions to withdraw, 'Major-Generals Nott and Pollock' he said 'have not a grain of military talent'. Whereas a retirement immediately after the relief of Jalalabad would have enabled the troops to leave Afghanistan with a British victory fresh in everyone's mind, a withdrawal after several months' inaction could not be disguised as anything but a retreat before the face of the enemy.

This was, in essence, Pollock's own view, and he knew that the longer he postponed the retreat to India the greater the chance of Ellenborough allowing him to march on Kabul. At the beginning of July this policy succeeded. Ellenborough ordered that, as Pollock insisted that several more months must elapse before the weather was cool enough for him to return to India, and as he had a large and successful army at his disposal, he should occupy the time in gaining a fresh victory, by advancing to Kabul. At the same time Nott was given permission to march his own army to Kabul, if he thought this a feasible operation with the resources at his disposal. Nott, if he went to Kabul, was then to withdraw to India along with Pollock's men. The orders, and options, sent to Nott were kept secret, even from Sir Jasper Nicolls, the Commander-in-Chief India.

Once Ellenborough had overcome his reluctance to initiate the return to Kabul, he adopted the idea with enthusiasm. The aim of the expedition, he instructed Pollock in a despatch of 23 July, 1842, was to exhibit British strength in the place of the British defeat, to inflict just but not vindictive punishment, to recapture the lost guns and regimental colours, to rescue the prisoners and to give every proof of British power consistent with British humanity and the usages of war. Nevertheless, he added, 'after so exhibiting that power you are, without allowing yourself to be diverted there from by any object, to obey the positive orders of your government to withdraw from Afghanistan'.

Nott himself was in no doubt of his ability to make the rendezvous. At the end of May, during the absence of one of his brigades, sent to bring in the defenders of Kalat-i-Ghilzai, he had routed with less than 2,000 of his own troops an attack by more than 8,000 Durranis. His losses amounted to one killed and fifty-two wounded. 'How I should like to go to Caubul!' he then wrote. 'It is wonderful that the people in Hindustan should be so panic-struck.' Referring especially to the 42nd and 43rd Bengal Infantry,

'The British encampment outside Kabul, late September 1842'. In the background are the city of Kabul and the hill surmounted by the fortress of the Bala Hissar. The lines shown here are those of Major-General Nott's army from Kandahar. (Lithograph by R. Carrick, after Rattray.)

he remarked, 'Our sepoys are noble fellows,' and reckoned that 5,000 sepoys would easily defeat five times that number of Afghans.

Three thousand camels arrived from Quetta, collected in response to Ellenborough's earlier instructions to retire. Nott now had the means of either advancing or retiring. He did both. Two squadrons of the 1st Shah Shuja's Cavalry, three regiments of Shah Shuja's infantry, and all the Bombay troops except the 3rd Light Cavalry, the 1st troop of Horse Artillery and the 3rd Company of 1st Foot Artillery, marched back through Baluchistan to Sind. The rest marched for Kabul on 10 August, 1842. In addition to the Bombay contingent mentioned above, this force included another troop of horse artillery from the Bengal army with two companies of Bengal foot artillery, manning a field battery of 9-pdrs and the 18-pdr siege train, originally brought up by Sir John Keane with the Army of the Indus three years previously. There were eight squadrons of irregular horse, two battalions of British infantry, five of Bengal infantry and one of Shah Shuja's Contingent.

He was to need every man of these units before his march was finished. At first he was unopposed, though Durrani bands hung upon his flanks in case he left an opportunity for a sudden attack. On 28 August Nott's cavalry rode out to meet a body of Afghan horse. Badly handled, the Bombay light horse lost two officers killed and three wounded before they, with their irregular comrades, galloped back to the protection of the infantry, having suffered seventy casualties in the mêlée. Encouraged by this, the Ghilzai Sirdar Shams al-Din, commanding at Ghazni, assembled a force of some 10,000 men and met Nott at Karabagh on 30 August. Nott attacked with vigour. The Afghans maintained a steady *jezail* and artillery fire, but were outmanoeuvred by Nott's trained soldiers and, unable to stand against the crashing volleys of the running, cheering infantrymen, eventually drew off, leaving behind their guns and camp equipment.

Nott reached the outskirts of Ghazni on 4 September. There he drove the Afghans from the surrounding heights and his artillery engaged and silenced the great 48-pdr Ghazni gun called 'Zabbar Jang'. Before the siege guns could be turned against the walls, Shams al-Din and his army abandoned the city and fled during the night of September. Three hundred and twenty-seven men of the 27th Bengal Native Infantry, taken prisoner when Ghazni fell to the Afghans, were found and released from captivity.

Before leaving the city, Nott's engineers blew up the citadel and collapsed the city walls. Nine centuries before, the Sultan Mahmud, Mahmud the Iconoclast, Mahmud of Ghazni, had carried away the gates of the sacred Hindu temple of Somnath in Kathiawar and had brought them home to Ghazni, where they were installed as the gates of his own tomb. This had been a constant reminder to Hindus during the following centuries of their national and spiritual humiliation at the hands of their Muslim conquerors, and in 1833 Ranjit Singh, the chief of the last Indian kingdom to push back the Muslims, had tried, albeit without success, to make the restitution of these gates a condition of his support for Shah Shuja. Now, nine years later, Ellenborough ordered their removal. The gates of Mahmud of Ghazni's tomb were dismantled, secured to an 18-pdr gun carriage and led away with the British *en route* to Kabul. After three more brushes with ineffectual Ghilzai opposition, Nott reached Kabul on 17 September, finding, to his disappointment, that Pollock had beaten him there by two days.

Pollock had left Jalalabad on 20 August and, using his tactic of crowning the heights on either side whenever his advance was opposed, pushed on steadily. On 24 August he drove the Afghans out of Mamu Khel, for the loss of seven killed and forty-five wounded. At Jagdalak on 8 September he lost six killed and fifty-eight wounded, mostly from long-range *jezail* fire, and came upon the site of the 44th's last stand. On 12 September he reached the pass of Tezin, where Muhammad Akbar Khan awaited him with 16,000 men.

During the evening and the night there were several daring raids against the British camp, which, though driven off, boosted Afghan enthusiasm for the coming battle. Early on the 13th, Pollock resumed his advance and entered the pass. Afghan horsemen surged down upon the baggage train bringing up the rear, which was still in the open country. Pollock had anticipated this and the Afghans found waiting for them a strong rearguard – the 3rd Light Dragoons, the 1st Bengal Light Cavalry and the 3rd Bengal Irregular Cavalry. The well-drilled cavalrymen, at last catching their opponents on favourable ground, succeeded in pressing home a charge, killing large numbers of the Afghans, scattering the rest and capturing one of their standards.

While the blue-coated cavalry were winning this fight in the open, the red-coated infantry inside the pass had a more difficult battle. At one point the vanguard advanced ahead of the flanking troops, which, struggling along the heights, had necessarily a slower rate of progress than the main body going along the road below. As infantry from the main column deployed and began to climb up towards their enemy, the *Ghazis* threw away the advantage of height and range and rushed down to meet them, as, the previous winter, they had rushed down on the frozen and broken remnants of the Kabul garrison. But this time the troops were well fed, well led, well organized and, more important than all, had seen their dead of the last winter's massacre. Bitter fighting took place all over the hillsides, bayonet against Khyber knife, and at last the *Ghazis*, their own religious fervour matched by the martial spirit of English and Indian soldiers alike, were driven back. The Afghans made a final rally on the peak of Haft Kotal, but were dislodged and mercilessly pursued by the Gurkhas of Shah Shuja's sappers and miners under their valiant commandant, Captain Broadfoot, the engineer whose works had so successfully protected Jalalabad. The Afghans lost over 1,000 dead, and all three of the guns they had committed to the battle. The British lost thirty-two killed (among them the gallant Haidar Ali, Commandant of the Afghan *Jezailchis* in the British service) and 130 wounded.

This was Muhammad Akbar Khan's last serious effort to stop the British advance. He made a number of harassing attacks on Pollock's flanks and rear, on 9, 10 and 11 September, causing losses of six killed and fifty-nine wounded, but otherwise drew away to the north. The British were now marching over the killing grounds of the Khurd Kabul Pass, growing more and more enraged as they passed the bodies of those killed in the retreat from Kabul, many still recognizable as soldiers from the rags of the various regimental uniforms which the skeletal remains still wore. 'The bodies,' wrote Backhouse of the mountain artillery (another veteran of Sale's brigade) 'lay in heaps of fifties and hundreds, our gun wheels crushing the bones of our late comrades at every yard for four or five miles.'

A few marches from Kabul Pollock was joined by Fateh Jang, the Durrani prince to whom Muhammad Akbar Khan was Wazir. Disguising himself in ragged clothes, Fateh Jang slipped past the Wazir's guards and rode alone to the safety of the British camp. Pollock reached Kabul on 15

September and established his camp on the site of the race-course laid out by the British garrison in happier days. On the 16th the British re-entered the Bala Hissar and hoisted their colours on the ramparts.

With Kabul re-occupied, Muhammad Akbar's army defeated and British military reputation restored, there remained only one task to complete. This was the rescue of the European hostages and prisoners of war from Kabul and the other garrisons that had fallen. The hostages had at first been kept in overcrowded and uncomfortable accommodation, male and female together, suffering from fleas, which they called 'light cavalry', and lice, which they called 'the infantry'. But they were allowed to make contact with Jalalabad before it came under siege, and Lady Sale's husband sent up various boxes of clothes and useful things. Captain Colin Mackenzie, one of the diplomats who had been taken prisoner at the time of MacNaghten's murder, tried all his diplomacy on Lady Sale to try and persuade her to lend some of the needles her husband had sent her to the other ladies, who had none, but retired without a single needle. A younger lady, Mrs Mainwairing, was more generous when her husband sent up her boxes from Jalalabad, and shared the contents with the other wives without hesitation, much to their relief.

In the middle of April they were made to march for Kabul, leaving most of their possessions behind. Lady Sale hoped that the Afghans might try using some of her bottles of medicine, as one contained Caustic soda and another nitric acid. On 24 April General Elphinstone died, broken in body and spirit by the destruction of his army. His body was sent to Jalalabad for burial on the chivalrous orders of Muhammad Akbar. On 10 May Captain Anderson's little daughter Mary was restored to her parents. After she had been carried off in the Khurd Kabul Pass she was taken to Kabul, where Lieutenant John Connolly, one of the hostages left with Shah Zaman Shah, bought her in the bazaar for Rs 4,000 (after some haggling). She was thereafter looked after with Zaman Shah's own family. At the end of that month the captives were installed at Kabul and were able to borrow money from local bankers for clothes and necessities. Their mails passed freely to and from India, and Lady Sale's letters were being read and widely published in London while she was still in captivity in Afghanistan. In Kabul they found thirty-five European rank and file, left behind sick by Elphinstone when his column had marched out. One child, the two-year-old Seymour Stoker, son of a soldier of the 13th Foot, Lady Sale's regiment, died after being placed in the care of, but neglected by, that incorrect personage Mrs Wade. Other children were born, including in July two little girls, one to Mrs Trevor (her eighth), one to Mrs Sturt (her first). Sadly, both mothers had been widowed during the fighting of the previous January.

As Pollock and Nott approached, the captives were moved from the comfortable quarters they had been given at Kabul to the harsher

'The approach to Jagdalak 8 September 1842'. General Pollock and his army near the site of the last stand of the 44th Foot the previous winter. In the distance Muhammad Akbar Khan gathers his forces to oppose the returning British. (Lithograph by Hulme, after Rattray.)

conditions of Bamiyan. They adopted Afghan costume, to avoid attracting attention from fanatics. Muhammad Akbar Khan, despite his reverses in the field, remained courteous, and protected them against suggestions from some of his followers that the English might fetch a good price if taken to the slave markets of Bokhara and sold there.

At Bamiyan, while Muhammad Akbar was engaged in battle with Pollock at Tezin, Eldred Pottinger (the senior British political officer) conversed with Salah Muhammad, who was the commander of their guards. Salah Muhammad had previously been a subahdar in Shah Shuja's infantry before joining the Barakzai party. Now he was willing to turn his coat again, as the British looked like winning. Moreover, Mohun Lal, the ever resourceful Indian political assistant, had sent him a message that General Pollock was prepared to pay him Rs 20,000 cash down and a pension of Rs 12,000 annually for the restoration of the prisoners.

Pottinger at once took advantage of this and opened negotiations with local chieftains, securing their friendship with promises of lavish grants in return for their support. But Salah Muhammad feared that Akbar Khan might hear of this and try to recapture the prisoners. He smuggled in a few muskets and some ammunition to the prisoners, on a camel, and asked for some of the European NCOs and men to be formed up as an advance guard to make a show. 'Now my lads,' said Captain George Lawrence, 'here's Salah Muhammad Khan has brought arms and ammunition for some of you: who volunteers to take muskets?' But the English soldiers, after nearly a year in prison, behaved disgracefully. None spoke. None moved. Lady Sale offered to take a musket herself; but the men could not be shamed into their duty even by this. 'It is sad,' she wrote, 'to think that the men were so lost to all right feeling.'

The situation was now dangerous for both Salah Muhammad Khan and his prisoners, as a strong force of Afghans under Sultan Jan, Akbar Khan's cousin, was not far away. At two in the morning a horseman arrived with a message from one of Pollock's political officers, Sir Richmond Shakespear (the rescuer of the Russian captives at Khiva), saying he was coming to their rescue with 600 Qizilbash horsemen. Hastily, the British party marched out to meet them. At 3 p.m. Shakespear and his men arrived, to be greeted with a hearty welcome by everyone except Brigadier Shelton, because Shakespear had stopped to acknowledge the ladies' thanks as he passed, instead of reporting immediately to Shelton, the senior British officer.

But the Qizilbashis were still not enough to meet Sultan Jan if he appeared, and so Pollock at Kabul asked Nott to move up to meet the rescued prisoners coming out. Nott declined to move, on the grounds that his men were exhausted and that the government had given him no orders to move north from Kabul to rescue any prisoners. He would only march under protest. Rather than press him, Pollock sent Sale, on his sixtieth birthday, with his own brigade, including his old regiment the 13th Foot. Sultan Jan's men exchanged a few shots with outlying patrols, but on 20 September, 1842, Sale's troops made contact with the former prisoners, who included his own wife, daughter and baby granddaughter. 'It is impossible to express our feelings on Sale's approach,' wrote Lady Sale. 'To my daughter and myself happiness so long delayed as to be almost unexpected was actually painful, and accompanied by a choking sensation which could not obtain the relief of tears.' When the party reached the cheering line of infantry, the men of the 13th pressed forward to welcome, each in his own style, their colonel's wife and daughter, and at last Lady Sale was able, while she tried to thank her soldiers, to enjoy the luxury of a good cry. Backhouse's mountain guns fired a salute and two days later they all rejoined Pollock at Kabul. All told, there were liberated some twenty-two British officers, two civilian clerks, thirty-five soldiers, twenty-two children, ten ladies and two soldiers' wives, including the unfaithful and by now notorious Mrs Wade.

Akbar Khan was now out of reach, but his confederate Amanulla Khan was located at Istalif, in Kohistan, and a strong brigade of all arms under Major-General M'Caskill was sent against this chief. Istalif was seized and burnt and Amanulla's force was defeated. M'Caskill also attacked and punished the town of Charikar, where the massacre of Shah Shuja's Gurkha

'The Kabul Hostages'. A group of the British hostages in Afghan hands, 1842. Most of them wore Afghan costume to avoid attracting the attention of fanatics. Apart from the absence of a face veil, the day dress of early Victorian ladies, decently covering them down to their wrists and ankles, was quite within the bounds of Islamic propriety. (After V. Eyre.)

regiment had taken place at the beginning of the rising a year before. Pollock ordered the great Bazaar of Kabul, one of the architectural gems of Central Asia, to be blown up as a mark of retribution, selecting it as the site where MacNaghten's remains had been exposed after his murder. Fateh Jang having declined to resume his throne, he and the old blind Zaman Shah Durrani, and others identified with the British cause, decided to return to India. Another son of Shah Shuja, Shahpur, ascended the throne, though Muhammad Akbar still hoped to do a deal with the British. But Ellenborough had sternly warned Pollock to have nothing to do with Afghan politics and stressed that his mission was now only to withdraw to India.

Thus on 12 October, 1842, the British marched out of Kabul. Nott, bringing up the rear, found himself engaged several times during the withdrawal, in the Haft Kotal Pass, on 14, 15 and 16 October, at Jagdalak on the 18th, and at Gandamak on the 19th. At Jalalabad the army regrouped and then headed down the Khyber for Peshawar. The rearguard was still harassed by the local tribesmen, who decided to speed the departing British on their way. At Ali Masjid several men were killed and more wounded, among them Lieutenant Neville Chamberlain of the Shah's cavalry.

From Peshawar the army marched to Ferozpur, where another large force, styled the Army of Reserve, had assembled. This, commanded by the Commander-in-Chief India, Sir Jasper Nicolls, had been formed to overawe the increasingly restless Sikhs and ensure that the army returning from Kabul would be granted unmolested passage. There Lord Ellenborough was waiting for them, and after a grand review of the combined armies – 40,000 men and 100 guns – he dispersed them to their peacetime stations amid a shower of honours, rewards and general celebrations. Shah Shuja's Contingent was disbanded, except for the 3rd Infantry, the Regiment of Kalat-i-Ghilzai, which was added to the Bengal Line as a mark of esteem.

Ellenborough issued proclamations marking the end of the war. In one to the princes of India, couched in such highflown terms that some of its recipients regarded it at first as a forgery, he referred to the recovery of the gates of the temple of Somnath, for centuries the memorial of India's humiliation by the Afghans, now proof of India's military superiority over the Afghans, and 'the proudest record of your national glory'. Unfortunately the effect of this, which may have offended as many Muslims as it conciliated Hindus, was partly lost when experts pronounced the gates which had been brought back to be modern reproductions and not the original gates at all.

Another proclamation declared that the Government of India had marched into Afghanistan only to expel an unfriendly ruler and restore a friendly and popular one. As that ruler had in practice proved unpopular and was suspected of being unfriendly before he was murdered, the British would withdraw and 'leave it to the Afghans themselves to create a government amidst the anarchy which is the consequence of their crimes'. This was rather hard on the Afghans, who had certainly not invited the British into their country. It could be argued, indeed, that the anarchy was the result not of Afghan crimes but of the British destruction of the Barakzai regime and their failure to stand by the Sadozai dynasty they had restored.

The British, said Ellenborough, would recognize any Afghan 'ruler capable of establishing himself and desirous of maintaining friendly relations. But otherwise, the Government of India would be content with its natural frontier, the Indus and Sutlej. Attacking the policy of the previous ministry, he continued by saying that the enormous expenditure required for the support of a large force in a false position at a distance from its own frontier and its resources would no longer absorb revenues needed for internal improvements within British India.

Clearly, the whole of the Afghan policy had proved a failure. The myth of British invincibility had been broken. The rolling wave of British expansion had for the first time been thrown back. The effect of the invasion had been to make the Afghans anti-British, not anti-Russian and, unsatisfactory though the extent of British influence in Central Asia and Afghanistan might have been before the war, it was even worse after it.

'Florentia, Lady Sale. 1787–1853.' This indomitable matron, the wife of Major-General Sir Robert ('Fighting Bob') Sale, was the senior army wife with the Kabul garrison and became the heroine of the retreat and subsequent captivity. (Painting by V. Eyre.)

It had been, strictly speaking, an unlawful war, in that no official declaration of war was ever made. The Afghans, previously neutral or even well disposed to the English as individuals, had suffered all the disastrous accompaniments of a foreign invasion, occupation and war of liberation. India lost 15,000 officers and soldiers killed, with unknown numbers of camp followers. Some £20 million of Indian revenue was spent with nothing to show for it. Fifty thousand camels were lost, with a corresponding ill effect on the commerce of the surrounding areas.

Even Herat, where in 1842 Yar Muhammad, tired of being the power behind the throne, murdered Kamran Shah and usurped his crown, owed its continued independence as much to Russian as British influence. Early in 1842, as the British grip on Afghanistan weakened, the Shah of Iran turned once more to his old dream of conquering the city, which Yar Muhammad had offered to him previously as part of the policy of playing off the Iranians against the English. But the last thing the Russians wanted was a move which might, after all, persuade the new British Government that its national interest obliged it to remain in Afghanistan to defend Herat. Therefore the Russian Ambassador in Tehran, Count Medem, supported the diplomatic pressure of his British colleague in restraining the Shah.

The Russians persuaded Peel and his foreign secretary, Lord Aberdeen, that they only wanted peace and had no further territorial claims in Central Asia. Britain and Russia jointly mediated in a dispute between Iran and the Ottoman Empire, and the Russian Ambassador in London, Baron Brunnow, made great play with the useful impression this would make on the minds of oriental peoples, who, he said, constantly and mistakenly speculated 'on the supposed jealousy of England and Russia'.

Shortly after this, under threat of a renewed expedition from Orenburg, the Khan of Khiva made substantial concessions to the Czar's representatives, and in 1844 the Russians established a base on the Aral Sea, giving them access to the mouth of the Oxus. In the same year the Czar made a visit to England to mark the achievement of an Anglo-Russian *détente*. The room in Buckingham Palace where he stayed is still known as the 1844 Room.

In India, on the other hand, British power soon advanced from the rivers to the foot of the mountains. In 1843, seeing that the British were not, after all, planning to evacuate their country, the Amirs of Sind at last took up arms. The intense heat of the Sind summer might have been as vicious as the cold of the Afghan winter. The Sind desert might have proved as disastrous for British troops as the Afghan mountains. The Baluch fighting men were certainly as brave and as skilled at arms as their Afghan opposite numbers. But the Amirs of Sind were not Muhammad Akbar Khan, and above all, the British general, Sir Charles Napier, was not General Elphinstone. Self-confident, vigorous, professional and determined, Napier smashed the Amirs in a lightning campaign which brought the frontiers of British India up to those of the Khan of Kalat by the middle of 1843.

In December 1845, the Lahore government, unable to control its troops, sent them over the frontier to attack British India. A number of bloody battles followed and for a time the issue seemed in doubt. But by the spring of 1846 the British were masters of the Punjab. They did not actually annex the state until 1849, following the conclusion of the Second Sikh War (when the Koh-i-Nur diamond passed to the British crown), but effectively the British Indian Empire had now a common frontier with that of the Amir of Kabul.

That Amir was, once again, Dost Muhammad Barakzai. He had passed up through the Punjab as the British armies from Afghanistan had passed down it. He waited for a time while his son Muhammad Akbar dispossessed the last of the Sadozais, Shahpur, and then, satisfied that his return would be welcomed by a sufficiently powerful group of supporters, resumed his interrupted rule. Muhammad Akbar, who became his Wazir, was, however, not content to return to subordinate rule in the state, and was frequently on bad terms with his father. Akbar died in 1847 and was remembered by his fellow countrymen in song and story as a great paladin, the hero who defeated the Sikhs at Jamrud and wiped out the Kabul garrison sparing only one man to tell the tale.

VI

Masterly Inactivity and the Forward Policy
England, Russia, and Afghanistan 1854–78

The Anglo-Russian *détente* of 1844 was of strictly limited duration. Ten years after Queen Victoria had entertained Czar Nicholas at Buckingham Palace, the soldiers of the two monarchs were fighting one another in the Crimean War.

At Kabul, Dost Muhammad was intrigued to hear that the British were once more prepared to part with ready money to counter a Russian threat. In 1855 he sent his son and heir, Ghulam Haydar, to meet the British Chief Commissioner of the Punjab, John Lawrence, at Jamrud Fort, to ask for military aid in case Russia or Iran attacked Herat. Lawrence was not empowered to go so far, and was, indeed (as he remained), averse to any undertakings in Afghanistan. Instead, the Amir was sent a substantial cash grant to use for defence purposes, and the two sides exchanged assurances of perpetual peace and friendship.

The fall of Sebastopol in September 1855 was virtually the end of major operations in the Crimea, and peace was signed in Paris the following March. But meanwhile, with Russian encouragement, the Iranians had renewed their claims against Herat. The Russian aim of embroiling England in a war with Iran was achieved, but too late to influence the outcome of the Crimean War. It was not until December 1856, after Herat had fallen to the Iranians, that the Anglo-Iranian war actually began. An army from Bombay, commanded by James Outram (by this time a General), defeated the Shah's forces in the Persian Gulf, and in April 1857 the Iranians agreed to withdraw from Herat.

Paradoxically, the effect of this war, intended by the Russians to weaken the British position in the north-west of India, was actually to strengthen it. The Khan of Kalat was given British arms and money to repel Iranian movements against his western borders, in Makran, and accepted a British Agent at his court. Similarly, the Amir of Afghanistan agreed to the British keeping a Vakil, or Indian Envoy, at his court to maintain a channel of communication between the two governments. Thus, in this unexpected fashion, was established the friendship which the British might have enjoyed twenty years previously, had they not then preferred that of Maharaja Ranjit Singh.

During the Indian Mutiny of 1857, even at the very time when Lawrence was proposing to his superiors that they abandon Peshawar, which he always regarded as an intrusive Afghan element in his otherwise Sikh-dominated province, Dost Muhammad remained neutral. His reward was to be allowed to make himself master first of Kandahar and then of Herat, which he took by storm in May 1863. There, at the end of the following month, he died, leaving twelve of his sixteen sons to fight for the succession. His death, after a reign of thirty-seven years, could hardly have been unanticipated, but it was still a bad time for the British to lose a friend, for the continued expansion of Russia across the steppes of Central Asia had brought the Czar's troops ever closer to Afghanistan.

Prince Gorchakov, the Russian Foreign Minister, issued a memorandum on 21 November, 1864, in which he justified this expansion. The position of Russia in Central Asia, he said, was that of all civilized states in contact with half-savage wandering tribes. To repress the pillaging propensities of tribes within the frontier, these had to be reduced to submission. But these tame tribes then became exposed to attacks by wild ones beyond the frontier. The government had to defend the former and punish the latter. When the soldiers withdrew at the conclusion of an expedition it was regarded as a sign of weakness, and soon the operations had to be repeated.

With some justification, Gorchakov compared the Russian problems in Central Asia with those then being faced by the United States Government in the Western Plains, the French in Algeria, the Dutch in the East Indies and the British on the North West Frontier of India. Nevertheless, he continued, the Czar desired no further conquests or annexation and had decided to restrict 'the extent of the countries subject to his sceptre within reasonable limits'. The Russians, he said, sought only to prove to their Central Asian neighbours that although aggression would be punished their independence would be respected, and that peaceful and commercial relations would be far more profitable than disorder, caravan raiding, pillage and reprisals.

Despite these high-sounding phrases, the forward movement continued. Tashkent was captured and annexed by the Russians in 1865. At the end of 1865 war broke out with the ruler of Bokhara, who had imprisoned a Russian diplomatic mission, just as Stoddart and Connolly had been imprisoned twenty-one years before. But the Russian army was near enough to help the Russian diplomats. Samarkand was seized and annexed in 1868. In 1869 Bokhara accepted Russian suzerainty, and Russian influence had reached the Upper Oxus.

The prestige value of the conquest of these ancient, though decaying, cities had an immense effect in India. Two schools of thought grew up on the British side about how to counter this apparently unstoppable advance, one school advocating the 'Forward' policy, the other urging 'Masterly Inactivity'. Each school had its extremists and its moderates, its doves and its hawks. Of the Forward school, the extremists wanted to advance to the Hindu Kush, or even the Oxus itself; the moderates desired the most strategically advantageous frontier that could be had by the least possible advance. The 'Inactivity' extremists wanted no further movement under any circumstances, unless it were a retreat to the Indus. Their moderates, on the other hand, though prepared to contemplate some advance, demanded proof beforehand that the Russians constituted any real threat.

The most influential of the 'Inactive' school was Sir John Lawrence, who became Governor-General of India in 1864 and who readily complied with instructions from the Liberal Secretary of State for India, Lord Halifax, to remain strictly neutral in the struggle for succession to Dost Muhammad's throne. Lawrence's view was that the British could best defend India by winning over the hearts and minds of its chiefs and people, and by spending money on internal improvements rather than on military adventures on the frontier. Then, if the Russians did attempt an attack, the British could meet them with a contented population at their back. The farther the Russians had to march, he said, the weaker they would be when they arrived. Why go forward to meet them in the midst of a probably hostile country?

Dost Muhammad was succeeded by his third son Sher Ali. In 1866 he was driven out by his brother Afzal Khan, but by 1868 had regained his throne at Kabul. Lawrence, about to leave India, renewed the recognition formerly given to Sher Ali as *de facto* ruler and made him a gift of money and arms as a goodwill gesture.

In 1869 Sher Ali came to India to visit Lawrence's successor, Lord Mayo, at Ambala. Mayo had been appointed by the short-lived Conservative government of 1868, but before he reached India this government was defeated at the polls and replaced by a Liberal ministry with William Gladstone as Prime Minister and the Duke of Argyll as Secretary of State for India.

Argyll's policy, as Lawrence had advised, was to settle the Central Asian question by negotiating directly with Russia. By January 1873 an agreement was made with the Russians that a region of neutral territory should be left between the British and Russian empires, and that Afghanistan (meaning all the territory ruled by Amir Sher Ali) lay outside the Russian, and inside the British, sphere of influence.

Mayo's successor, Lord Northbrook, proposed to send a British Mission to the Amir to announce the results of British arbitration between him and the Shah of Iran over their disputed Sistan border, and to report to him the new Anglo-Russian accord. Sher Ali replied, in effect, that he did not want British officers to enter his country, least of all to tell him about Sistan, where the arbitrators had given the best areas to the Shah. Instead he sent his representative, a trusted and experienced minister, Said Nur Muhammad, to meet Northbrook at Simla in July 1873. Northbrook suggested that the Amir, in view of the Anglo-Russian understanding, might now like to spend less on defence, in particular on the large standing army he had raised, and to support which he had introduced conscription, an unpopular measure in any country. Nur Muhammad replied that his master had no faith in Russian promises nor in British assurances of support, for if they would not stand up for him in Sistan against Iran, which was weak, how could they be expected to do so elsewhere against Russia, which was strong. Rather he would rely on his own efforts to defend himself. The Russians, in that very year, had defeated the Khan of Khiva. Khivan refugees who crossed into Afghan territory might easily decide to carry on the war from there, which would give the Russians an excuse to interfere in Afghanistan. His own nephew, Abdur Rahman, the son of Afzal Khan, who had reigned briefly at Kabul during the war of succession, was a pensioner of the Russians at Tashkent. Who was to say that, if it became necessary, the Russians might not use him just as the British had used Shah Shuja-ul-Mulk?

His exasperation towards the British was increased still further by the case of Sirdar Yakub Khan. Yakub was Sher Ali's eldest son, whose generalship had played a significant part in Sher Ali's recovery of his throne. He became estranged from his father after the nomination of the Amir's favourite son Abdulla Jan as heir. After a series of defiances and reconciliations, Yakub was recognized as Governor of Herat, but continued to show signs of dissidence until the beginning of 1874 when he was placed under arrest, after having gone to Kabul on a promise of safe conduct. Northbrook was moved by this act of treachery to intercede in the hope of ameliorating Yakub Khan's treatment, but was admonished by Sher Ali for intervening on behalf of a son whose misdeeds his own father was ashamed to repeat. The Afghan Amir, replying to Northbrook's assurance that he had written as a 'friend and wellwisher', said that 'sincere and intelligent friends do not like, under any circumstances, to put their faithful friends to such shame'.

Meanwhile, in England the wheel of parliamentary fortune once more revolved. The general election of January 1874 turned out Gladstone and the Liberals and restored Disraeli and the Conservatives. The Marquess of Salisbury replaced the Duke of Argyll at the India Office. Along with the rest of the Cabinet he felt that the agreement with the Russians, by which Argyll and his friends had set such great store, was not to be relied upon.

As the British did not know what the Russians were really up to in Central Asia, Salisbury proposed to establish intelligence agents at Herat and Kabul, openly if possible, secretly if not. 'Of course, it would need a large expenditure of Secret Service money,' he told Northbrook 'but it would be well laid out. You may be sure the Russians are not stinting it.'

'Edward Robert Bulwer Lytton, 1st Earl of Lytton, 1831–1891'. Governor-General of India 1876–1880. During his period of office Queen Victoria was declared Empress of India with much pomp and ceremony. But behind the butterfly glamour of Lytton's viceregal court, India, weakened by famine, financial incompetence and military unpreparedness, lacked the means to support the war which he began against Afghanistan.

Northbrook was opposed to the idea of establishing British Missions in Afghanistan, but Salisbury continued to insist that some kind of British diplomatic presence be established. In an official despatch of January 1875 he argued that if the Amir were really a friend of the British, he could have no objection to the idea. Northbrook and his council demurred. Salisbury, in a despatch of November 1875, ordered them to proceed with his instructions. They were to open negotiations with Sher Ali to establish a British Resident at his court, who would advise him on internal and external affairs, and thus discourage him from unpopular oppressive acts at home, or ill-considered aggressive acts abroad.

Rather than implement such measures, Northbrook resigned. His last official letter on the subject denied all Salisbury's arguments. The Amir's rule, if not universally popular, was strong and, with Yakub in custody, unchallenged. The Amir in his foreign policy had hitherto complied with British wishes and he showed no desire to seek the friendship of the Russians. But the thing he dreaded most of all was any possible interference in his internal affairs, such as would be signalled by the arrival of a British Resident. 'We deprecate, as involving serious danger to the peace of Afghanistan and to the interests of the British Empire in India, the execution under present circumstances, of the instructions in your Lordship's Despatch,' said the departing Governor-General.

Disraeli and Salisbury greeted Northbrook's resignation with some relief but had some difficulty finding a suitable successor. Eventually they appointed a career diplomat, Edward Bulwer Lytton, the first Earl Lytton, whose views in foreign affairs seemed to coincide with their own. Brilliant, witty, a gifted writer, but intolerant of opposition and contemptuous of those whose intellect he regarded as inferior to his own, Lytton's own character played an important part in the events which were to follow. He was warned that in introducing the Forward policy he would face a strong rearguard action by all those in India or Whitehall identified with Masterly Inactivity. Salisbury had previously written to Northbrook that 'the iron of 1842 has entered into their soul'. To Lytton he described them as 'men who in their youth have seen the Afghan ghost and have never lost the impression'. (Sir John Lawrence's brother George had been one of the Kabul hostages.)

To assist him in dealing with any entrenched attitudes that he might find among his official advisers from the Indian military establishment, men whom he later described as 'the powers of military darkness', Lytton was given, on his personal staff, an officer of the new school of soldiering, Colonel George Pomeroy Colley. He was a member of the 'Wolseley ring', the group of officers associated with Sir Garnet Wolseley, that very model of a modern major-general. Colley was impressed by the influence on the conduct of war of the rapidly developing technology of his time, and especially of the introduction of the breech-loading rifle. A single British regiment, he declared, armed with breech-loaders, and plentifully supplied with ammunition, should be able to march at will throughout the length and breadth of Afghanistan. To Major-General Ross, commanding the frontier division at Peshawar, he wrote that his views differed from the officers whose experience was of Indian Wars because 'until I came out here I had been living principally with officers fresh from the great breech-loading battles in Europe'. His French and German army friends, he said, had convinced him that without prior artillery bombardment it was utterly impossible to dislodge even the worst troops, if they were armed with breech-loaders and had plenty of ammunition.

Just before Lytton left London for India in February 1876, he was invited to call at the house of Count Shuvalov, the Russian Ambassador. Shuvalov showed him a letter from General Kaufmann, Governor-General of Russian Turkestan, complaining of British unfriendliness. Britain, Kaufmann had written, should join Russia in disarming the Central Asian Khanates and dividing their territories. Thus European civilization would replace Islamic barbarism. The British would be the gainers, for such a plan would weaken the turbulent Muslims of north-west India. If there was any serious trouble in India, the British would have a friendly Christian neighbour at hand ready to come to their assistance. Kaufmann proposed to show his own goodwill by sending a complimentary letter to Calcutta to await Lytton's arrival, routing it via Afghanistan and instructing the Amir to forward it to Peshawar.

Lytton refused to have anything to do with this sort of contact, or to join in any sort of crusade. On the contrary, he promised he would support the Muslim frontier states as portals of the Indian Empire. As for Kaufmann's friendship, why had he recently prepared a column ostentatiously aimed in the direction of India when tension was rising between England and Russia in Europe? And how could he give instructions to the Amir? But Shuvalov's diplomacy was equal to this. He was evasive about the Amir, and said that Kaufmann, as a patriotic soldier, had only done what he thought would be of service to his country. Now that the international tension caused by the current Balkan crisis had lessened, the force had been demobilized. But Lytton had been convinced that the Russians had more influence at Kabul than the advocates of Masterly Inactivity supposed.

Salisbury's new plan was to put a British Agent into Afghanistan under the guise of a special Mission sent to announce formally, to the Amir, that Queen Victoria had assumed the new title Empress of India. The Mission, led by Sir Lewis Pelly, an experienced member of the Bombay Political Service, would go to Kabul and once there would invite the Amir to enter confidential discussions on any subject he might choose. The Mission would also go to Kalat, which would become of increased importance if the Amir proved difficult.

When Lytton arrived in India, he was considerably irritated to find a mission already on its way to Kalat. This was led by an ambitious frontier official from the Punjab, Captain Robert Sandeman, who had gone into Baluchistan the previous year to negotiate with the Marri tribe. On his arrival he had claimed that the country was on the verge of a revolution, and had marched with the rebels to Kalat itself. By July 1876 Sandeman had succeeded in obtaining the agreement of the various contenders to a new arrangement in the country, whereby the Khan would be bound by British advice, and allow appeals by his Sirdars against alleged oppression to go to a British Agent for decision. Lytton was glad to know that British influence had been re-established in Kalat, but felt that, in view of the Amir's suspicious attitude, Sandeman had gone too far. What would be the effect on the Amir when he saw his neighbour the Khan reduced to a political nonentity as the first result of British intervention? More than local questions had to be considered, he told Sandeman, and ordered him to rescind the arrangements allowing British arbitration in internal disputes. 'Potentates such as the Khan of Khalat or the Ameer of Kabul are mere dummies or counters,' Lytton wrote to Sandeman, 'which would be of no importance to us were it not for the costly stakes we put on them in the great game for empire we are now playing with Russia.'

PUNCH, OR THE LONDON CHARIVARI.—November 30, 1878.

"SAVE ME FROM MY FRIENDS!"

"IF AT THIS MOMENT IT HAS BEEN DECIDED TO INVADE THE AMEER'S TERRITORY, WE ARE ACTING IN PURSUANCE OF A POLICY WHICH IN ITS INTENTION HAS BEEN UNIFORMLY *FRIENDLY* TO AFGHANISTAN."—*Times, Nov. 21.*

'The Amir of Afghanistan flanked by the Russian Bear and the British Lion'. Amir Sher Ali's predicament was elsewhere likened to that of an earthen pipkin between two iron pots, or corn ground between the upper and nether millstones.

Under Colley's supervision, Sandeman negotiated a new treaty, re-establishing a British Agent at Kalat, and handing over Quetta, long the goal of the Forward school, to a British garrison.

The final seal was set on the restoration of British control over Kalat by the attendance of the Khan and his suite at the grand Imperial Assemblage at Delhi. There, in the former capital of India, the seat of the Mughal Emperors, and the Afghan Sultans, in the presence of the chiefs, princes and high officials of all India, the Queen of England was declared Empress of India, with much pomp and ceremonial. The Khan's party, finding an unfamiliar substance labelled 'Pears' provided in their tents, translated the word too literally, and so ate the soap.

But while the British cause prospered in Baluchistan, in Afghanistan it made no headway. The Amir acknowledged the Queen's new title, but said that he had no need of a British Mission to notify him of it. If he accepted a mission from the British, he said, he could expect a similar request from the Russians, which he could not then refuse without offending them. Nor could he guarantee the safety of English officers in his kingdom. His own commander-in-chief had just been assassinated in the midst of his army.

With memories of 1842 still strong, there was always a chance of some big-oted, ignorant tribesman from the hills killing an Englishman. If he tried to bring the murderer to book he would be involved in difficulties with the tribe concerned. If he failed, his relations with the English would suffer.

But nothing would alter Lytton's belief that closer ties between Afghanistan and the Government of India were essential as a counter to the Russian threat. In July 1876 he told his council that while no doubt the Afghans would welcome British help if Russia attacked, it was not a Russian attack on Afghanistan he feared but a Russian alliance. Then, in times of Anglo-Russian war, or risk of war, what Afghan, encouraged by Russian aid, would be able to resist the ancestral urge to sweep down on the rich plains of India, to pillage, rape and burn? Regarding Russia, he quoted and endorsed what Palmerston had written in 1853.

> The policy and practice of the Russian Government has always been to push forward its encroachments as fast and as far as the apathy or want of firmness of other Governments would allow it to go, but always to stop and retire when it met with determined resistance, and then to wait for the next favourable opportunity to make another spring on its intended victim. ... If aggressions succeed locally, the St Petersburg Government adopts them as a *fait accompli* which it did not intend but cannot in honour recede from. If the local agents fail they are disavowed and recalled.

In October 1876, Lytton summoned Atta Muhammad, the British Vakil at Kabul, to Simla. There, in a detailed discussion, the Governor-General likened the Amir's position between the Russian and Indian empires to that of an earthen pipkin between two iron pots. But if the Amir would accept the aid he had sought previously from the British, they would make him the strongest ruler that ever sat upon the throne of Kabul. In return for this, he had only to allow English agents and (a new proposal) travel-lers and merchants in his country, and accept special missions at his court from time to time.

Under British pressure the Amir agreed to a conference at Peshawar between his minister, Said Nur Muhammad, and Sir Lewis Pelly, the pro-posed leader of the Special Mission. Prolonged discussions were held between 30 January and 19 February, 1877, punctuated by all the face-saving delays of oriental diplomacy, and by time-consuming references back by despatch rider over the wintry mountains to Kabul. Nur Muhammad fell ill, further holding up the talks. His death at Peshawar on 26 March, 1877, signalled the end of the conference. Brought up in the conventions of European diplomacy, Lytton could not accept that any state wishing to be on even neutral terms with its neighbour would refuse to accept that neigh-bour's ambassadors. He ordered Pelly to declare the proceedings at an end and to dissolve his Mission. Vakil Atta Muhammad was recalled from Kabul, and Lytton decided to 'let the Amir (if I may use a coarse but expressive phrase of Prince Bismarck's) stew for a while in his own gravy'.

But in 1877 there were other events to distract attention. In London Lord Salisbury became Foreign Secretary and was succeeded at the India Office by Lord Cranbrook. In Bulgaria the Turkish authorities continued to oppress their Christian subjects with that degree of severity which had led William Gladstone, the previous year, to return to politics and demand their expulsion 'one and all, bag and baggage' from the province, regardless of the fact that the departure of the Turks might well be followed by the arrival of the Russians. In April 1877 Russia declared war on Turkey over Bulgaria. Turkish resistance collapsed, and with the Russian steamroller moving towards Constantinople the Sultan signed the Treaty of San Stefano, yielding independence to a Greater Bulgaria on terms which made it virtually a Russian satellite.

Disraeli, now Lord Beaconsfield, refused to recognize the treaty. A British fleet was sent to the Bosphorus and the first-line strength of either side, British sailors and Russian soldiers, each lay within reach of Constantinople. The Army Reserve was embodied, not in itself a force which would have given any Russian general a sleepless night, but bringing the Regular Army up to war strength. An army corps, with Sir Garnet Wolseley as Chief-of-Staff was mobilized. Parliament voted increased credits for the defence votes. Patriotic citizens joined their local Volunteer Corps to protect their hearths and homes against the Russian Bear. A new word, Jingoism, was coined, as from every music-hall audiences declared that: 'We don't want to fight, but by Jingo if we do, we've got the men, we've got the ships, we've got the money too.' An unauthorized line, added by critics of this brave attitude, ran: 'We won't go to the front ourselves, we'll send the mild Hindoo,' for Beaconsfield had, in a typically flamboyant gesture, played an oriental card, and in April 1878 sent a division of Indian troops to Malta as evidence of England's might in the East.

Unfortunately, the Russians trumped the card with a Central Asian ace. General Kaufmann mobilized three columns, totalling 15,000 men. Starting separately from Tashkent, from Petro-Alexandrovsk and Ferghana, they were to head for the Upper Oxus and unite there. Ahead of them he sent a mission to the Amir of Afghanistan. The columns made slow and painful progress and were still far from their destination when they were stopped because of fresh news from Europe. There the German Chancellor, Bismarck, had declared himself the honest broker, and summoned the great powers to the Congress of Berlin, where all the outstanding disputes between the various European nations were to be resolved. Beaconsfield and Salisbury attended, and returned declaring that they had secured 'peace with honour'. The Russians, on 13 July, signed the Treaty of Berlin in agreement with the British, and a new spirit of *détente* was in the air.

'Amir Sher Ali dictating his reply to the British Viceroy, November 1878'. The court of Kabul as imagined by the British public. The Amir dictates his defiant answer to the Government of India's ultimatum prompted by a Russian Colonel. Behind him are his ministers and generals, while the shrouded figure in the doorway asserts the presence of petticoat influence.

The diplomatic mission, led by General Stolietov, with six officers and an escort of twenty-two Cossacks, had left Tashkent at the end of May. Brushing aside a message sent to him by Sher Ali as he passed through Bokhara, that his visit would be premature, Stolietov entered Afghan territory, finally reaching Kabul on 22 July, 1878. No-one knew there that the Treaty of Berlin had been signed nine days previously. Stolietov did know, from couriers sent racing after him, that the Congress of Berlin was being arranged and that the crisis might blow over, but this he did not pass on to his reluctant hosts. All that Sher Ali knew was that three clouds of dust, rumoured to have 80,000 Russians inside them, were moving in the direction of his country and that it would be as well, as he had alienated the British, to be polite to its advance party.

It is not clear precisely what Stolietov's instructions were. He handed over letters of friendship from his own superiors to the Amir and offered vague assurances of support and co-operation. Possibly, had things gone differently in Berlin, Stolietov might have been given greater encouragement from St Petersburg in his efforts to, at least, make trouble for the British, at most, extend Russian influence across the Hindu Kush. As it was, his masters sacrificed him on the altar of their European foreign policy and, in deference to British protests, he was recalled. He left Kabul on 24 August and was back at Tashkent just over three weeks later, though the staff of his mission stayed on at Kabul. From there he wrote to Sher Ali in general face-saving terms, informing him that he had been instructed to report personally to the Czar. 'If God wills, everything that is necessary will be done and affirmed. I hope that those who want to enter the gate of Kabul from the east will see that the door is closed; then, if God wills, they will tremble.'

But those who wanted to enter the gate of Kabul from the east were already on their way. Lytton, since the collapse of his policy at the Peshawar conference, had grown steadily more extreme in his views. He described Sher Ali as 'a savage with a touch of insanity' who apparently believed he was so valuable to the British that he could play the Russians off against them with impunity. Now Lytton toyed increasingly with the ideas of somehow replacing Sher Ali by a more reasonable candidate, or of breaking up his kingdom into smaller, more easily controlled petty states, or even of conquest and annexation to secure Balkh, Maimena, Herat and the Upper Oxus for the outer line of British control. The arrival of Stolietov gave him the opportunity he was awaiting. The Amir, having received a Russian Mission, must now accept a British one. Lytton began to plan accordingly.

Throughout June and July, Lytton telegraphed to London the reports reaching him of Stolietov's progress towards Kabul and urged that, now the Amir was accepting a Russian Mission, he could no longer be permitted to refuse a British one. At first the Cabinet was inclined to treat the matter purely as an Indian one, and at the beginning of August Lytton was authorized, now that Stolietov's arrival in Kabul was beyond all doubt, to prepare to send a British Mission there. Lytton was also invited to say what action he proposed to take if the Amir still refused to accept it. Lytton replied, on 8 August, that failing the achievement of a satisfactory understanding with the Amir the British should occupy the Kurram valley and Kandahar. On the 9th he telegraphed that he had nominated General Sir Neville Chamberlain, a distinguished frontier soldier, and a member of the 'Lawrentian' school of thought, to lead the Mission. Chamberlain was known personally to Sher Ali and had been one of the last British officers to be wounded, in the Khyber, during the British evacuation of Afghanistan in 1842. The Mission, said Lytton, was assembling and would leave Peshawar within the week, irrespective of the Amir's consent, with orders to turn back only if opposed by force and to insist, if the Russians were still in Kabul, that the Amir dismiss them before the British began negotiations.

Meanwhile, in London, Lord Cranbrook had been persuaded by the head of his political department, Colonel Owen Tudor Burne, to secure further diplomatic action. Burne, an influential member of the political department at the India Office, had long been an advocate of the Forward Policy. He had gone to India as Lytton's private secretary, and was identified with Lytton's views, which he, like Colley, had helped to mould. Now back in London, he saw himself as Lytton's ally, driving on the ageing and reluctant Cranbrook to take the decisions necessary to ensure Lytton received the support he needed. A formal remonstrance at Stolietov's proceedings was sent from London to St Petersburg on 19 August. But neither Cranbrook nor Burne told Lytton.

The anti-Russian tone of Lytton's instructions to Chamberlain therefore caused some consternation to the British Government.

Cranbrook warned Lytton that no great power would endure so great an affront as the insistence of another that an independent monarch should dismiss its envoy to his court. Chamberlain's mission was to be delayed a further five days, to see what reply came from St Petersburg and while the problem was considered by the Cabinet. Disraeli was considerably irritated. After the Berlin Congress he had announced to the British public that he had brought back peace with honour. Now, he told Salisbury, Lytton might start a war, and the public might well suppose that as there was no peace, there was no honour either. He also let Cranbrook know, in no uncertain terms, that Lytton should have been informed of the note sent to St Petersburg.

In India, Lytton was determined not to lose the opportunity which Stolietov's presence in Kabul had given him. Following the recent international crisis, British prestige was high and British nerve was strong. Every day that passed reduced the war fever and strengthened those who wished for more peaceful policies. His own period of office in India was nearly half over. The chance of another surge of patriotic feeling, another wave of Jingoism strong enough to carry the British Empire into Afghanistan, was being steadily diminished by all this talk of 'peace with honour'. Justifying himself subsequently by the claim that the mission to Kabul was necessary, in its own right, irrespective of whatever reply came from St Petersburg, and that, if a satisfactory reply came, there would be time to send Chamberlain fresh instructions before he met the Amir, Lytton pushed on the arrangements for the Mission.

The death of his heir Abdulla Jan, a dynastic as well as a personal tragedy for Amir Sher Ali, was not allowed to interfere with this arrangement. The Vakil, sent ahead of the Mission, was received on 12 September, as soon as the period of court mourning ended, and announced as instructed that Sir Neville Chamberlain would be leaving Peshawar within the week. Lytton had also instructed Major Pierre Louis Napoleon Cavagnari, the Commissioner of Peshawar, to write to the Amir and his officials along the intended route that any act of delay or opposition would be regarded as hostile. The Amir protested at this derogation of his authority and publicly refused to accept the Mission if it came without his consent. Privately his Wazir told the Vakil that if the British would give the Amir a chance to save face, he would not bow to the inevitable, as he had with Stolietov.

On the frontier, tension grew. The Afghan governor of Ali Masjid discovered that some Afridi headmen were at Peshawar, discussing with Cavagnari the price of allowing the Mission to cross their tribal territory. The governor, Faiz Muhammad, ordered these putative subjects of the Amir to return to the hills at once, or else face the displeasure of the Kabul authorities.

Lytton decided to bring matters to a head. Chamberlain was told to notify Faiz Muhammad that he was starting immediately. If Faiz Muhammad would guarantee his safe passage through the Khyber, the British would send the Afridi headmen away. If not the British would make their own arrangements. Faiz Muhammad replied that if the Amir so ordered it, he would himself escort the Mission. If not, it should not pass. It was, he said, for Chamberlain to decide whether to wait at Peshawar or try to come at once without the Amir's consent, and thus by force.

Chamberlain's orders from Lytton had been to advance as soon as possible, despite all attempts by local officials to stop him. Only in the event of armed force being used, or the clear intention of it, by the Amir's officers was he to return to India. Now he was as sure that force would be used as if half his escort had been shot down in front of him. He proposed that the next day his Mission move forward to Jamrud, and that the day after a small party under Cavagnari should put to the test, in a symbolic way, the Afghan determination to resist.

Lytton agreed, and as he had promised told the home government of his plans. But the amount of time he had allowed was too short for any consideration. Nor indeed was there any reason for such a close time limit to have been imposed. Chamberlain, having waited more than a month, could have waited a few more days. The urgency had passed with Stolietov's recall. But this indeed may explain Lytton's own anxiety to move so rapidly. As it was, the telegram reporting his intentions arrived on 20 September in London to find the whole Cabinet dispersed about the country, many of the ministers being in the Scottish Highlands for the shooting. By the time the telegram had been retransmitted, and delivered by messengers from rural post offices to remote country houses, any chance of replies reaching India in time to cancel Lytton's plans was safely past.

Thus, on 21 September, 1878, Cavagnari's party rode across the Afghan border. About a mile from the fortress of Ali Masjid they were stopped by Faiz Muhammad, who had ridden out to meet them. Cavagnari urged Faiz Muhammad, in the interests of friendship between their two nations, not to oppose the Mission's progress. Faiz Muhammad replied that he stood as a sentinel at his post. Without his master's orders, the Mission should not pass. As for British friendship, what friendship was it that tried to force an entry in this way, and stirred up dissent among the Afridis?

Sensing an increasingly ugly mood among the Afridis with the Afghan party, Cavagnari asked for a plain answer – would Faiz Muhammad oppose the Mission by force. 'Yes I will;' was the reply 'and you may take it as kindness, and because I remember friendship, that I do not fire upon you for what you have done already.' 'You have had a straight answer,' he said, as the Englishmen shook hands with him and mounted their horses to return to India.

When Beaconsfield realized what had happened, he was furious. Writing to Cranbrook on 25 September, he said that Lytton had been told to 'wait until we had received the answer from Russia to our remonstrance. I was very strong on this, having good reasons for my opinion. He disobeyed us. I was assured by Lord Salisbury that, under no circumstances, was the Khyber Pass to be attempted. Nothing would have induced me to consent to such a step.'

But the Cabinet agreed that, despite Lytton's reckless conduct, something would have to be done to restore British prestige after his emissaries had been repulsed by the Afghans. Lytton was allowed to assemble troops on the frontier, and to issue a proclamation stating that, though the Government of India had no wish to interfere in Afghan affairs, it would occupy the Khyber Pass to protect the Afridis, who were being persecuted by the Amir's levies for having shown friendship to the British. But Lytton was told to stop at Ali Masjid and not to occupy the Kurram valley or any other Afghan territory. There was to be no act of open hostility pending a reply from the Amir establishing beyond all doubt that Faiz Muhammad had acted entirely in compliance with orders.

On 19 October Lytton telegraphed that the Amir had replied in insolent terms. He asked for a declaration of war. But the Cabinet was well aware that Parliament, despite a comfortable government majority in the Commons, would never vote supplies for a war on the Amir simply for refusing to admit a British Mission to his own country. Salisbury spoke with some bitterness on the subject of Lytton trying to dictate the conduct of foreign policy and forecast that unless he were curbed, he would bring about some terrible disaster.

Disraeli proposed a compromise. Suppose the British occupied the Kurram, not as an act of war, but as a reprisal. This would be perfectly admissible in international law, and would avoid the necessity of recalling Parliament. All agreed except Cranbrook, who, as Disraeli subsequently told the Queen, suddenly startled everyone by saying he was for war, immediate and complete. Cranbrook seems to have been thoroughly disenchanted with Indian affairs. He had never wanted to go to the India Office, and now he had been blamed for failing to control the headstrong Lytton. One reason why he wanted war, he said, was that it was the only way Lytton could be made to heed the advice of his own Commander-in-Chief and the proper military authorities. As it was, guided by others (he meant Colley and Burne) Lytton seemed to be risking hostilities with forces that, in the opinion of the Indian military, were inadequate. The rest of the Cabinet, stunned by the outburst, acquiesced. Lytton was ordered to demand, in temperate terms, an apology from the Amir, amnesty for the Afridis and the reception of a permanent British Mission at Kabul, but, failing a satisfactory reply by 2 November, the Amir was to be treated as a declared enemy.

However, as Chamberlain put it, the Amir had no more intention of apologizing than of turning Christian and applying for a bishopric. As no reply was received from the Amir, three British columns invaded Afghanistan at dawn on 21 November. '*Jacta est alea*' wrote Lytton, the die is cast.

Note on the dialogue between Faiz Muhammad and Major Cavagnari at Ali Masjid, Khyber Pass, 21 September 1879

The meeting between the advance party of the British Mission and Faiz Muhammad, the Afghan Governor of Ali Masjid, came to an end when

Cavagnari asked for a plain answer to a plain question. If the British Mission entered Afghanistan without the Amir's permission, would Faiz Muhammad use force to stop its progress? Faiz Muhammad replied that it would be his duty to do so, and that he would do so, even if he were only a single sentinel. 'You may take it as kindness', he added, 'and *because I remember friendship* that I do not fire on you for what you have done already.'

The words here italicized have been taken by several writers to mean that Faiz Muhammad was on terms of personal friendship, or at least acquaintance, with Cavagnari, his opposite number on the British side of the border. Thus he is portrayed rather romantically as saying, in effect, 'It is only because I remember our past friendship that I do not fire on you'. A poignant scene is established of two old friends, obliged by their duty to their respective governments to become enemies, and Faiz Muhammad chivalrously refraining from firing on Cavagnari for old times' sake.

But the present writer has been unable to find any other evidence of personal friendship between these two officers. A more prosaic, but more credible, explanation of Faiz Muhammad's words is that he is using *friendship* in exactly the same way as it had been used by both sides earlier in this dialogue, to mean 'international goodwill'. Cavagnari had been putting pressure on Faiz Muhammad not to place at risk the *friendship* between the Afghan and British governments by opposing the entry of the Mission without direct orders from the Amir. Faiz Muhammad had asked Cavagnari to explain how the British reconciled *friendship* with their behaviour in dealing directly with the Amir's own subjects, the tribes along the Khyber. So the context clearly shows that Faiz Muhammad was really saying that, although the British might have set out to create an international incident by crossing the Afghan border without permission, and indeed contrary to the expressed wishes of the Afghan government, he at least remembered the importance of maintaining friendly relations between the two states, and would not be provoked by this border violation on the part of the British. What should be adduced from this dialogue, therefore, is not that the relationship between the two men was one of personal friendship between individuals, but rather that it was one of professional courtesy between two diplomats.

VII

The Queen's Pawns
The British invasions of Afghanistan 1878–79

The invasion of Afghanistan in 1878, unlike that of 1839, was made on three fronts. Now the British war aim was not to march on Kabul and dethrone the Amir, but rather to detach from his rule the important frontier districts, and in the process to destroy the army that he had built up. One column, under Lieutenant-General Donald Stewart, marched from Quetta against Kandahar and consisted of two divisions, with a total of seventy-two guns (including a siege train), one squadron of British hussars and six regiments of Indian cavalry, three battalions of British infantry, ten of Indian infantry, a battalion of pioneers and four companies of sappers and miners. The second, under Lieutenant-General Sir Samuel Browne, the one-armed inventor of the Sam Browne belt, marched from Peshawar to take the Khyber Pass. This also consisted of two divisions, and amounted to forty-six guns, one and a half British cavalry regiments, three regiments of Bengal Lancers, the Corps of Guides (a combined cavalry and infantry unit), four companies of sappers and miners, six British infantry battalions and ten Indian infantry battalions. The third column, sent into the Kurram Valley, formed a central front. The commander here was Major-General Frederick Roberts. He had a squadron of the 10th Hussars, the 12th Bengal Cavalry, eight guns of the Royal Horse Artillery and eight mountain guns from the Punjab Frontier Force, a company of sappers, a battalion of pioneers, two British infantry battalions and five Indian infantry battalions.

There was violent disagreement between Lord Lytton and his Commander-in-Chief, General Sir Frederick Haines, over the relative, indeed the absolute, strengths of these columns. Lytton's view was that the Kandahar force should be limited to one division, without brigade headquarters, to save money. Colley had already pointed out that the British had failed to hold Afghanistan in the last war not because of military defeat but because India was going broke from the cost of maintaining a large army there. His faith in the superiority conferred on the British troops by their new breech-loaders led him to the conclusion that the number of troops sent could be reduced to a minimum. Haines pointed out that the force marching on Kandahar might easily run into 15,000 Afghan regulars, with artillery, and supported by tribal levies. The British force would be weakened, not only by inevitable sickness and battle casualties but by the need to guard ever lengthening lines of communications as it advanced deeper into hostile territory. Any reverse, he pointed out, 'would make painfully apparent the true economy which inadequate preparation in the commencement confers on all military ventures in their issues'. Lytton said he would take full responsibility in the event of failure, on the grounds that the military problems were less serious than the current financial and political ones. Haines replied that this was not a responsibility of which, by the terms of his own appointment, he could divest himself. Lytton, rather than face a constitutional crisis, had to give way, though without any confidence in Haines's arguments. To Cranbrook he later wrote:

> Sir F. Haines had an *idée fixe*, from which no argument or remonstrance could detach what he is pleased to call his mind, that whatever might be our agreed policy and intention, the Afghan War would necessitate a huge campaign against Herat which it was his hope and determination to lead himself, and with this proposal before his mind's eye he insisted ... on making the Candahar Force about three times larger than it need have been. ... Our Commander-in-Chief and his whole staff are a coagulation of mediocrities and inveterately obstinate stupidities, and they have weighed upon me and upon India like a horrible incubus throughout the war.

Haines had also expressed reservations about the size and composition of the Peshawar Force, and secured the addition of a second division to this (though not a corps headquarters to command the whole) by pointing out the difficulty of the country and the ferocity of the inhabitants, which required large numbers of troops to guard the supply lines. The only force he did not ask to be enlarged, was Roberts's column in the Kurram valley.

Roberts was by now known to be one of Lytton's favourites. As Quartermaster-General of the Bengal Army, he had prepared a paper on the situation on the North-West Frontier and Central Asia in response to orders given, ultimately, as a result of Salisbury's demands for more intelligence of developments there. Lytton had read this and approved its contents, and following a chance meeting, added Roberts to his circle of intimates.

The result of these disagreements was to delay the granting of authority for expenditure on the increased forces, and in particular the logistic support which they needed. Transport, commissariat, ordnance and medical services all suffered as the result of continued postponement of decisions. In the summer of 1878 the Government of India's Military Department, then headed by Sir Sam Browne, had even sold off 'surplus' transport from the depot at Rawalpindi. 'A most ill-timed measure' noted the Commander-in-Chief, of whom the Military Department was entirely independent.

The movements of the Kandahar force were very like those of the Army of the Indus forty years previously. Most of the troops assembled at Multan in the Punjab, and then went up through Baluchistan and the Bolan Pass to Quetta, experiencing the same extremes of climate and geography as their predecessors, and suffering the same illnesses and privations. The major difference was that Khodadad Khan, unlike his father Mehrab Khan, was demonstratively pro-British, and assisted Colonel Sandeman's attempts to lay in supplies of food and warm clothing. The troops moved up steadily towards Kandahar throughout December, and on reaching that city on 8 January, 1879, discovered that the Afghan garrison had already withdrawn.

On the Khyber front, General Sam Browne's campaign began badly. Starting from Jamrud, two brigades were sent into the hills, on a night march, at last light on 20 November. One brigade was to crown the Rohtas heights, which looked down upon Ali Masjid, and the other to take up a position on the far side of the fortress, thus cutting its lines of communication with Jalalabad. At first light on the 21st the two remaining brigades of Browne's division began to file into the Khyber Pass itself; heading directly for Ali Masjid. There the defiant Faiz Muhammad awaited them at the head of 3,000 regular infantry, 600 levies, 200 cavalry and twenty-four cannon, protected by a series of skilfully sited field fortifications. An artillery duel that began about noon did little to shake the defenders, even when the elephants of the Royal Artillery's heavy battery hauled their 40-pdr guns into action. By 2 p.m., with their reserve wagons jammed far behind them in the supporting columns trying to struggle up the pass, the British artillerymen began to run short of ammunition and had to reduce their rate of fire, while the Afghans, who had previously registered the range of all likely target areas, kept up a constant bombardment. Cavagnari, accompanying Browne, pointed out that there were large numbers of Afridis under arms watching the fight, and argued that unless Browne attacked the fort, the Afridis might well attack him. Browne ordered forward his infantry, though there was still no sign of the two brigades he had sent out the previous night. During the afternoon the infantrymen slowly fought their way up the lower slopes of the Afghan position, but it became clear that there was no chance of reaching the crest before the end of the winter day and they were recalled in some confusion.

General Sir Samuel Browne, said Lord Lytton, should have been tried by Court Martial, having blundered, neglected every duty of a commander

'The Fort of Jamrud, at the entrance to the Khyber Pass'. Ranjit Singh's fortifications, constructed to defend his newly conquered province of Peshawar against Afghan counter-attack, successfully defied Muhammad Akbar Khan's army in 1837. Its distinctive outline was used for the reverse side of the British Army's 1908–35 Indian General Service Medal.

and achieved the thorough demoralization of his own troops. Browne spent an uncomfortable and anxious night, his two infantry brigades with their cavalry and artillery support lying scattered and disorganized at the foot of the Khyber cliffs.

But at dawn it was discovered that the two flanking brigades, starving, exhausted and frozen, had at last made their presence felt. Wandering about for two nights and a day, losing contact with the main force, with each other and with their own transport and rear echelons, these two formations knew nothing of the progress of the battle at Ali Masjid other than what they could guess from the muffled sound of distant gunfire. But their presence was reported to Faiz Muhammad, who appreciated that once they were in position, as eventually they were bound to be, his own defence could not be sustained. Accordingly, under cover of darkness, he and his men abandoned the works they had defended with such tenacity and retired towards Jalalabad. The British followed up this retreat and occupied Jalalabad on 20 December.

The third column, under Roberts, advanced rapidly from Thal, on the Indian side of the frontier, and by 27 November had occupied the whole of the Kurram valley. The head of the valley was blocked by a line of Afghan defences, centred on Peiwar Kotal (*Kotal* is a topographical term, meaning 'saddle' or ridge between two hills) and extending along the crests for about two miles on either side. The Afghan garrison, commanded by

Karim Khan, one of the Amir's best generals, consisted of seven regular regiments with seventeen guns, a total of nearly 5,000 soldiers, though for lack of trained artillerymen only nine of the guns could be served at a time. Roberts's intelligence was that the defences were held only by the three regiments he had been pursuing from their original position on the frontier and that their artillery had either been abandoned or bogged down at the foot of Peiwar Kotal. He ordered his whole force forward to reconnoitre and, if the chance occurred, to rush the defences. But as the British made camp on the night of 28 November, the whereabouts of at least some of the Afghan artillery became only too apparent, as their shot began to fall among the British lines. A hasty scramble to get out of range followed, and a further two days were spent to give men and beasts a chance to recover from their exertions of the previous week.

At dusk on 1 December, Roberts led out the bulk of his force on a night march to turn the Afghan left. With him he took the 72nd Highlanders, 5th Gurkhas, the 2nd and 29th Punjab Infantry, the a 23rd Pioneers, six mountain guns carried on mules and four light field guns carried on elephants. The rest of the force (eight field guns, two battalions of infantry and two squadrons of cavalry) was ordered to guard the camp and to make a frontal attack on the Afghan position in support of the flank attack when this developed. During the night Roberts's main force pushed on through the hills over rough and frosty ground.

They experienced the usual difficulties of keeping contact with each other and of finding the correct route. The elephants, the Pioneers and the 2nd Punjab Infantry took the wrong road altogether and were two miles away heading directly away from their objective before they were found and recalled. As the rest of the flanking force neared the Afghan position, two shots were fired by men of the 27th Punjabis, a regiment composed half of Sikhs half of Pathans. But Roberts was lucky. Although an Afghan sentry heard the shots and reported them to his officer, no further action was taken on their side. Just before dawn, the Gurkhas and Highlanders together rushed the defences and succeeded in dislodging the Afghan troops, despite a fierce counter-attack that the Pathans of the 29th did little to oppose. At 7.30 a.m. Roberts heliographed to his camp in the valley, 2,500 feet below, to begin the frontal attack.

Roberts himself pushed on towards Peiwar Kotal, only to be stopped by the discovery that the ridge was not a continuous feature, but bisected by a precipitous ravine with only a narrow causeway joining the two sides. He also found that he was accompanied only by the unreliable 29th Punjabis, as the Highlanders, Gurkhas and mountain guns had disappeared over the crest in pursuit of the retreating Afghans. One after another, Roberts sent off his staff to try to locate his missing regiments. At last, even the chaplain, the Reverend J.V. Adams, was despatched, but without success. Roberts, anticipating an Afghan rush along the causeway to regain the

'The attack on the Peiwar Kotal, 2 December 1878'. Men of the 5th Gurkha Rifles and the 72nd Highlanders rushing the Afghan position. Engraving from the oil painting by Vereker Hamilton which now hangs in the Indian Army Memorial Room at the RMA Sandhurst. In this painting, the artist has altered the expression on the face of a dead Gurkha to a smile, at Roberts' personal request.

captured position, harangued the 29th and urged them to regain their lost honour by making an attack themselves. The Sikhs went forward, unsupported, but the difficulty of the terrain and the intensity of the Afghan fire obliged them to fail back.

By now, the Reverend Adams had discovered not merely the Highlanders and Gurkhas but also the rest of the force which had got lost during the night, and had directed them all up to Roberts's locations. Several Afghan charges along the causeway towards the British were repulsed and counter-attacks were launched against the Afghan barricades by the Pioneers, who had been put into the line in place of the 29th Punjabis. But these were repulsed in their turn.

Roberts now appreciated that the Afghan flank, defended by large numbers of men, guns and immense natural obstacles, was impregnable. He called off this attack and began another turning movement, which

'Peiwar Kotal, 2 December 1878'. This illustration from the Illustrated London News *shows the ridge north of the main Afghan position. Roberts's infantry and pioneers failed to break through the Afghan barricades, but the mountain guns, shelling the Afghan camp in the valley below, made a decisive contribution to his eventual victory.*

brought him to a position about a mile behind the Peiwar Kotal. There, at about 4 p.m. he halted. His men, exhausted after marching all night and climbing and fighting all day, bivouacked on a hill-top some 9,000 feet above sea level without tents, rations, water, or warm clothing. They huddled around fires of pine trees felled by the Pioneers' axes, and sought what protection they could from the frost.

The frontal attack, during this time, had met with more success. The British artillery, with its cavalry escort, moved up the valley floor and engaged the Afghan batteries in a brisk duel. The 2nd Battalion of the King's Regiment and the 5th Punjab Infantry took the high ground to the right, though the Punjabis subsequently swung too far right, and after climbing for some hours came up to the crest held by Roberts and the main force about 2 p.m. On the way up they passed through a point from which there was a line of sight, behind the Peiwar Kotal, down a gully, to where the Afghan camp and baggage lines were pitched. Two mountain guns were sent down from the ridge as soon as Roberts was informed of this and their shells, arriving unexpectedly in what was supposed to be a safe area, soon started a panic. Tents caught fire, transport animals stampeded, drivers, followers and camp guards all fled, followed by some of the neighbouring troops, who were holding up Roberts's flank attack. The English soldiers of the King's Regiment, during this time, worked their way ever closer to the Peiwar Kotal and from a distance of 800 yards silenced one Afghan battery by shooting down the gunners at their guns. The Afghan garrison, shaken by the spectacle of their camp being turned into a shambles below them in the rear, gave way before a further advance by the King's men, and by 2.30 p.m. their main position, their camp and eighteen guns were secure in British hands, though it was not until 8.00 p.m., long after dark, that a despatch rider eventually reached Roberts's camp with the news. Thus, for the loss of twenty-one killed and seventy-two wounded, the British gained the Peiwar Kotal and access to Central Afghanistan.

When it became clear that a British invasion was imminent, Amir Sher Ali turned to the Russians for support. But the Russians had no intention of going to war with England for the sake of Sher Ali, and his appeals for Russian aid fell on deaf ears. Kaufmann pointed out that in any case it was impossible for him to send an army southwards at the onset of winter, and urged the Amir to make the best terms with the English that he could. The Amir, in reply, referred to what he called 'the recent treaty concluded through General Stoletoff on the part of his Imperial Majesty', and said that 'should any harm or injury, which God forbid, befall the Afghan Government, the dust of blame will certainly settle on the skirt of His Imperial Majesty's Government'.

On 30 November, the Amir's reply to the British ultimatum was delivered. He offered to accept a temporary British Mission, but declined to apologize for Faiz Muhammad's refusal to let Chamberlain's Mission pass, or to guarantee an amnesty to the Afridis, who had given Cavagnari safe conduct through the Khyber. This answer was rejected by the British and their advance continued. After the fall of Peiwar Kotal his army began to crumble and his authority grew less. On 13 December he released Yakub Khan, now the heir apparent, and left Kabul *en route* to Russian Turkestan, accompanied by remaining members of the Russian Mission.

His plan was to go to St Petersburg and ask the Czar to bring his affairs before a congress. The Congress of Berlin, he knew, had saved the Sultan of Turkey from the Russians at the behest of the English, so it would not have been entirely unreasonable for him to suppose that the Amir of Afghanistan might similarly be saved from the English at the behest of the Russians. He failed to realize that it was not so much the congress as a British battle fleet which had saved the Sultan, and that without a Russian army, which was not forthcoming, no congress would be called to save the Amir.

Thus, after reaching Mazir-i-Sharif on his northern frontier with Bokhara, Sher Ali discovered the bitter truth that the Russians regarded his likely presence as an embarrassment. Kaufmann invited him to come to Tashkent, but pointedly added that no instructions had been received to make arrangements for any journey onwards to St Petersburg. Sher Ali, always a man of violent moods, gave way to despair. His dream of playing off one great power against another had faded. He had abandoned his capital, with all that this entailed in lost prestige, in a gamble that had failed. Already sick in body he now refused food and medicine, and died on 21 February, 1879, aged fifty-six, having reigned, with interruptions, for some fifteen years.

The difficulty in which Lytton found himself was that although he had won the war he could not end it without a peace treaty, and he could not make a treaty when there was no Afghan government to agree to it. He could not recognize a government that did not exist; he could not recognize one which was unfriendly; he could not set up one overtly dependent on British protection. He authorized Cavagnari to offer recognition and support to any friendly government which could succeed in establishing itself. He thought of adopting the policy that had been tried successfully in Kalat, of associating the Sirdars in any agreement with their ruler and thus persuading the chief men of the country that they would benefit from British influence. Yakub Khan, who had taken over at Kabul when Sher Ali fled, seemed, Lytton told Cranbrook, to have inherited his father's perversity and hatred of the British, and in a few short weeks had acquired all Sher Ali's unpopularity with none of his power. He was 'a very slippery customer whom we shall be well rid of if he disappears. ... He could not maintain himself without our support and our support could not be given to a more unpopular and incompetent ruler.'

Once more he mooted the idea of dismembering Afghanistan. A local ruler could be installed at Kandahar, dependent on British goodwill and overawed by the British from Quetta. The Iranians should be allowed to take Herat after all and would thus be converted into British allies. The Kabul state, reduced to an insignificant size and posing no threat to India, might be taken by Wali Muhammad Khan, a younger brother of Sher Ali, who had some local influence and with whom Cavagnari was in negotiation. The region between the Hindu Kush and the Oxus, he mused with astonishing placidity, might as well be left to the Russians and the border between the Russian and British empires or their vassals might be established along the natural mountain frontier.

The advantages of this last proposal were entirely lost on a British Cabinet which had become involved in a war in order to keep the Russians out of any part of Afghanistan. The government's Liberal opponents, the guardians of the Nonconformist Conscience (at this time a formidable electoral power) were objecting to an unjust war and the dissenting chapels were praying for a British defeat. Its own supporters would not be enthusiastic about an unsuccessful war, especially if it became expensive. The electorate, ready to cheer the news of British victories, did not like to hear of commissariat failures such as were being reported from the Kandahar front, nor of any battlefield reverses, such as that which had just been reported from South Africa. There the British High Commissioner, Sir Bartle Frere, a former Governor of Bombay and a strong advocate of the Forward Policy, had, on 11 January, 1879, following an unanswered ultimatum, declared war on the King of the Zulus for refusing to accept a British Resident. On 22 January, at Isandlawana, the Zulu *impis* had massacred a strong column of British and colonial troops, killing more British officers that day than the French had done at Waterloo. Lytton was told that the idea of abandoning Afghan Turkestan to the Russians was unthinkable and that, if necessary, he must end the war by a unilateral proclamation.

Yakub wrote to Cavagnari from Kabul on 26 February that Sher Ali had thrown off the dress of existence and relinquished the robe of life. 'As my exalted father was an ancient friend of the British Government, I have out of friendship sent you this intimation,' he concluded, with that blithe disregard of historical accuracy common in diplomatic overtures of this nature.

Lytton, for his part, was only too glad to seize the chance of talks with Yakub Khan. The British armies were positioned in difficult country, at the end of protracted supply lines and harassed by increasingly restive local tribesmen, who cut the telegraph wires and menaced road convoys. Instead of a quick and inexpensive campaign, he was now faced with the possibility of a costly occupation such as had ruined the British cause during the First Afghan War. His Commander-in-Chief, he complained, had no regard for financial considerations and was to blame for the starving condition of the Kandahar force by bloating it to a size far beyond the capacity of the inadequate transport service to feed, with the result that as soon as supplies arrived there they were immediately consumed. As for the force at Jalalabad and along the Khyber line, his generals had 14,000 troops, but were unable to advance because of the frightful mortality among their camels. If they did advance, it would be through country where a few resolute men might easily inflict a severe disaster on a larger force, or so Lytton was advised by Chamberlain, and the risk of another Isandlawana was not something any British politician was prepared to accept.

At this time the Viceroy had an added distraction caused by the arrival in India, on a world tour, of General Ulysses S. Grant, victor of the American Civil War and ex-President of the United States. 'That bore,' wrote Lytton

'The Guard of Honour for Amir Khan'. Men of the 10th Hussars, and a battery of field artillery, lined up to receive Amir Yakub Khan, on his arrival at the British camp, Gandamak, 8 May 1879. The hills in the background are those in which the last remnants of Elphinstone's retreating army had been destroyed in the retreat from Kabul, January 1842.

on hearing of his imminent approach. In fact, the visit was anything but boring, for at a grand ball given in his honour by the Lieutenant-Governor of Bengal the General, as Lytton reported to an interested Lord Cranbrook, got as drunk as a lord, 'ran after all the ladies with intent to ravish them, kissed these, pinched those, drove the others into hysterics, and after generally behaving like a mad elephant was finally captured and carried on board by six sailors, a sodden mass of spirits and tobacco.' The Lieutenant-Governor fumigated his ball-room and the Viceroy proceeded on his way to the summer capital at Simla.

In Afghanistan, after all the delays of oriental diplomacy, the treaty of Gandamak was signed on 26 May by Yakub Khan, Amir of Afghanistan, on the one side and Major Cavagnari, on behalf of the British Government, on the other. The usual assurances of perpetual peace and friendship were exchanged. Yakub agreed to an amnesty for those who had collaborated with the British. He agreed to British control of his foreign policy, in return for the promise that British troops, arms and money would be available to assist him repel any unprovoked aggression. He accepted a British Agent at Kabul, and assented to the presence of British officers on his frontiers when necessary. Both sides agreed to promote trade and commerce. A telegraph line was to be built from Kabul to Kurram. The British restored Kandahar and Jalalabad, but kept the Khyber Pass. Kurram and the Afghan enclaves around Quetta and along the Bolan were 'assigned' to the British, a term which satisfied the sensibilities of the Afghan patriots and English liberals alike, as it implied that the districts were not permanently annexed, and the excess of revenue over civil expenditure was handed over to the state of which in international law they still formed part. Finally, the Amir and his successors (rather than his heirs, for the British Cabinet still would not give the dynastic guarantee) would receive a subsidy of six lakhs of rupees per annum. The British occupation forces were to be withdrawn as soon as the climatic and medical conditions allowed (there was a cholera epidemic in the Khyber), but meanwhile the Afghan civil governors should resume the local administration without British interference.

Congratulations and rewards were now the order of the day. Regiments were awarded battle honours. Soldiers were awarded campaign medals. Generals received decorations and were voted the thanks of Parliament. Lytton received glowing letters of tribute from Beaconsfield, Salisbury and Cranbrook. Cavagnari, now very much one of Lytton's protégés was awarded a knighthood, though Lytton felt obliged to persuade him to be Sir Louis, rather than Sir Napoleon Cavagnari.

To Cavagnari went the appointment of British Agent in Kabul, or rather, as it was entitled by Royal approval at Lytton's request, British Envoy Extraordinary and Minister Plenipotentiary at the court of the Amir. 'This is a great chance for you, Cavagnari,' said Sir Frederick Haines as the new Envoy left Simla. 'Yes sir, it is a case of man or mouse,' Cavagnari answered. Avoiding the plague-ridden Khyber route, he jour- neyed to the Kurram and was escorted to the Shutargarden Pass beyond Peiwar Kotal by the newly gazetted Sir Frederick Roberts. Roberts had a gloomy view of the Mission's prospects. His father, Sir Abraham Roberts, had been the Commandant of Shah Shuja's Contingent before being replaced by the ill-fated Brigadier Anquetil, so he had an intimate knowledge of the way British political agents were regarded in Kabul. He was invited, at a farewell dinner in camp, to propose the health of Cavagnari's party, but, he later recorded, 'somehow I did not feel equal to the task; I was so thoroughly depressed, and my mind was filled with such gloomy forebodings as to the fate of these fine fellows, that I could not utter a word'. The next day, 16 July, as they rode to meet the Afghan escort awaiting the British Mission, Cavagnari noticed a solitary magpie. Remembering the old adage about magpies, 'one for sorrow, two for joy', he pointed it out to Roberts and asked him not to mention it to Lady Cavagnari, who was sure to take it for a sign of ill omen. The two men parted, then turned back, shook hands again and went their separate ways.

'The Amir Yakub Khan, August 1879'. On his right are Sir Louis Cavagnari and his assistant, William Jenkyns, both in the new diplomatic uniform, invented by Lord Lytton of the Political Service. On the Amir's left are his Commander-in-Chief, General Daoud Shah, and his 'financial secretary', the Mustafi Habibulla Khan.

Cavagnari's letters from Kabul were cheerful enough. But he drew a vivid picture of intrigue and mutual distrust between the various parties at Kabul, and noticed the sinister influence of several regular regiments that had arrived from Herat and which swaggered about letting it be known that they had not been defeated by the Frankish invaders. Nevertheless, he wrote to Lytton on 30 August: 'I personally believe Yakub Khan will turn out to be a very good ally, and that we shall be able to keep him to his engagements.'

He was a trifle disappointed that so little notice had been taken in the British newspapers of his Mission's arrival in Kabul, especially as this was the achievement of a declared aim of the British Government during the past years. 'I am afraid,' he told Lytton, 'there is no denying the fact that the British public require a blunder and a huge disaster to excite their interest!'

Still, the growing turbulence of the regiments from Herat was worrying enough to make Sirdar Wali Muhammad (the Barakzai prince whom his nephew, the Amir, had earlier threatened to impale for corresponding with the British) warn Cavagnari that something was afoot. Cavagnari, the Sirdar later reported, 'remarked in reply that it was the habit of a rabid dog to bite, be the person bit however innocent'. Another warning came from an Afghan-born officer in the Indian cavalry, who was at this time on leave in his home village near Kabul. 'Never fear,' said Cavagnari in the Persian idiom, 'keep up your heart, dogs that bark don't bite.' 'But these dogs do bite,' replied the officer, 'there is real danger.' Cavagnari would not be swayed. 'They can only kill the three or four of us here,' he said, 'and our deaths will be avenged.' In a telegram to Simla dated 2 September, 1879, he reported 'all well', just as the last British Envoy to Kabul had once reported the country all quiet from Dan to Beersheba.

The next day the Herati regiments came into the Bala Hissar to receive the three months' arrears of pay due to them. The revenues not having been fully collected due to the war, they were offered only one month's wages. A riot broke out and one of the officers, pointing to the British Residency 100 yards away, tried to divert what was fast becoming a mutinous mob by saying that as Cavagnari was now running the country and the British were rich, they should go and ask him for what was due to them. Cavagnari, like Alexander Burnes a generation before, appeared on his balcony and harangued the mob. He told them that they were servants of the Amir and their pay was no concern of the British Government. Someone fired a shot and the mutineers went off to fetch their rifles from the cantonments two miles away.

The Amir made some attempts to stop the trouble, though, as had been the case with Shah Shuja in the previous war, there were conflicting reports about how hard he tried. The Afghan Commander-in-Chief, Daoud Shah, came down from the palace to try and restore order, but was stoned, unhorsed and trampled on by his own soldiers, who, joined by the city mob, had returned to the Bala Hissar and begun an attack on the Residency.

Cavagnari was among the first to die, hit in the forehead while firing a rifle from the Residency roof. Soon the roof was occupied by the mutineers and the defenders driven below. The defenders of the Residency were seventy-five Indian soldiers of the élite Corps of Guides from the Punjab Frontier Force, commanded by Lieutenant Walter Hamilton, who had won the Victoria Cross during the fighting in the Khyber. The other Britons were Surgeon-Major Kelly and William Jenkyns, of the Bengal Civil Service, each of whom died leading desperate sallies against Afghan cannon.

Fighting continued for several hours, the numbers of the escort steadily dwindling as they fell at their posts. When all the English were known to have been killed, the Afghans offered a chance of surrender to the remaining men of the Guides. Jemahdar Jewand Singh, the senior officer left, replied, much as had the Spartans after the fall of Leonidas at the battle of Thermopylae, or the English after that of Byrtnoth at the battle of Maldon: alive or dead, they stayed with their chief. Then he and his five surviving comrades sallied out to their deaths in one final charge, the Jemahdar being the last to fall, after killing eight men before he went down.

Roberts was at this time in Simla, attending a committee on army reform set up to examine the lessons of the recent campaign. At about one o'clock

on the morning of September he was awakened by his wife telling him that a telegraph man had been wandering about the house downstairs, trying to deliver a message. It was from the political officer in the Kurram, reporting that one of Cavagnari's secret agents had arrived with news that the Embassy was under attack and defending itself against artillery.

The Governor-General's council met in the dawn. It was decided that all troop movements out of Afghanistan were to be stopped at once, pending confirmation of the news. When it was confirmed, later in the afternoon, the Kurram Valley Field Force was ordered to advance a mountain battery, a pioneer regiment and an infantry battalion to the Shutargardan Pass. Roberts's column was not only the nearest to Kabul but also the only one capable of resuming operations quickly, as Browne's divisions had been broken up and most of Stewart's men had already been sent back from Kandahar to India.

Colonel Sir George Colley, Lytton's confidential military adviser, was at this time far away in South Africa, whither he had been summoned by Sir Garnet Wolseley to join him in the restoration of British military prestige there. Early in 1878, when on leave in the United Kingdom, Colley had married Edith Hamilton, a general's daughter whom he had met some years previously. She was left in India at Lytton's court when her husband sailed for the Cape, and her account of how the news of Cavagnari's death was received at Simla, written to her absent husband, gives an idea of the shattering effect it had on the Viceregal circle.

We had to keep up appearances, even when the look that passed over H. E.'s face when he read the telegram told us pretty well that there was little hope left. Then, just at the end of dinner (which was half an hour earlier for the theatre), in came Z [Roberts?] talking in gallant style – but a look about his eyes which to me made it ghastly. Nothing was to be shown as yet so Lady L went to the theatre. ... I was so thankful I had declined before; I don't think I could have sat through it. Oh Geordie, it is all too dreadful! I sometimes think I feel it more than anyone except Z. Cavagnari's face haunts me, and all our last talks, and the poor little wife at home.

To Roberts, who within thirty-six hours of receiving the telegram at his house was heading back to his men in the Kurram, Lytton poured out a whole series of violent instructions in a private letter of September. The general was to march on Kabul. He would have unfettered freedom of action when he reached there, but its duration could not be guaranteed so he must take advantage of it quickly. 'There are some things which a Viceroy can approve and defend when they have been done, but which a Governor-General in Council cannot order to be done.' A price was to be put on the head of all persons concerned in the attack on the Embassy. All such persons captured or denounced were to be promptly executed in a manner most likely to impress the populace. Preliminary trials or enquiries were 'wholly out of place'. The Afghans would denounce anyone for money and 'it is highly probable that your informants will denounce only their personal enemies and that some comparatively innocent persons may suffer by this course'. But that could not be helped. 'Every Afghan brought to death I shall regard as one scoundrel the less in a nest of scoundrelism.' Some rough and ready authority such as a drumhead Court Martial might be necessary to satisfy English sentiment, but the enquiries should in each case be limited 'to the question of whether the exactors of retribution are satisfied that it is desirable that the alleged culprit should be put to death'. Retribution, not justice, was to be the watchword. The object was to strike terror swiftly rather than set up a reign of terror. 'There will be more clamour at home over the fall of a single head six months hence than over a hundred heads that fall at once.' The Kabulis were to be disarmed and after due warning, anyone found in arms 'should be killed on the spot like vermin'. Lytton considered burning Kabul to the ground, but rejected it for practical difficulties, the houses being mostly of non-combustible material.

The Ameers of Kabul and their people have hitherto read history in the dark and they have read it wrong. They need light. ... It is our present task to shed such a glare upon the last blood-stained page of Afghan annals as shall sear the sinister date of it deep into the shamed memory of a smitten and subjugated people.

In another letter, written a week later, which he ordered Roberts to burn when read, Lytton ordered him to press on, not to bother about his lines of communication and seize every possible strategic point 'before the political weathercock at home has shifted'. Roberts replied that he would be there all the sooner for ensuring all was ready before he started. The Afghans, he said, were arrant cowards. The problem would be getting them to stand and fight. But for lack of transport Roberts could not move forward until the end of the month. Then he marched with four cavalry regiments, three British and four Indian infantry battalions, one pioneer battalion, a company of sappers and miners, two Indian mountain batteries, one field and one horse artillery battery and two gatling guns. All told, he had some 7,000 men under command, and twenty-two guns, from which he had to find a garrison for the Shutargardan Pass.

At first, both sides preserved the fiction that Roberts was marching to assist the Amir in putting down disturbances and restoring order in his capital. The Amir's two chief ministers, the Wazir, Shah Muhammad, and the Mustafi, Habibulla Khan (equivalent to the Prime Minister and Chancellor of the Exchequer), arrived in Roberts's camp on 15 September with a message from their master. The Amir proposed that Roberts spare his Queen's soldiers the hardships and privations of a march with the winter approaching and leave it to the Afghan authorities to punish the mutineers. Roberts believed that this was a ruse to enable the Amir to rally national resistance against the British. He sent the ministers back with the reply that the British nation would not rest satisfied, in view of what had passed, 'unless a British army marched to Kabul and there assisted Your Highness to inflict such punishments as so terrible and dastardly an act deserves'. He also expressed himself glad to inform the Amir that two other columns, one from Kandahar and one from the Khyber, had already started for Kabul, and that 'the Viceroy of India, in His Excellency's anxiety for Your Highness's welfare and safety, issued orders that each of the three armies ... should be strong enough to overcome any opposition Your Highness's enemies could possibly offer'.

When Roberts reached the top of the Shutargardan Pass, on 17 September, he received what he called 'the rather embarrassing information' that the Amir, accompanied by his young son Musa Khan, and Daoud Shah, the Afghan Commander-in-Chief, had arrived at the British advanced positions near Ali Khel and were in camp there awaiting his arrival. Yakub Khan repeated his regret and distress at Cavagnari's fate, and bewailed his inability to prevent it, as he had already done in letters to the Viceroy. Roberts suspected that Yakub's real motives were to forestall any friendly approaches by his uncle, Sirdar Wali Muhammad, who had already joined Roberts's camp, and to delay the British advance. The Amir vainly pleaded with Roberts to stop, saying that he had left the ladies of his family in the Bala Hissar with only one loyal regiment left to guard them.

The mob might attack them if the British approached. Nor had any of the citizens yet made arrangements to move their own families to safety, not expecting the British arrival to be so imminent. Roberts's only concession was to issue a proclamation that innocent people should leave Kabul and either join his camp or make other arrangements for their own safety, and that all women and children should be evacuated from the city. Complying with further instructions from Lytton, he issued an order to his officers, impressing on them the need for constant vigilance in preventing 'irregularities likely to arouse the personal jealousies of the people of Kabul who are, of all races, most susceptible as regards their women'. Lytton had noted earlier in the year, when writing to the Duke of Cambridge, Commander-in-Chief of the British Army, that 'immaculate chastity is not one of the many virtues of the British soldier', and there was certainly some anxiety among the British authorities lest there be a repeat of the indiscretions which had caused such animosity during the First Afghan War.

But Howard Hensman, war correspondent of the Allahabad *Pioneer* and the London *Daily News*, who accompanied Roberts's force, noted that the feeling in the camp was that there were two sides to the old stories from Kabul and that the order ought to be translated into Persian for the Afghan ladies' benefit. 'Until then, the virtue of our brave soldiers must tremble in the balance.'

Officials and military men from Kabul continued to pass in and out of the British camp, ostensibly to wait upon the Amir as he accompanied Roberts to Kabul. 'The camp is over-run with wild-looking Afghans,' Hensman recorded. 'Our soldiers bear them no good will. ... Tommy Atkins is on the whole a very honest sort of fellow, and his ire is now raised against these swaggering cowards who were in Cabul when our Embassy was attacked.' One Sirdar, Nek Muhammad, returned to Kabul after a long and secret interview with the Amir, ostensibly with instructions to quieten the troops there. But shortly afterwards he reappeared with thirteen regiments of regular troops, supported by tribesmen, and took up a strong position on the heights of Charasia, blocking the British line of advance. Roberts felt that to delay an attack would only encourage resistance, so the following morning, 6 October, 1879, he repeated the plan which had been successful at the Peiwar Kotal. The cavalry, field guns and one battalion of Highlanders guarded the camp and made a frontal demonstration, while the veterans of Peiwar Kotal, the 72nd Highlanders, 5th Gurkhas, 5th Punjabis and 23rd Pioneers, made a flanking attack along hill-tops. The plan once more succeeded and the Afghans fled with the loss of twenty guns and several hundred men. Nek Muhammad had his horse shot under him, but escaped in the confusion and made his way to Russian Turkestan. The British losses were twenty killed and sixty-seven wounded. The gatling guns, used in action for the first time by the British

'Lieutenant-General Sir Frederick Roberts and his staff inspecting the captured Afghan artillery, Sherpur, October 1879'. In the background is the ridge of Bemaru. Sherpur, the Aldershot of Afghanistan, was built by Amir Sher Ali on the site occupied by the British cantonments during the First Afghan War.

Army, fired 150 rounds between them, one jamming after the first ten shots.

Two days later, the Kurram Valley Field Force reached the outskirts of Kabul, and on 3 October it held a victory parade through the streets of the city. 'Now I am really King of Kabul,' wrote Roberts to his wife. 'It is not a kingdom I covet and I shall be right glad to get out of it.'

The kingdom really had devolved on Roberts, for on 12 October Amir Yakub Khan had abdicated, stating that he had conceived an utter aversion for his people. As long as he was a successful general he had been popular, he said. When he became Amir they turned on him for making peace with the British.

> Now I detest them all, and long to be out of Afghanistan for ever. It is not that I am unable to hold the country. I have held it before and could hold it again, but I have no further wish to rule such a people, and beg you to let me go.

Roberts tried to make him reconsider, but it is clear that Yakub Khan's spirit would not endure being a British puppet, nor the hatred of his people, which, as Sher Ali had so often said, was inevitably accorded to any Amir who failed to keep the British out of the country.

This ended the fiction that the British had entered Afghanistan to come to the Amir's assistance and that those who fought against them were rebels in arms against their sovereign and his allies. Roberts nevertheless issued a proclamation declaring that all who had resisted the British invasion were to be regarded as traitors, liable to the death penalty. Anyone carrying arms within ten miles of Kabul would be punished by death. Anyone involved in the attack on the Embassy was proscribed. A price of five rupees was put on the head of anyone who had carried arms against the British since September, seventy-five rupees for a captain or subaltern of the regular army, 120 rupees for a field officer. He arrested the Wazir, the Mustafi and various other of the Amir's advisers, and told them that they would remain in custody until their conduct had been investigated.

On 16 October, a series of explosions destroyed much of the Bala Hissar. The British blamed Afghan irreconcilables. The Afghans blamed British frightfulness. It was probably an accidental detonation in one of the powder magazines inside the old palace-fortress, which Roberts had noted as a potential hazard, and for which reason he had decided against accommodating any of his troops there. As it was, a number of British casualties were sustained, including twelve killed, and the 5th Gurkhas lost all their stores and personal belongings. Their comrades of the Peiwar Kotal, the 72nd Highlanders, hearing of this, insisted on handing over their greatcoats to give the Gurkhas some protection from the autumn weather. Roberts ordered the ruins of the Bala Hissar to be dismantled, leaving only the desolate stone walls, and set up his army two miles to the north in the newly built cantonment of Sherpur, the Aldershot of Afghanistan, created by Amir Sher Ali to house his modern regular army and its ordnance depots.

There was subsequently a great deal of controversy over Roberts's proceedings at Kabul during this period. There were newspaper reports of every sort of atrocity. He was accused of shooting men who were unaware of his proclamation and who were carrying side arms merely in accordance with the custom of their country; of hanging soldiers who, though they had borne arms, had done so in defence of their homeland and not against their Amir, and who should have been treated as prisoners of war; and of the indiscriminate execution of anyone denounced to him as having been involved in the attack on the Residency, even by those who were simply using this as a pretext to settle private feuds. There were also reports that men under his command had tortured prisoners, or had given no quarter to men wishing to surrender.

Roberts's answer was that most of these reports were based upon stories filed by journalists with some unjustified personal grudge against him, or on rumours current in the camp and narrated by junior officers in their letters home. As an instance of the type of rumour to which ready credence

was given in his camp, he cited one which he was constantly being asked about, that Lady Cavagnari had returned to India to murder the ex-Amir. As for giving no quarter, he said that by the usages of war the Afghans had forfeited any right to quarter, as they themselves gave none, but that nevertheless his orders were to allow men to surrender, and in fact many Afghan wounded had been treated by British medical officers. Concerning the quasi-judicial proceedings, he reported that no-one was punished for bearing arms alone, but only in conjunction with other offences and after due trial before a military commission presided over by a general officer. He said that not more than eighty-seven persons were executed, among them the Kotwal or Chief Magistrate of Kabul and a ruffian who had carried Cavagnari's head to the bazaar. (The remains of the British officers were never found; those of the Guides were thrown into the city ditch by the Kotwal's men.) This view is supported by Hensman, who reported at the time (with no great indication of approval) that in any case of doubt the tribunal remanded prisoners for further evidence.

But despite these assertions, the fact remains that war cannot be made with kid gloves. No free man worthy of the name can be expected to treat the invaders of his homeland other than with the most terrible ferocity.

No soldier of an invading army, be his cause never so just, can be expected to show invariable mercy to men who a few moments previously have been trying to kill him or actually have killed his comrades. The readiness of wounded Afghans to kill those who did offer them succour and the reports, not always accurate, of tortures inflicted on British and Indian wounded and prisoners, only made some soldiers the less willing to offer quarter if not under the direct eyes of a senior officer.

To English readers it may seem that Roberts was a conscientious and patriotic soldier who did his duty as he saw it according to the standards of his age. And compared to the way the Russian generals behaved in their conquest of Central Asia, Roberts's policy was mildness itself. But the Afghans saw his behaviour in the same way that English readers would regard a German general who, in 1939, had invaded Kent and marched to London to avenge the murder of the German Ambassador, his close personal friend and political ally; treating all members of the Army and Home Guard who opposed the march as outlaws; burning villages near the scenes of any fighting; hanging the Lord Mayor and other citizens for being members of the Resistance; and arresting Mr Neville chamberlain (namesake of the frontier general) and the rest of the British Cabinet, all in the name of assisting King George VI to restore order in the streets of his capital; and then blowing up the Tower of London and sending the ex-king to exile in Germany.

Certainly at the time there were protests against the conduct of the war. William Gladstone, stumping the Scottish Lowlands in his famous Midlothian campaign, denounced every aspect of the government's policy, including its having become involved in two fruitless wars. He spoke of the fate of thousands of Zulus, shot down by British troops for no other offence than having had the courage to defend with their naked bodies their own hearths and homes from a foreign invader. As for the Afghan War, he told his enthusiastic audience: 'Remember that the sanctity of life in the hill villages of Afghanistan, amid the winter snows, is as inviolable in the eyes of Almighty God as can be your own.' Beaconsfield dismissed this as 'rhodomontade', but not all his wit could disguise the fact that while the British taxpayer might applaud a speedy, successful campaign demonstrating the superiority of the British Army over its savage foes, and the bravery and dash of its soldiers in heroic battles, he was not so keen on reports of British regulars wiped out by Zulu *impis* of British Envoys murdered in their own Residencies, of commissariat failures, of alleged atrocities, nor, most important of all, being asked to foot the bill with nothing to show for his money. The country was at this time in the throes of an industrial slump. Five wet summers in a row (for which the electorate, as is customary, held the government to blame) had ruined the farmers and sent the cost of food soaring. It was not to be wondered at that the Prime Minister felt the stars in their courses were fighting against him.

VIII

The Two Knights

British Generals in action 1879–80

While Sir Frederick Roberts and his men were establishing a British military government around Kabul, two other British armies were operating at opposite ends of Afghanistan. At Kandahar, Sir Donald Stewart hastily reassembled his field force and recalled units from their way back to India, just as Nott had in the previous war. By the end of September the British position around Kandahar had been secured, and during October a force was sent to make a demonstration in the direction of Ghazni. A garrison was thrown into Kalat-i-Ghilzai while the rest of Stewart's force returned to Kandahar for the winter. During these movements there were a number of brushes with the Ghilzais, who had assembled in response to a call for holy war then being taken up with increasing vigour among the Afghan tribes.

On the Khyber front a force was mobilized under Major-General Bright, who took command at Peshawar on 13 September. 'Thank God,' wrote Lord Lytton, 'we have got rid of Sir Samuel Browne.' Unfortunately for the rapidity of this column's advance, he had also got rid of all its transport. The reason, as Sir Frederick Haines explained to the Duke of Cambridge, was 'an overwhelming desire to assume an aspect of perfect repose at as early a date as possible. In fact there is always a desire to do something either before Parliament rises or before it assembles, which sadly militates against the logical sequence of military plans.' Even more fatal than the commissariat failures were the breakdowns in the medical arrangements. The dreaded *comma vibrio*, the cholera bacillus, which had decimated the regiments returning from Kandahar, also lurked in the camping places of the Khyber defiles, a better defence against the returning British than the *jezails* of those bold spirits among the hillmen who, scorning British gold, took up arms to join the holy war now being preached by their spiritual leaders. Several regiments were so reduced by sickness that they were unfit even to guard the lines of communication and had to be sent back to the plains. But Bright pushed his men on, reaching Gandamak on 2 November. On the 6th, at Kata Sang, he met a detachment of troops sent out from Kabul under Brigadier-General Macpherson and then returned to Gandamak. A force under Brigadier-General Charles Gough was at Jagdalak on 15 December when his signallers reported an urgent message flashed from Kabul by heliograph that it was to march at once to Roberts's aid.

During these months national and religious feeling against the British had been growing. There was economic hardship, as Roberts appropriated the government share of the crop to feed his troops. As in 1841, the high prices paid by British commissaries on the open market caused inflation and shortages. The occupation of Kabul, from which the British had, in popular memory, been driven in the previous war, was an affront to national dignity. The deportation of Amir Yakub Khan to India was another. Roberts's 'Black Assize', with the gallows standing ready before the ruins of Cavagnari's Residency, was a challenge that no Afghan of spirit could refuse to take up. But irrespective of any of these incidents there was the unquenchable desire of the Afghan people not to have foreigners, and still less unbelievers, in control of their country, or even in it at all.

The cry of *jihad*, or holy war, was raised early. The most eminent leader to call on all true Muslims to rise in arms against the infidel invaders was Mir Din Muhammad, usually known by his honorific title, Mashk-i-Alam, the Perfume of the Universe. He, at this time aged about ninety, was a man held in great reverence and esteem and noted for his piety and learning. Many of the religious and legal officials in the country had been educated at his feet, and readily responded to their old professor's call to encourage their people to take up arms. The local religious leaders, or mullahs, many of them ignorant, bigoted men, preached *jihad* with the same eloquence as their superiors, and a growing combination of national and religious sentiment suddenly placed the unsuspecting British in a very critical situation.

The first signs of trouble seemed easy enough to disregard. An attack by Ghilzais on 2 October on the garrison left behind on the Shutargardan Pass was beaten off with little loss to the British. So was another one on 14 October, though it was noticed that a simultaneous attack was then made on the garrison at Ali Khel. On the 16th, the Shutargardan garrison was surrounded, and was once more attacked on the 18th, though relief came from Kabul the next day and the tribesmen dispersed. After this, the Kabul to Khyber route having been opened, the Shutargardan was abandoned and its garrison moved to Ali Khel and Kabul.

But by early December, it became clear that a serious rising, aimed at the British occupation forces in Kabul, was imminent. Roberts, roused from his pipe dreams of a peerage, or a large cash reward such as had been voted to Sir Garnet Wolseley for the Ashanti War, ordered up the Corps of Guides from the Khyber force to reinforce Kabul.

Roberts's intelligence reported that there were now three Afghan armies in the field, approaching Kabul from the north, west and south. He decided to forestall their attack by defeating and dispersing each of these forces before they could unite and combine against him. Accordingly he sent out two columns, each of about 1,000 men of all arms. One such battle group, under Brigadier-General Macpherson, moved out north-westwards on 8 December, halting after three miles at Kila Ashar. The other, under Brigadier-General Baker, marched southwards on the 9th, ostensibly towards Charasia, but with orders to turn west in the direction of Argandah, about twenty miles away in the direction of Ghazni. Then it was reported that the Afghan forces from Ghazni were moving to join up with those from Kohistan, north of Kabul. Roberts ordered Macpherson to leave his cavalry and horse artillery, under Brigadier-General Massy, at Kila Ashar and move quickly against the Kohistanis. Macpherson complied, and on the morning of the 10th succeeded in breaking up a large concentration of tribesmen with little loss to his own troops. The battle was not decisive, however, and Massy failing to intercept them with the cavalry from Kila Ashar, the Afghans variously dispersed into the neighbouring hills and villages, or moved off towards their allies in the direction of Arghandah.

Roberts then ordered Macpherson, now some nine miles north-west of Sherpur, to march early on the 11th towards Arghandah, where the force from Ghazni, under the leadership of Sirdar Muhammad Jan, was thought to be. Baker was by this time about twenty miles south-west of Kabul. He too was told to push on towards Arghandah. Thus, if Muhammad Jan resumed his march on Kabul, he would find Baker in his rear, Macpherson on his left and the balance of Roberts's force, some 3,000 men, in his front. If he stayed where he was, he would be attacked simultaneously from opposite directions. Massy was ordered to move his cavalry directly along the road from Kabul to Arghandah, keeping in communication with Macpherson over the hills on his left, but not to join battle until Macpherson himself was engaged.

Massy had gained something of a reputation as the commander of a smart cavalry regiment in the United Kingdom, and had been sent to India specially to take command of a horse brigade. But Roberts formed the opinion that Massy was slothful and incompetent, and employed him only with reluctance. Rather than move along the Kabul-Arghandah road, Massy decided to cut several miles off his journey, by marching across country south-westwards from his position at Kila Ashar, on the city's western outskirts. Thus he was about five miles away from Macpherson and much closer to Arghandah than either of the other two columns when his scouts reported the presence of large numbers of Afghans, occupying the village of Kila Kazi, much nearer to Kabul than had been expected. Massy's first reaction was to suppose that these were fugitives from Macpherson's victory of the previous day and continue his advance, though there was now a considerable noise of drumming, dust and general commotion to his front.

'Our Life for Our Queen'. A fanciful impression of the cavalry action outside
Kabul, 11 December 1879. Brigadier-General Dunham Massy, commanding 213
men of the 9th Lancers and forty-four men of the 14th Bengal Lancers, with four

guns of the Royal Horse Artillery, encountered an overwhelming Afghan force under Sirdar Muhammad Jan, and was driven back towards Sherpur.

As he topped a small rise he was astounded to see Muhammad Jan's entire army, some 10,000 tribesmen, spread out in an arc before him, opposed to his own puny force of 300 lancers and four light field guns. He opened fire with his artillery, but had no effect on the advancing horde. Steadily forced back, Massy dismounted a troop of the 9th Lancers and ordered them to use their Martini-Henry carbines, but the tribesmen came on in their hundreds and the thirty cavalrymen made no impression on them. Four miles away, at Sherpur, Roberts had heard artillery firing and, aware that something had gone wrong with his plans, galloped out with his personal staff as fast as their horses would carry them.

When Roberts reached the scene of the action, he sent messages back to Sherpur for two companies of Highlanders and asked Massy to try to delay the Afghans as long as possible to give Macpherson time to arrive. But the attackers came on in waves, with no infantry to stop them, and in order to try to get the guns away Roberts ordered a cavalry charge. This, delivered over broken ground against odds of forty to one, lance against Khyber knife, failed to check the onslaught and riders and horses went down together. Roberts made a stand with the guns in the small village of Bhagwana, but, the ammunition running low, was obliged to retreat under cover of a second charge. The villagers emerged and joined the fight against the hard-pressed British. Their headman attacked Roberts himself, who was only saved by the intervention of an unhorsed trooper of the 1st Bengal Lancers. The chaplain, the same Reverend Adams who had brought up the reinforcements at the Peiwar Kotal, was in this fracas too, dragging two British soldiers of the 9 Lancers from beneath their fallen horses by sheer strength and giving up his own mount to a wounded lancer. This warlike and powerfully built man of God was awarded the Victoria Cross for his valour in this fight.

But for the British the day was now lost. The guns stuck fast in an irrigation ditch and were abandoned. The cavalry re-formed and retired, firing, by alternate squadrons for three miles back to a narrow gorge, the Deh-i-Mazang, from which the road led straight down into Kabul. There the Highlanders were waiting, and they with a few volleys checked the Afghan pursuit as soon as the exhausted horse soldiers filed past. Macpherson, meanwhile, hearing the sound of battle, had marched directly to the sound of the guns, arriving on the battlefield about an hour after the fighting ended, to find the mutilated bodies of the British dead and to wonder what had happened to his comrades. He exchanged shots with the Afghan rearguard and reached the Deh-i-Mazang at about 7 p.m. Baker arrived at Arghandah, the original concentration area, the same night. The next day, 12 December, discovering what had happened to the rest of the army, he returned to Sherpur.

The fact that Muhammad Jan had outmanoeuvred the British general, captured his guns, defeated his cavalry and was now on the outskirts of Kabul was soon common knowledge in the surrounding hills. Those already in arms against the British took new heart. Those who had been waverers now flocked to join the struggle. In the earlier battles of this war the Afghans had been the attacked rather than the attackers, and had been led by regular officers who knew enough of their profession to worry about their flanks and lines of communication. Roberts's previous successes had been largely attributable to this and he had come to underestimate the abilities of his enemy. Now he had divided his forces in the presence of a fast-moving enemy once too often, an error which cost many of Massy's horse soldiers their lives and their commander his reputation.

Sir Frederick Haines, who, despite Lytton's ill-founded criticisms, was as professional a soldier as could be wished for, relieved Massy of his command on reading Roberts's despatches. Roberts tried to mend matters by suggesting he be given another brigade somewhere in India, but Haines replied that if Massy was unfit to command, that was the end of the matter. Massy was sent back to England in disgrace, though there was a strong body of opinion among his own friends that he had saved Sherpur by intercepting the Afghan force, which had slipped through the arms of Roberts's pincer movement, and that a vindictive Roberts had made him a scapegoat for the failure of a faulty plan.

Muhammad Jan's men took up a position on a ridge on the south west side of Kabul known as the Takht-i-Shah. Roberts's first attempt to dislodge them, made on 12 December, petered out in the face of stubborn resistance, the Afghans manning their defences with determination and greeting every British shell with cries of derision, or waving their knives and rifles in defiance. The next day, the 13th, Baker's column having rejoined, the British tried again and succeeded in capturing the ridge, though not without a bitter struggle.

On the 14th, large numbers of Afghans appeared on the Asmai-Koh, a high hill north-west of Kabul covering the Deh-i-Mazang defile. A British force was sent against this position and captured the crest, only to be driven back by the Afghan counter-attack with the loss of two mountain guns. Simultaneously, another Afghan force gathered at Siah Sang, a hill on the east side of the city, and although cavalry sent against them by Roberts forced them to stay on the hill, it was clear that the plan, to which he had continued to pin his faith, of bringing to battle and defeating each section in turn of the forces opposed to him was now unworkable.

Roberts confessed to having had no idea, before the afternoon of the 14th of either the numbers that had been assembled against him, or of their ability to stand up to regular troops. He had suffered casualties in four days. Shaken in his confidence in the ability of his own relatively small force to deal with this threat in the open, he decided to abandon the city and retire inside the defences of Sherpur.

During the afternoon the outlying forces were withdrawn from the surrounding hills. As each position was abandoned by the British it was occupied by exultant Afghans, growing in confidence as the troops pulled back, everyone remembering that this was how it had been in 1841. But the soldiers, though closely pressed and at times involved in hand-to-hand fighting when the tribesmen grew bold enough to try a rush, came down in good order and each unit was greeted personally by Roberts as it marched in.

With the withdrawal of the British into Sherpur, law and order in Kabul collapsed and the victorious tribesmen, joined by the city mob, surged in to take revenge on all those who had collaborated with the British. Some went to the house of Sirdar Wali Muhammad, known to have been on good terms with the British. But that prince, along with various other notables, had made his way into Sherpur in some haste when he saw what was happening. The ladies of his *harem*, whom he had left behind, were subjected to the indignity of being stripped and searched by a group of hypothetical patriots for any valuables concealed about their persons. Other groups made for the Hindu and Qizilbash quarters to claim the traditional victors' rewards of loot, pillage and rape. These two communities, forming the commercial and middle-class elements of Kabuli society, were rich enough to be worth robbing and held heterodox religious views, so could the more readily be accused of disloyalty.

Thus, in December 1879, the British at Kabul appeared to be in a position very similar to that of their predecessors in December 1841. Their Envoy had been murdered. Their troops had been driven from the city and the hills by a wave of national feeling. The winter had set in with its usual severity. Their supplies from the surrounding countryside had been cut off. Their troops were too few to garrison their cantonment and take the offensive simultaneously. Their nearest supports were miles away on the Jalalabad road.

But there were many ways in which the position was different. Sherpur, unlike Elphinstone's peace-time cantonment, was defensible, with thick mud walls on three sides of it, one of them on the Bemaru ridge itself. Roberts had built up, during the previous weeks, more than a month's supply of food and three months' forage for his beasts. All this, plus ample stocks of firewood from the ruins of the Bala Hissar, was inside his defences. Elphinstone's supplies had been abandoned outside and he had been dependent on local purchase for maintenance. Roberts's men were given four blankets each to beat the cold and had a good supply of warming and nourishing drinks. Elphinstone's men had been demoralized for lack of food and warm clothing.

Above all was the matter of leadership. Elphinstone, caught by the outbreak on the point of moving to India, literally scarcely knew if he was coming or going. Roberts knew he was staying. Elphinstone had a poor second-in-command and was able to inspire neither the affection nor the confidence of his command. Roberts was generally popular and trusted by officers and men alike. Elphinstone had been old and sick. Roberts was active, mentally and physically. Elphinstone had been burdened with all the wives, families and civilian employees inseparable from a peace-time army. Roberts's force was a mobilized army, on campaign, with essential followers only and no dependants to worry about. Roberts enjoyed political and military authority, unlike Elphinstone, who in political matters had to defer to MacNaghten and his successors. Finally, just as there was now good leadership on the British side, there was poor leadership on the Afghan side, no-one emerging with that combination of diplomatic skill and generalship which had characterized Sirdar Muhammad Akbar Khan.

With the British shut up inside Sherpur, facing the problem of defending four miles of wall with some 6,000 men, the leaders of the insurrection, who by this time included the ex-Amir's wife, and the late Sirdar Muhammad Akbar Khan's daughter, discussed what to do next. Roberts was offered terms for a withdrawal to India. He would be allowed to go on condition that Amir Yakub Khan was sent back with honour to his people and two senior British officers given as hostages. If not, he was told, 'We have a lakh of men. They are like dogs eager to rush on their prey. We cannot much longer control them.' But everyone knew what happened to the last British army to retreat from Kabul through the December snows, and Roberts's refusal to treat was predictable. They turned to other subjects. The Mashk-i-Alam was appointed Kotwal of Kabul, the British military governor having fled into Sherpur. All the citizens of Kabul were ordered to demonstrate their patriotism and religious fervour by handing over their stocks of grain and food to replenish the pouches of the *jihadis*. Ex-Amir Yakub's mother handed over her jewels and personal fortune to buy supplies for the 'troops' (there was by now only one regular regiment, the Amir's Bodyguard, still in being) and in return secured the nomination of Yakub's infant son, Musa Khan, as Amir, supported by the powerful Sirdars, who saw themselves as exercising power in his name.

At 5.30 on 23 December, 1879, a flaring beacon lit by the Mashk-i-Alam himself was the signal for a desperate assault against Sherpur's defences by the whole Afghan force, inspired by the preaching of their mullahs to destroy the infidel invaders once and for all. Shouts of *Allah-il-Allah* (the opening of the Muslim creed, 'there is no God but God') and of *Din Din* ('The faith, the faith') filled the air, together with the beating of innumerable *tom-tom* drums. Wave after wave of tribesmen swept against Sherpur. But against modern weapons and strong defences, the bravest men, the most devout of believers, had little chance. Only a mistake by Roberts would have let them win, and Roberts was making no more mistakes. Without artillery (all the Amir's proud guns had been captured in their arsenal and were still inside Sherpur) the attack was bound to fail. Even the darkness that was to hide the attackers' approach was broken by star-shells fired by the British gunners to illuminate their targets.

And, a completing touch, a spy had warned Roberts the preceding night of the plan of attack, down to the very time and place of the signal fire. As the torch was applied, the British were already standing in their embrasures and on their fire-steps. Colley's faith in the defensive power of the breech-loader proved fully vindicated. By midday the attack had failed. A sortie by the British cavalry ended the fighting and the Afghans fell back, carrying most of their casualties away, but leaving about 1,000 dead on the battlefield. British casualties during the siege totalled eighteen killed and sixty-eight wounded, including five killed and twenty-seven wounded during the final assault.

On 24 December the reinforcements for which Roberts had telegraphed at the beginning of the siege arrived, and the British reoccupied Kabul on Christmas Day 1879. The ex-Amir's ladies were placed under British surveillance, but the other leaders of the insurrection escaped into the hills, promising to return in the spring. The tribesmen melted away to their villages and the snow-covered countryside around Kabul assumed an aspect of quietness and peace. Sirdar Wali Muhammad was appointed Governor, and an amnesty was extended to those who had been involved in the rising.

The collapse of Yakub Khan's Amirate convinced the British Cabinet that there was now no alternative to the dismemberment of Afghanistan. Sovereignty over an independent Kandahar, 'protected' by a British garrison there or at Quetta, was offered to a Barakzai prince, Sher Ali, whose father, Mir Dil Khan, a brother of Dost Muhammad, had been one of the Sirdars of Kandahar driven out in 1839. Sher Ali had been appointed Governor of Kandahar by Amir Yakub Khan after the Treaty of Gandamak. After cautious negotiations and several assurances that Afghanistan would never be reunited, and that the British would never withdraw from Kandahar, he accepted the British offer and was formally installed as Wali or Ruler in the middle of May 1880.

Herat proved less simple. The Foreign Office, headed by Salisbury, took the view that to set up Herat as an independent state, or to bring it under direct British control, would alienate the Iranians, who had never really abandoned their claims to this province. It would have the effect of driving them into the Russian camp, and they might then be prepared to let the Russians take Merv, abandoning their own claims to it in return for Russian help in taking Herat. Reversing the policy of half a century, the British Cabinet indicated to the Shah that if he could succeed in occupying Herat, the British Government would not object, and on further evidence of the Shah's friendship (assuming this to be forthcoming) might recognize Herat as Iranian territory. This, it was thought, would ensure that Iran became a firm ally of the British, while sparing the British themselves the expense and embarrassment of trying to hold a region so far from their Indian base.

'An attack on a baggage train, Second Afghan War'. An artist's impression, from the Illustrated London News, *of British and Indian troops ambushed by Pathan tribesmen. In a country with scarcely any roads fit for wheeled traffic, nearly all the baggage was carried by pack animals, and a successful raid could secure not only the baggage but the valuable animals which carried them.*

Afghan Turkestan, between the Oxus and the Hindu Kush, would be left as a neutral zone. One idea advanced at the beginning of November by Major Oliver St John, who had previously been in Cavagnari's party at Ali Masjid and had replaced him as Lytton's favourite political officer, was that it could be given to Amir Sher Ali's nephew, Abdur Rahman.

Sirdar Abdur Rahman was at this time, as he had been during the previous twelve years, a pensioner of the Russians. He had never given up hopes of gaining the Amirate of Kabul, which his father had once held, for himself, but the Russians had always prevented him, at first because they did not wish to break the promises of non-interference in Afghan affairs they had given the British, and later because they wished to cultivate the friendship of Amir Sher Ali.

But at the end of 1879 the situation changed, and with Russian encouragement and financial aid, together with a loan of 200 breech-loading rifles (valued by the Russians at twenty-five roubles each), 2,000 rounds of ball ammunition and field equipment for 100 cavalry and 100 infantry, Abdur Rahman marched south to claim his inheritance.

Certainly from the Russian point of view, Abdur Rahman's arrival in Afghanistan at this time amply repaid the money they had spent on his pension. With no one able to take Yakub's place at Kabul (for the anti-British Sirdars had fled and the pro-British ones had no following) the British might have been tempted, even forced, to establish direct government there. This would not have suited the Russians so well as an independent local ruler, who might, in due time, become more friendly to them than to the British. This would explain the haste with which Abdur Rahman was sent off. 'The Russians pressed me most strongly to leave. They said I could not leave soon enough,' he wrote. And Abdur Rahman was not ungrateful. He told the British officers in Afghanistan as much.

> I am bound to them by no oath or promise, but simply by feelings of gratitude, and consequently I should never like to be obliged to fight them. I have eaten their salt, and was for twelve years dependent on their hospitality.

Lytton, for his part, was desperately trying to find someone to whom he could hand over the government of Kabul. At the end of February 1880 he sent to Kabul a member of the Indian Foreign Department, Lepel Griffin, with orders to 'set about the preparation of a way for us out of that rat-trap' as soon as he arrived there.

Otherwise, he thought, his policy had been successful enough. The Khyber and the Bolan passes were secure in British hands. Baluchistan was peaceful and friendly. So was Kandahar under Wali Sher Ali. British officers could now enter most parts of Afghanistan. And the Afghan state, with its military power a threat to India rather than a buffer, had been broken up. All that was necessary now was for the Kabul government to be settled and the British troops could go home. This last was increasingly important, for as in the First Afghan War, what had been intended to be a short, swift and decisive campaign had turned into an unpopular, prolonged and increasingly expensive war.

Lytton's attempts to blame the generals, for over-insuring against defeat by demanding unnecessarily large and costly forces, were beginning to backfire. He had complained that neither Haines nor any of his staff had ever been able to grasp the effect of the breech-loader on warfare. 'And as they have never read a book they can neither imagine nor believe anything which they have not themselves seen.' Beaconsfield, to whom Cranbrook passed on Lytton's private letter, was driven to protest to Salisbury:

> I remember, with alarm, 50 or 60 thousand camels have already been wasted … General Sam Browne according to Lytton, ought to have been tried by court martial, and he goes through them all with analogous remarks. And these are the men whom, only a few months ago, he recommended for all these distinctions. I begin to think he ought to be tried by a court martial himself …

The appearance of Abdur Rahman on the scene, in early March 1880, and his letting it be known that he was prepared to treat with the English, was therefore greeted by Lytton with enthusiasm. 'A ram caught in the thicket,' was the phrase he used to Cranbrook at the India Office. Cranbrook and the rest of the Cabinet, on the other hand, were by no means happy at the thought of handing over Kabul to a prince who might well be under Russian influence, and it was only reluctantly that approval was given for Lepel Griffin to open negotiations with him.

In the spring of 1880, as the defence of Kandahar had been made the responsibility of the Bombay Army, Lieutenant-General Sir Donald Stewart handed over the city to Lieutenant-General Primrose, and marched with the Bengal regiments towards Kabul. The despatch to Kabul of an officer considerably senior to Roberts was regarded, in some quarters, as a consequence of the allegations of British atrocities there. 'All this is unpleasant for me,' Stewart wrote to his wife 'as I daresay some people may think I have had a hand in the matter.'

He reached Kalat-i-Ghilzai in early April, and heard the news from England that the first returns from the general election had been most unfavourable to the Conservative government. 'The news received from him about the elections has put a sad damper on our spirits,' he told Lady Stewart. 'We think it quite possible that there may be complete change of policy.' A week later he wrote again: 'All we know is that the elections were going against the Government. ... I suppose Lord Lytton will resign at once.'

But soon more immediate problems took his attention. The Hazaras taking advantage of the collapse of Afghan military power, came down in great numbers from their own districts and accompanied Stewart's line of march, burning and looting deserted Afghan villages, desecrating graves and enslaving any non-combatants they could find 'The fact is they are all cut-throat barbarians,' be told his wife. 'I shall not have anything to say to the Hazaras, and shall decline their co-operation if they offer it.' Other bands also followed his line of march, some made up of *jihadis*, who had assembled near Kandahar others of local men. Stewart's appreciation was that they were heading for Ghazni and would try to combine against him with the Sirdars there.

On 19 April, concerned by the increasing number of hostiles hanging about his flanks and rear, Stewart decided to protect his baggage and heavy artillery by placing it in the centre of his column, with one of his two brigades at the front and the other bringing up the rear. When his cavalry reported a large gathering of horse and foot in front of him at Ahmad Khel, some twenty miles west of Ghazni Stewart at first assumed this to be another band of Hazaras. But it almost at once became clear that he was opposed by a strong force of Ghilzais and others.

Stewart at once formed a line, while his guns began to play upon the Afghan masses on the heights to his front. In the centre he placed one battery of horse artillery (six 6-pdrs) and one of field artillery (six 9-pdrs) with their respective cavalry and infantry escorts. On the right were six squadrons of Indian cavalry. On the left were the infantry, the 59th Foot, the 3rd Gurkhas and the 2nd Sikhs. On the extreme left rode a squadron of the 19th Bengal Lancers. In reserve were the 19th Punjab Infantry, with two companies of Bengal sappers and miners, while Stewart's Divisional HQ was defended by one troop of Indian cavalry, a company of Indian infantry and a company of the British Army's elite 60th Rifles. The rest of the division, consisting of a mountain battery, a squadron of Punjab Cavalry, one British and two Indian battalions, was far to the rear, separated from the battle line by all the logistic support units, the hospital, the ordnance field park, the paymaster's treasure chests, by long strings of baggage camels and by a siege train. This battery alone, two 40-pdrs and two 6.3-inch howitzers intended for use against the walls of Ghazni, took up a mile of road, each gun with twenty yoke of oxen trudging slowly along.

The gunfire provoked a furious rush by a horde of Afghan swords men all along the British front. 'Down they came,' wrote Lieutenant-Colonel E.F. Chapman, Stewart's Chief-of-Staff 'at least 3,000 in number, sweeping over the intervening ground with marvellous rapidity and quite regardless of our fire … right and left, to get round the flanks, rode horsemen with standards; the whole hill seemed to be moving.' On the British left a squadron of Bengal Lancers was routed and galloped to the rear, colliding with the 19th Punjabis. 'Some of the cavalry did not do well,' noted Stewart in his diary, 'nor did some of the other troops.' The next day, writing to his wife, he was more plain: 'The Ghazis came on sword in hand and a part of the line gave way before them, and to make matters worse, there was a stampede of a part of the cavalry and everything was swept before it.' The stampede swept over the medical dressing station and reached within ten yards of Stewart's own headquarters, where his staff drew their swords ready for personal combat. But then the fire of the HQ defence companies diverted the Afghan rush and the cavalry rallied as the pursuit slackened.

In the centre of the line the Afghan attack seemed almost irresistible. The 59th Foot had only just deployed, and some companies had not had time to fix bayonets before the *Ghazis* surged down on them. Two companies on the left were ordered to fall back to protect the flank, and for a time it looked as though the rest of the battalion would give way altogether. The horse gunners, unable to stop the tribesmen even with case shot at thirty yards, limbered up and galloped to take up a new position farther back. The Gurkhas formed rallying squares and held firm. The 3rd Sikhs, with the advantage of a few minutes to get ready to receive the attack, stood like rocks and the crisis of the battle passed.

Stewart committed his reserves, including his sappers, fighting as infantry, his divisional HQ defence companies and the 19th Punjabis.

'The Return of the Fore and Aft'. A scene from Rudyard Kipling's short story 'The Drums of the Fore and Aft', said to be based on an incident at the Battle of Ahmed.

Gradually the fire of the breech-loaders and the artillery, joined by the two 40-pdrs, which came into action from a distant hillside, began to have their effect. Some elements of the rear brigade appeared in the distance. The British line steadied. The Afghans lost heart as the impetus of their rush slackened and fell back before a cavalry charge on the British left. Some, wounded or shamming dead, cut desperately up at the troops as they passed, determined to give their lives in defence of their religion and their homeland. After two hours' fighting the Afghan force, some 15,000 strong, of whom about 5,000 had actually been involved in combat, broke up and retreated.

Stewart reported a body count of 800 Afghans and a loss to his own men of seventeen dead and 120 wounded. The Afghans themselves said they lost 1,100 dead, with at least an equal number wounded. Once their initial rush had failed (and it very nearly succeeded) there was only one outcome possible in a battle between men with swords and shields and men with rifles and artillery. Some of Stewart's officers grumbled that he should have increased the number of enemy dead in his report, but regardless of the effect it had on their future careers, Stewart refused to exaggerate.

Others in his force, once they had recovered from the shock of the battle, paid tribute to the courage of their ill-armed foes – 'Their bravery was magnificent,' was Chapman's phrase. Another officer, Captain Elias, wrote in similar vein:

Anyone with the semblance of a heart under his khaki-jacket could not help feeling something akin to pity to see them advancing with their miserable weapons in the face of our guns and rifles, but their courage and their numbers made them formidable.

At Kabul, Roberts heard the reports of Stewart's progress without enthusiasm. He wrote to Lytton saying that there was no need for Stewart to come to Kabul and expressing the earnest hope,

that he will not be allowed to finish the operations which I commenced. To be superseded now, when matters are I hope progressing towards a speedy and satisfactory conclusion, would be a mortification and a blow to my reputation that I could never recover.

Lepel Griffin offered to resign rather than serve under Stewart, in order to strengthen Roberts's claim to have, if not military, at least political charge at Kabul.

On 21 April the British column reached Ghazni, which surrendered without a fight. In the clear atmosphere a heliograph was seen winking from forty miles away, where a brigade from Kabul was on its way to meet them. On the 23rd a gathering of Afghan tribesmen at Arzu, seven miles to the south-east, was attacked and broken up by Stewart's men, leaving 400 dead for the loss of two killed and eight wounded on the British side. A few days later, despite a last effort by Roberts to persuade him to keep away, Stewart camped his division at the Shutargardan Pass and left to take supreme command at Kabul. He arrived there to find his earlier anticipations proved correct. The British electorate had turned the Conservatives out of office. William Gladstone was back in No 10 Downing Street. Lord Cranbrook had gone from the India Office, to be replaced by Lord Hartington. Lord Lytton had sent in his resignation.

IX

Stale-Mate

The ending of the Second Afghan War 1881

Even before the change of Government at Westminster, the British had determined on a withdrawal from Kabul. In a memorandum dated 2 April, 1880 Lytton had argued that, now Kabul had been pacified and British military power demonstrated, the aim must be to establish a friendly local ruler there, subordinate to and in alliance with the Government of India. Such a ruler was not to be dependent on British aid, for if he were, he would never succeed in establishing his own power in the country and the British would be committed to an expensive and indefinite period of occupation. Therefore, said Lytton, the British troops should be withdrawn as soon as the climate allowed.

In an absolute reversal of his earlier policy, Lytton urged that the British should withdraw to avoid provoking a Russian advance. The Russians, he said, might fear that from Kabul the British would march to the Oxus and stir up the Turkestan tribes. Possibly this fear might induce the Russians to move first, into Afghan Turkestan, between the Oxus and the Hindu Kush. But if the British gave assurances that they were leaving Kabul, the Russians would have no excuse for moving. Against the contingency of an unprovoked Russian move he would rely upon the government in London to use pressure elsewhere.

Abdur Rahman's position grew stronger as it became known that he was negotiating to take over Kabul from the British. His partisans in Afghan Turkestan levied forced contributions from the caravans and merchants to raise money for his troops, although he himself kept out of it, playing the role of the benevolent prince. Stewart wrote home that Abdur Rahman,

> like all his family, thinks the people are made for the sole purpose of supplying him with men and money. They are a vile race, and we shall never make anything of them. The more I see of them, the more hateful does their character appear.

Lytton began to worry that Abdur Rahman was trying to protract the negotiations knowing that the British wanted to withdraw. This, he told Cranbrook on 27 April, was an attempt to put the British in the position of 'gamblers sitting down at 10 o'clock to break the bank with the knowledge that whether they win or lose, they must leave off playing at 12 o'clock.' He ordered Griffin to inform Abdur Rahman that the British, having achieved all the safeguards they needed on their frontier by establishing themselves at Kandahar and in the Kurram, no longer needed any treaty relationship with the ruler of Kabul, nor (almost an aside) to maintain agents at his court, and therefore the troops would return to India in October next. Griffin did so, but persuaded Lytton to omit the mention of Kandahar, knowing that Abdur Rahman could never openly accept this, and to omit any specific date.

He also, without authority, referred to 'the establishment of a strong and friendly Amir', contrary to his instructions, which were that the British were not setting up any sort of Amir, nor did they need to, but were simply notifying Abdur Rahman of their position and intentions.

Sir Donald Stewart assumed political as well as military control on his arrival at Kabul, though not without a struggle. Lytton telegraphed him, while he was still on the march, that Griffin was not to be overruled without prior reference to the Foreign Department. Stewart, who had read the history of the First Afghan War, refused to accept command without political power and offered to stand down in favour of his friend Roberts, whom he knew enjoyed Lytton's confidence. Lytton assured the general that it was never intended that Griffin should be independent of him, and a telegram from the new Secretary of State directing that Stewart be given full political powers placed the matter beyond all doubt. 'Lord L. is somewhat put out about this,' noted Stewart, 'and thinks that someone at Cabul must have been telegraphing home about this without the knowledge of the Government of India. ... I know that I did not dream of doing anything so disloyal.'

Stewart was more than a little concerned for his friend Roberts, who was so closely identified with the outgoing regime. To Lady Stewart he wrote: 'He is rather in a state of mind about his future, because he will have no appointment when this force returns to India. There is no telling what may happen after Lord Lytton goes. It will be a great shame if they don't do something for Bobs.' He went on to say that there was still ill-feeling against Roberts, and voiced the suspicion that his own division's victories had been so well received 'due to the nasty feeling that we have put the Cabul heroes a little in the background'. Roberts himself felt his fortunes were at a low ebb. He had written to Owen Tudor Burne the previous February that a commander had only the government he was serving to look to for support and justice. Now that there was a new government, formed by a party which had been so critical of him, he felt there was no point in remaining at Kabul and asked Lytton for permission to leave, though stressing he was not unhappy to serve with General Stewart. Lytton, in a personal telegram, expressed deep sympathy, but urged him to stay at his post until October, when the army would return to India in any case. 'Your premature retirement,' he wired, 'would be generally misinterpreted to your detriment.' So Roberts stayed at Kabul, and Stewart was glad to have him there. 'He is very true to me, and is of great use to me in many ways, and if there is to be fighting he will be my right hand.'

And at this time it looked as though there was a good chance that there was to be fighting, for Lepel Griffin had reached the conclusion that Abdur Rahman's position in the country was so strong that, unless the British gave him all he wanted, their army would not be able to withdraw in safety. He had therefore expressed his communications to Abdur Rahman in conciliatory terms, which that prince at once used to try and secure further concessions from the British, including a guarantee that there would be no British Agents anywhere in his state (not just in Kabul his capital); that he would not be asked to join an anti-Russian pact; and that Kandahar should be reunited with the rest of Afghanistan.

Griffin now suggested that the British should try to establish a strong and friendly ruler at Kabul; if not Abdur Rahman, then someone else. But any idea of making commitments to a future ruler of Kabul was anathema to Lytton. He now wanted unconditional withdrawal. 'I see but two courses open to the Government of India,' he wrote on June in his farewell minute as Governor-General. 'The course which has been recommended by Mr. Griffin to the Government, and the course which the Government has recommended, in vain, to Mr. Griffin. In adopting the first course we should be in my opinion, little short of insane.' It would, he continued, involve the indefinite retention of British troops in Afghanistan, with the probable dissolution of the Indian units, which would not accept garrison service so far away from home, and the certainty of prolonged and onerous military expenditure. 'I feel sure that my Colleagues will not fail to realise the very unsatisfactory results of the policy which Mr. Griffin has tried, and on which his future action, if not summarily stopped, will still be based.'

Lytton had every reason to be sensitive over the question of expenditure. From the beginning he had realized that an expensive occupation of Kabul could ruin his Afghan policy just as it had ruined Auckland's. It was, indeed, his plans for cutting corners and risking military actions on the cheap which had goaded Cranbrook into starting a formal war. Now in the final weeks of his administration it was discovered that the military accounts system had completely collapsed, and the war so far had cost twice as much as the published estimates had indicated. The reason was that the Military Accounts Department took note only of audited accounts, not of actual expenditure. Under the pressure of war, the auditors were considerably in arrears and, therefore, the published figures were a massive understatement. Lytton himself referred to this as a public scandal and reproach. His opponents referred to wilful deception and deliberate mendacity. The eventual cost of the war was to be £17 million instead of the £5 million in the estimates.

The new Governor-General, Lord Ripon, arrived at Simla, the summer capital of India, on 8 June, 1880. He was at first inclined to stop the negotiations with Abdur Rahman and consider the restoration of Amir Yakub Khan. He abandoned the idea, partly to avoid giving the impression that the British Government was inconstant in its actions, and partly because to break off negotiations with Abdur Rahman without good cause would put the British in the wrong. Moreover, Abdur Rahman was certainly in control in Afghan Turkestan and would remain there even if kept out of Kabul, irritated with the British and more pro-Russian than ever.

Stewart told Ripon, as he had told Lytton, that the army must leave Kabul by the autumn for reasons of morale, but that it could, in his view, march before then, whenever seemed politically desirable. He did not fear anything more than annoyance by the tribes as it withdrew. As for the political situation, he felt (as did Ripon) that the British, having destroyed the previous system of government, ought to leave some sort of settled regime behind, though he did not believe the country would collapse into anarchy if this could not be done. He was opposed to making a treaty with Abdur Rahman, as Lytton had been. His view, expressed to Ripon on 11 June, was as follows:

No man can expect to rule at Cabul till he has given proof of his ability to hold his own against all comers, and as a contest seems inevitable, it follows there is something to be said for leaving the Afghans to fight their quarrel out among themselves.

But he admitted that this course was opposed to both European and Indian sentiment, and so urged that Abdur Rahman's real intentions, for or against the British, should be established without delay. Stewart and Griffin were at this time both of the opinion that Abdur Rahman was preparing to lead a general rising against the English, just as Muhammad Akbar Khan had in the First Afghan War.

Ripon decided to answer Abdur Rahman's queries with a plain statement of his own policy towards Afghanistan. Kabul was to have no diplomatic relations with any other power but the Government of India. In return for the acceptance of British control over Kabul's foreign policy, British aid would be available against unprovoked foreign aggression. Kandahar would remain independent. The Afghan border areas given up by the Treaty of Gandamak would remain under British control. The rest

'George Frederick Samuel Robinson, 1st Marquis of Ripon 1827–1909 and his household'. Governor-General of India 1880–1885. Appointed by Gladstone's incoming Liberal government to replace Lytton, Ripon successfully withdrew the British garrisons from Afghanistan, and left the way clear for the accession of Amir Abdur Rahman.

of the country, including Herat, Abdur Rahman could have if he could take it. No British Agent would be installed in his country. These terms were sent on 14 June, 1880, with a request for a reply within four days.

Around Kabul the tension increased. Gatherings of tribesmen were reported making their way towards Abdur Rahman's camp across the Hindu Kush. The British began to experience difficulties in collecting supplies. The weather grew hotter daily. 'One thing is clear,' wrote Stewart to his wife on 20 June, 'a crisis is approaching and we shall have a settlement or a fight.'

On 27 June, the Afghan prince sent his reply. 'You have resigned to me Afghanistan up to the limits which were settled of old by Treaty with my noble grandfather, the Amir Dost Muhammad Khan,' he said, and announced the same to his followers. This was true so far as it went, except that he did not say which treaty. He certainly implied that he was his grandfather's true heir and that Sher Ali and Yakub had been usurpers, so no treaty between them and the British was binding on him. As for the treaties with Dost Muhammad, the one in 1855 had been concluded before he held Kandahar, but that of 1857 had been concluded after he had gained it.

Stewart and Griffin felt that this reply was deceptive, but Ripon decided to accept it at face value, and instructed them to request Abdur Rahman to come to Kabul. The British Vakil in his camp, Muhammad Afzal, reported personally to Stewart that Abdur Rahman could be trusted, if only because the Russians, having suffered a defeat in their campaign in Chinese Turkestan, could not offer him any further aid just then. Stewart was still inclined to be cautious, and it was not until 8 July that he accepted that Abdur Rahman really was to be trusted. On the 20th, Stewart was told to send him money and artillery and signify that the British accepted him as the *de facto* ruler of northern Afghanistan.

In a formal durbar held in Kabul, on 22 July, Abdur Rahman was declared Amir. The reading of the Friday *Khutba*, the formal prayer for the ruler of the country, included the name of Abdur Rahman for the first time, without any objection being raised by the congregations.

Abdur Rahman listened to what the British had to tell him, but made it clear that while well disposed, he would not himself enter Kabul escorted by British troops. Stewart wrote to his wife that all seemed ready for the army to leave Kabul on 10 August. 'I can hardly believe that we are to get out of this country without trouble, and yet everything looks bright and promising at this moment. Abdur Rahman seems sensible ... I hope he will be a success. It is a regular lottery, though.'

At the opposite end of the country the Sirdar Sher Ali had been installed as Wali or Ruler of the new independent state of Kandahar in May 1880. He was, in his ceremony of investiture, presented by General Primrose with a jewelled sword, and replied with conventional politeness that he looked forward to having an opportunity of drawing it against the enemies of the British Government.

Despite his new-found dignities, the Sirdar's position was by no means an enviable one, for he seems to have been surrounded by ladies of forceful character and outspoken ways. One such, the widow of his uncle, Kohen Dil Khan, who had ruled at Kandahar before the First Afghan War, told General Stewart with some scorn that Sher Ali was like wax. 'You might make an elephant or a horse, or even a donkey out of him.' After the investiture, the Sirdar was subjected to a violent outburst from his niece and from one of his father's widows, who abused him for joining the unbelievers and for having the temerity to compare himself to his Durrani ancestors. His favourite wife took the Sirdar's side and a violent scene followed. But this lady may have been protesting too much. Earlier Sir Donald Stewart had written to his own wife that the Afghan lady had been noticed looking on from the screens of her apartments at a reception given for the British officers, and later had sent a servant to make an assignation with a handsome Iranian youth in the service of the British interpreter. 'The lad told his master, who advised him to have nothing to say to the lady if he valued his head, and there the matter rests. I wonder what the Sirdar would say if he knew about this.'

But soon the new Wali had other things to worry him, in particular the news from Herat. The original British proposals for the future of this province had at first been rejected by the Shah of Iran, since all he was being offered, in return for what could well prove a costly campaign to capture it from Sirdar Ayub Khan (ex-Amir Yakub's brother), was an undefined tenure for only as long as it suited the British. After a delay of three months, when the Iranians re-opened the subject, they found a new government in office in Britain which was no longer interested in the idea. Thus, one of the basic premises underlying the establishment of the new state of Kandahar, that its northern frontier would be secured by a strong ally of the British, had failed to materialize. Instead, Herat was held by the anti-British Ayub Khan, supported by the remnants of his father's old regular army, well armed, well drilled, strong in modem artillery and with a number of skilful military engineers.

At the end of May there were renewed reports that Ayub would move south from Herat with his army, to make a bid for his father's throne before Abdur Rahman (his cousin) could establish himself at Kabul. But the view in the Indian Foreign Department, accepted by the new Governor-General, was that Ayub was neither a brave man nor a skilful commander, and that he would not leave his base. 'Ayub has cried wolf, wolf so often, he will never come,' said Ripon at a meeting of his council when these reports were discussed.

But Ripon had misquoted the fable, as Sir Frederick Haines remarked to a colleague after the meeting. 'Ayub is the wolf, we are the heedless shepherds. … Ayub *will* come, we shall have a disaster, and I shall be hanged for it.'

On 21 June, 1880, Colonel St John, in political charge at Kandahar, telegraphed that Ayub, who had declared himself Amir, had marched from Herat and the Wali had gone with a hastily assembled army (2,500 horse, 2,000 infantry and six guns) to watch his own northern frontier. Sher Ali had no confidence in his own men and repeatedly asked for the assistance of a British brigade. Primrose, influenced by St John, supported this request, and was told by Ripon (who by now had received confirmation from Teheran that Ayub really was in the field) that he could send a brigade to join the Wali, but it was not to go beyond the Helmand River. Haines appreciated that by dividing the British forces, he was leaving the Kandahar garrison dangerously weak, and began moving up troops along the long lines of communication from Bombay.

The brigade detached from Kandahar, under Brigadier-General G.R.S. Burrows, reached the Helmand on 11 July. It was decided to bring the Wali's men back across the river so that they could be disarmed, in view of their prince's gloomy opinion of their reliability. This was proved to be fully justified when, on 14 July, rather than be disarmed these men mutinied. The cavalry rode back towards Kandahar and the infantry and gunners marched to join Ayub, led by Nur Muhammad Khan, one of the

Wali's closest ministers, who, in Kandahar, had frequently entertained British officers as guests in his house. After some delay Burrows sent some of his own men after them and succeeded in capturing the Wali's battery, minus its ammunition wagons, whose teams had been ridden away by the mutinous artillerymen on the approach of the British.

Burrows then retired a short distance to Khushk-i-Nakhud and remained there until 26 July, with fresh orders to watch Ayub and to stop him from marching on Ghazni. The last thing the British Government wanted at this time was the appearance of a rival to Abdur Rahman. But no attempt was made to reunite the divided British forces. Hearing that Ayub had slipped past him to reach the village of Maiwand, from which he could move on either Ghazni or Kandahar, Burrows left his entrenchments and marched to meet him on the morning of 27 July. The opposing sides met at about 10 a.m., and it soon became apparent that the British had caught a Tartar. They could bring into battle two Bombay cavalry regiments, six guns of the Royal Horse Artillery and the six smooth-bores, manned by British infantrymen and officered from the Ordnance Field Park under the horse artillery's battery captain; the 66th Foot, the 1st Bombay Grenadiers, and the 30th Bombay Infantry, with a half company of Bombay sappers and miners; about 500 sabres and 2,000 rifles all told. But behind the heat haze Ayub had some 8,000 regular troops alone, in three cavalry and ten infantry regiments with thirty-two guns. To this could be added 3,000 other mounted men and at least 15,000 tribesmen and religious warriors, among them a contingent led by Azad Khan of Kharan, who had helped drive the British from Kalat in 1841.

Despite these odds, the British and Indian troops succeeded in pushing back the regulars opposed to them until halted by Ayub's artillery. The battle then became a fire fight, but this allowed the Afghan superiority in men and guns to have its full effect.

While Ayub's regular troops pinned the British firing line, the tribal contingents and cavalry moved round the British flanks and threatened the baggage train and logistic elements in the brigade's rear. This technique, perfected by Ayub, was known as the *killaband*, the besieging, or encirclement. He ordered his men to be ready to rush in without fear when the signal was given, as the British could not fire in every direction at the same time. Meanwhile, his artillery, skilfully manoeuvred and resolutely served, made good practice against the cavalry (which lost 149 horses out of 460), and began to demoralize the Grenadiers. Two companies of the 30th Bombay Infantry were detached to stop a *Ghazi*-led rush. They succeeded, but lost their two subahdars and their only British officer. Other officers in the Indian battalions, conspicuous by their sun-helmets, were picked off by enemy marksmen.

After more than four hours' fighting the end came suddenly. The smooth-bore battery, out of ammunition and with no wagons, went back

'Kandahar 1880'. The main city wall stretches across the middle distance, with the tower of the citadel inside. On the left is the suburb of Deh Khwaja, the scene of heavy fighting during August 1880. In the background is the eminence of Baba Wali dominating the north-western approaches to the city. (Lithograph after Lieut. J.F. Irwin.)

to the Ordnance Field Park to refill its limbers. Some of the cavalry rode in from a flank to drive off a group of *jihadis* who had got into the rear of the 66th Foot. This was the critical moment. A horde of *Ghazi*-led irregulars rose up from folds in the ground and rushed upon the left of the British line. The two detached companies of the 30th consisting mostly of recruits in whose inaccurate hands the breech-loaders could not realize their full value, and disheartened by the departure of the artillery and cavalry, were driven panic stricken towards the Grenadiers. Ayub then ordered his whole army to attack. The Grenadiers, with their colonel badly wounded, tried to form square, but became hopelessly clubbed and many men were cut to pieces by the *Ghazis* almost without resistance. The 66th stopped the rush upon their front with one volley, but when the sepoy units collapsed the English soldiers too abandoned their ground and fled to their right rear trying to escape the Khyber knives.

Though broken up into small groups, the English, with a few sepoys joining their ranks, managed to keep the tribesmen, here composed of Azad Khan's contingent from Kharan, at a distance until the retreating line reached a deep *nala* or ravine. There all semblance of order was lost as the men came down into it like an avalanche, the Kharanis hacking and slashing behind them. On the far side Colonel Galbraith rallied some of his men in the village of Khig, but was killed there with most of his battalion headquarters and with Major Blackwood of the Royal Horse Artillery. The rest, abandoning one of their Colours still in its case by the body of its dead ensign, fought their way to the other end of the village, where about 100 men made a last stand around their remaining Colour.

No British eyewitness survived the fight, but an Afghan artillery colonel reported that when only eight soldiers were left, led by one of their own officers and the adjutant of the Grenadiers, they charged and fought back to back, until they were shot down.

Elsewhere only the Royal Horse Artillery, which had lost two guns overrun by the *Ghazis*, and the sappers and miners, which had lost all their British personnel killed, were still fighting. In the logistic support area there was chaos as discipline broke down and soldiers and followers scrambled for transport animals on which to make their escape. Some found time to break into the liquor stores and into the treasure chest, perhaps reasoning that they might as well have it as leave it to the enemy. But not all were thieves. One party of Grenadiers faithfully guarded Rs 13,000 in silver through all the horrors of the retreat now just beginning. The cavalry were ordered to charge, but the troopers saw the day was lost and refused to ride to their deaths in a hopeless endeavour. Burrows rallied the 30th Bombay Infantry and stragglers from other corps and tried to make a rear-guard. But the Afghans gave him no respite, and after losing another 100 men he ordered the rest to retreat. He himself, having joined in the fighting with the greatest personal courage, gave up his horse to a wounded officer and walked after his men.

No horror was spared the beaten army in its flight. The men and animals were already wild with thirst. Most fugitives took the caravan road direct towards Kandahar, forty miles away, disregarding all attempts to turn them by Colonel St John, who knew that all the wells along it had dried up. Night fell, but to the hurrying men every rock or thorn bush was a *Ghazi*. When water was reached men and beasts fought each other for a few precious drops, before a panic drove them on again, many with thirst unslaked. The British lost about 1,000 dead, with only 168 wounded surviving, the ambulance-bearers having fled with the other camp followers when the battle line broke. Seven guns were lost, together with 2,424 baggage animals and all their loads.

The Afghan army too suffered heavy casualties. About 1,500 regulars were killed or wounded and some 3,000 tribesmen. After about five miles they abandoned the pursuit and returned to regroup and to loot the abandoned British baggage. But all along the road to Kandahar the villagers rose in arms, ambushing small groups and picking off stragglers, butchering many within a few miles of Kandahar itself.

At Kandahar, where for several nights the sentries had reported large beacon fires on the surrounding hills, the first news of the disaster arrived at 2 a.m. on 28 July, when an Indian officer of the 3rd Scinde Horse arrived to say that a major of artillery (Blackwood) had bidden him ride to Kandahar with news that the day was lost, and had given him his binoculars to show as proof of authenticity. The Jemahdar added that the whole force had been massacred, news which Primrose telegraphed to Simla and

'Saving the Guns at Maiwand, 27 July 1880', by R. Caton Woodville. Captain Slade, battery captain of E/B Battery, Royal Horse Artillery, bringing his guns out of action fifteen yards ahead of the advancing Afghan tribesmen. On his left, two guns were abandoned, and the gunners escaped with the limbers and teams only.

which was read out to a startled House of Commons at Westminster the same night.

But gradually others began to come in. First, the Wali Sher Ali and his escort appeared. A force was sent out under Primrose's second-in-command, Brigadier-General H.F. Brooke, to meet the remnants of Burrows's force. Burrows himself arrived, his voice gone, his sword tied up in a knot, in tears for the loss of his men. Father Jackson the Roman Catholic chaplain came in, who had throughout the battle and the retreat ministered to the wounded, consoled the dying and carried water to the thirsty men in the firing line when the *bhistis* (or water-carriers) were dead or had deserted. Captain Slade, the battery captain, brought in his remaining guns, the limbers crowded with wounded and drawn by cavalry horses. Galbraith's terrier also appeared, somehow having made his way home after his master's death.

Primrose, in a panic, ordered the abandonment of the cantonment and a general retreat inside the city walls. Brooke, before going out to meet Burrows, had ordered all the city gates save one to be barricaded, in case of a disaster. Now a traffic jam developed, as the wagons and litters bringing back the exhausted survivors of Maiwand converged on the single gate.

Sutlers and merchants trying to bring in their goods from the bazaar also joined the throng, as did the cavalry arriving from Maiwand and a wing of the 28th Bombay Infantry just arriving from Quetta with all its stores and equipment. The precipitate abandonment of the cantonments left them open to the city mob and all the engineer stores and tools were looted. Brook, on his return, organized handling parties to shift as much of the remaining material as was possible back into the city, despite repeated orders from Primrose to abandon the work and come in. At dusk the British retreated into Kandahar and closed the gates.

Stewart, during his period of command at Kandahar, had taken no steps to destroy the numerous walls or enclosures surrounding the town, nor in any other way to prepare it for a siege. One reason was that there was no money available to spend on the construction of field works; another was that to destroy the private property of the subjects of a friendly prince was scarcely a way of endearing the presence of his British allies to them; and the final one was that Stewart had never intended to defend the city, but instead planned to advance with his whole army and meet any enemy in the open field where he was confident of success. Only in the last resort would he have retreated into the citadel itself. Now that Primrose was shut up inside Kandahar, working parties had to be sent out to demolish walls and fill in ditches under fire from enemy sharpshooters. Despite the protection of covering parties, twelve men were killed and one officer and forty men were wounded while employed working as pioneers outside the walls.

Once inside the city walls the British position was reasonably strong, with thirteen guns and 5,000 men to defend 6,000 yards of wall, adequate supplies of water, food and ammunition, and well-sited defence works hurriedly laid out by the commanding engineer, Lieutenant-Colonel J. Hill. The possibility of a 'fifth column' attacking the British from within disappeared when, on the recommendation of his own officers, and with the hearty approval of the Wali (though contrary to St John's views) Primrose expelled the entire Pathan population of the city, some 15,000 souls, during the first week of the siege.

Ayub's main force arrived on 8 August. His artillery opened a continuous bombardment while his engineers began to construct a series of saps and parallels using all the techniques of up-to-date scientific siege warfare. On the 13th they occupied the suburbs of Deh Kwaja and Khairabad, from where they could enfilade the north face of Kandahar, thus denying the defenders freedom of movement in and out, and from where an assault could be made on the city by men with scaling ladders. Hill, alarmed by this, suggested a sortie, in force, to surprise the Afghans and destroy their new battery at Deh Kwaja. Primrose agreed, but handed over the task to Brooke, who reduced the number of men in the sortie, and by insisting on a preliminary bombardment destroyed the element of surprise.

At dawn on 16 August, Brooke led out 300 cavalry, four companies of the Royal Fusiliers and eight of Bombay Infantry, against Deh Kwaja. The British reached the village, but found every door blocked and every wall loopholed and defended. Man after man went down in the street fighting, while crowds of *Ghazis*, alerted by the half-hour cannonade preceding the sortie, hurried up to join the battle. Soon the men in the village were cut off from Kandahar and running out of ammunition. Brooke sent for fresh supplies and reported the position untenable. Primrose ordered his buglers to sound the recall from the ramparts, but refused Hill's request to be allowed to lead out a party to cover the retreat. Too many had been lost already, he said, not another man should go, and then, turning on Hill, 'It is all your doing.' 'I am damned if it is,' replied the sapper. 'You have done everything I told you decidedly and strongly was not to be done, bombardment, small force, separate attacks, and wrong end of the village, and you never informed me of all these changes.' While this wrangling went on on the walls, Brooke tried to fight his way out of the death trap which Deh Kwaja had now become. Colonel C.T. Heathcote, commanding the reserve column, refused to retire into Kandahar until Primrose's aide-de-camp arrived with a direct order to do so. Then, as Heathcote's men fell back, General Brooke's grey charger galloped riderless past them.

By 7.30 a.m. the British were back within Kandahar, having lost 106 dead and 118 wounded. Among those killed were Brigadier-General Brooke himself and six other officers, among them the Reverend G.M. Gordon, hit by a bullet while ministering to the wounded. Father Jackson too had been in the forefront of the battle, but once again his luck held and he returned safely to his flock inside the walls.

Away from Kandahar, the news that one brigade of British troops had suffered a disastrous defeat and another was shut up inside the city did not pass unnoticed.

Public opinion in England was outraged, and called for Sir Garnet Wolseley to be sent. ('Quite sickening,' wrote Stewart to his wife on hearing this.) The commodore at Rangoon offered a naval brigade. The Iranian minister in London expressed his regret, though pointing out in diplomatic language that it was the new British Government's refusal to resume negotiations with the Shah that had set Ayub's force free to march southwards. More troops were ordered out from England. The Bombay reinforcements, long delayed by floods which had washed away their railway in Kacchi and by a rising of the Marri tribe in Baluchistan, started to move forward from Quetta.

Stewart at Kabul had begun his diary for 28 July with the words, 'No news of importance from the country; all *seems* to be quiet.' Such words written by a senior British official in Afghanistan could only be followed by disaster, and the news of Maiwand reached him a few hours later.

'The withdrawal from Kabul'. Staff officers and their baggage descending the Kabul River to Jalalabad by means of local water transport. (From The Graphic, *a contemporary newspaper.)*

Haines telegraphed asking his views about sending troops from Kabul to Kandahar. Stewart replied that he could do so, though in his own opinion the movement was unsound politically, as liable to stir up the Afghans, and strategically, by dividing the force at Kabul when it was on the point of returning to India. But the Government of India still feared that Ayub would go to Ghazni and thence to Kabul, and in this case the reinforcements from Quetta, though they would relieve Kandahar as quickly as a force from Kabul, would not be able to intercept Ayub. Ayub would then arrive with a victorious army at Kabul after the British there had left for India, and might easily defeat Abdur Rahman, thus replacing a putatively neutral Amir by an avowedly anti-British one.

Stewart therefore was ordered to prepare a strong force of all arms to march for Kandahar via Ghazni. But the sole aim was to be the destruction of Ayub. The greatest care was to be taken not to provoke the inhabitants along the column's line of march. Announcements were to be made that the British Government's intentions to withdraw from Kabul remained unchanged. Nothing was to be done to risk the renewal of a major war, which the Indian Army was no longer in a state to wage. He proposed that Roberts should command, to which Haines and Ripon gave their assent. This gave Roberts a perfect chance to restore his laurels, somewhat

'The fort of Kalat-i-Ghilzai'. The chief city of the Ghilzai tribe, this fortress commands the route between Kandahar and Ghazni, and in both the First and Second Afghan Wars was held by British Garrisons despite strong local opposition.

tarnished since he had been chased into Sherpur the previous winter. He was allotted the pick of the Kabul garrison, some of whose regiments were by now distinctly home-sick and war-weary. (Many men who had survived two years of war and had expected to be on their way to India were less than enthusiastic at the idea of marching against Ayub.) Roberts was given all the best pack animals to make him independent of the roads. He was given the 9th Lancers, two battalions of Highlanders and one of the 60th Rifles. He was also given three regiments of Indian cavalry, three battalions of Gurkhas, three of Sikhs and three of Punjabis, one of which was a pioneer battalion and was in place of sappers. Many of these units had been with Roberts since the beginning of the war and were seasoned troops. Only in artillery was he weak, with no field guns and only three pack batteries, but Stewart felt this was adequate. 'Bobs is eager to go,' he told Lady Stewart, 'and I don't wonder … his force in fighting power will be nearly twice as strong as my Division, good though it was. Still it is only fair to give him the best of everything and risk as little as possible.'

Stewart dispatched Roberts on 8 August, 1880, and then two days later marched out of Kabul himself with the rest of the army, heading for Peshawar. He read Lady Sales's memoirs and was glad that his own journey was a very different one. Abdur Rahman took over at Kabul and did all he could to ensure that the two British armies left his dominions as speedily as possible, with no provocation to return as they had under Pollock and Nott. On 29 August, Stewart's diary reads, 'Jamrud. Got out of Afghanistan today with some pleasure.'

Stewart's generous act in giving Roberts command of the Kabul–Kandahar Field Force was the making of Roberts's future reputation. In twenty days he covered 280 miles, one of the most rapid marches in military history. It was a triumph for Roberts's expertise, as an administrator and quartermaster-general. He himself felt that his previous march, from the Shutergardan Pass to Kabul, passing through enemy country and fighting a major engagement on the way, was far more noteworthy. Stewart too thought that unnecessary fuss was made about the Kabul to Kandahar march, which took place at harvest time through the territory of an ally over a recently traversed route, while his own men had done it in weaker strength, surrounded by enemies, after a lean winter and through unknown country. But Stewart's march took place during a general election, when the British public had excitement at home. Roberts's march took place when attention had been focused on the defeat at Maiwand and had all the drama of a rescue bid. It also had the ready pen of war correspondent Hensman. Stewart earlier had expressed regret that his own men had not had a good correspondent to report their doings, though his own prowess had been given a very favourable press, at Roberts's expense. 'I am very disgusted to find that people continue to compare Bobs and myself,' he had written. 'I know it must vex him and it certainly vexes me.'

Roberts reached Ghazni on 15 August, Kalat-i-Ghilzai on the 23rd (where he picked up the British garrison and added it to his own force) and Kandahar on the 31st. He reported that the greater part of the garrison was demoralized, and that they had not even hoisted the British flag until three days before the arrival of the relieving column, by which time Ayub had abandoned the siege and taken up a defended position on the heights of the city. Roberts may well have been right about Primrose and the other generals. But his views as to their troops may have been coloured by his own prejudices as a Bengal officer writing about the Bombay army, especially with a view to the inevitable post-war reorganization and reductions, though he paid tribute to the Bombay sappers. But Hensman too remarked on the poor morale of the garrison: 'Not a band turned out to play us in, not a cheer was raised to welcome us ... the prevailing tone among General Primrose's troops was one still of depression and want of *heart*.' As to the Bombay sepoys, he commented on their slight physique as compared to that of the Afghan tribesmen, though adding, 'It is dangerous to say a word against the Bombay regiments, as a swarm of eager defenders will at once spring up to justify them.'

Following Roberts's reports of what he found at Kandahar, which were fully accepted by Sir Frederick Haines, Primrose was relieved of command and eventually sent back to England in disgrace. Roberts, on orders from the Indian Government, assumed command of all the troops in southern Afghanistan on 1 September. The Bombay division under Major-General Robert Phayre was still some days away, but Roberts felt that he had enough troops available at Kandahar to cope with Ayub Khan, who had now been joined by the young Prince Musa Khan and his suite. A reconnaissance in force, carried out on the afternoon of 3 August, one of the few occasions in this war when the British actually did carry out a successful reconnaissance, gave Roberts an idea of the ground, while the British withdrawal with this vital information encouraged the Afghans to believe they had won another victory.

Roberts decided to use the tactics he had employed with success earlier in the campaign. He would feint against the Afghan left, a saddle called the Baba Wali Kotal, with the artillery and Bombay troops, while concentrating his main effort on the Afghan right, the village of Pir Paimal. This plan was executed perfectly, though there was very bitter fighting, in which the battalion commander of the 72nd Highlanders was killed, before the village was taken. From there the British troops turned the Afghan flank, and by midday were threatening to take the whole position in the rear. The Afghans attempted to form a new line, but no longer had the advantage of the skilfully constructed defensive positions they had prepared. Their left still rested on the Baba Wali Kotal and here large numbers of *Ghazis* made a determined stand. A charge by the 92nd Highlanders, supported by the 2nd Gurkhas and 23rd Pioneers, carried this position by storm and the Afghan battery covering the position was overrun by the 3rd Sikhs. The Afghan troops then abandoned their position and dispersed, leaving behind their entire camp and all their artillery. Ayub himself fled back to Herat with his cavalry and gunners, while his infantrymen threw away their uniforms and, together with the tribal irregulars, hastily assumed the guise of innocent cultivators. The British cavalry, from the mountainous nature of the ground, arrived too late to intercept the retreat, but had the satisfaction of putting to the sword about 350 *jihadis* who were overtaken before they had dispersed. The British losses were forty killed and 228 wounded. Six hundred Afghan dead were buried by the victors, and Roberts estimated another 600 carried away by their own side.

The question was now, what was to be done with Kandahar. As early as 21 May, Hartington had questioned the wisdom of the existing policy and asked Ripon to see whether the British promises of support for Wali Sher Ali could be withdrawn without breaking faith. But they both had to accept that as the Wali had only accepted office on guarantees of British protection, and as, if this protection were withdrawn, he would be at the mercy of those who felt he had been wrong to co-operate in the partition of Afghanistan, there was no help but to continue to support him.

'The Battle of Kandahar, 1 September 1880'. The 92nd Highlanders fighting their
way through the village of Pir Paimal. In the left foreground, in addition to the

usual, and familiar, 'studio props', the artist has painted a 'doolie' or covered stretcher, used for the evacuation of battlefield casualties. (Anon.)

'Baba Wali Kotal, Kandahar'. A contemporary photograph after the battle of Kandahar, 1 September 1880, showing the position occupied by the Afghan artillery.

But now, if he had been proved to be a man of straw, the British might abandon him with a clear conscience. This at least was the view of Alfred Lyall, Secretary in the Indian Foreign Department. But Hartington and Ripon, with all the soul-searching associated with the Gladstonian Liberals and determined not to copy what Ripon called Lytton's 'terrible want of moral sense in political affairs', were not so readily convinced. Did one outbreak of mutiny prove that the Wali could never establish himself? Was the Wali's lack of independent authority (which he had never claimed to have, or even desire) in itself a reason for abandoning him? In early October 1880 he sent Lyall to Kandahar to see if the Wali would abdicate of his own free will. On arriving in Kandahar the previous month Hensman had told his readers that he heard that the Wali's only anxiety was to retire to India on a pension, but by October Sher Ali seemed to have recovered his spirits and was not immediately prepared to abdicate. But after five days' arm-twisting by Lyall, he agreed to abide by whatever the British Government suggested and accepted the offer of comfortable exile in Karachi.

'Amir Abdur Rahman with British diplomats and officers', during his state visit to India, at Rawal Pindi, March 1885. The review of the Rawal Pindi garrison held in his honour forms the setting for Rudyard Kipling's Jungle Book *story 'Her Majesty's Servants'. During the Amir's absence, Afghan and Russian troops clashed at Panjdeh. Faced with clear evidence that the British would resist any further advance by force, the Russians accepted a compromise which allowed them to consolidate their gains at Panjdeh in exchange for border adjustments elsewhere.*

Ripon's councillors were strongly in favour of simply annexing Kandahar. It was, Haines argued, British by right of conquest, was a healthy site for a garrison, strategically important and within easy reach of Quetta. Indeed, 165 miles of railway already had been laid from Quetta in the direction of Kandahar.

But the idea of annexing Kandahar was unacceptable to a government elected to put an end to Imperialist adventures. Even among the military the strategic value of a garrison at Kandahar was questioned. Indeed it was opposed by no less an authoritative figure than Sir Garnet Wolseley. In November 1880, therefore, Hartington sent a despatch saying that the British Cabinet had decided to withdraw from Kandahar, and Amir

Abdur Rahman was told that if he wished to incorporate the province into his dominions he should lose no time in preparing to do so. The Amir protested that he had not the arms and ammunition to establish control over the area. The British, unwilling to see Kandahar go by default to Ayub, provided both these commodities, and five lakhs of rupees.

On 16 April, 1881, the Sirdar Muhammad Hashim arrived at Kandahar to take over the city on behalf of the Amir of Kabul. On the 21st the British garrison commander handed over the city to him and marched for Quetta. The transport and commissariat departments were by now working at full efficiency, and the withdrawal was effected with the loss of one sepoy and one horse. On 4 May the last British troops left Afghanistan and the Second Afghan War was over.

Ayub Khan, when the British had gone, made another and this time successful attempt to seize Kandahar, but this provoked Abdur Rahman to take the field in person. A fierce battle took place outside Kandahar on 22 September, 1881. Ayub was defeated, and on returning to Herat discovered that in his absence it had been captured by another army sent by Abdur Rahman from Afghan Turkestan. He fled to Iran and eventually, in 1888, accepted asylum in British India.

The Second Afghan War was as disastrous for British India as the first. The transport herd of north-west India was destroyed, and those dependent on it for their livelihood, or the movement of their produce, were ruined. The Indian treasury suffered the loss of lakhs of rupees with nothing to show for it. The army suffered an estimated 50,000 casualties, killed, wounded or invalided, including the deaths of 140 expensively trained officers. A few former Afghan districts in Baluchistan were gained, but both the Khyber Pass and the Kurram valley were in effect abandoned to the tribes. The inhabitants of Afghanistan had been given every reason to hate the British, and a ruler had emerged at Kabul who was no more likely to become a British ally than his predecessor.

But Abdur Rahman proved as shrewd and as powerful as had been his grandfather Dost Muhammad. He consolidated the Afghan state, and accepted British diplomatic aid to secure its frontiers against the Russians and to resolve border disputes with his neighbours. He crushed internal rebellion with terrible cruelty and ruled his turbulent subjects with a rod of iron. Malefactors were impaled or stoned to death, robbers hung in cages and left to die at the scene of their crimes, unjust tradesmen had their ears nailed to the entrance of their shops in the bazaar. But he did much to modernize the administration of his state and to encourage commerce. His death in September 1901 was greeted with a mixture of regret and relief.

X

The King's Move
Afghanistan and India 1919

In 1901 the Amir Abdur Rahman was succeeded by his eldest son Habibulla, the first Afghan monarch to come to the throne without dispute for more than 100 years. But the change of ruler did allow the anti-British party, which during his lifetime Abdur Rahman had kept firmly in check, to emerge and make its presence felt, while the Russian Government took the opportunity to renew the suggestion it had made the previous year that the time was right for the establishment of direct communications with Afghanistan. This suggestion, indeed, was not unreasonable, since Afghanistan's northern boundary now touched Russian territory, either directly ruled by the Czar's own officers, or indirectly by his feudatory, the Amir of Bokhara. It was, to say the least, inconvenient that correspondence between border officials whose districts adjoined each other should have to be conducted via St Petersburg and London. But the British feared that any direct links between Russia and Afghan officials would soon be followed by the establishment of a Russian Mission in the country, from which a British Mission was still excluded. Accordingly, they opened negotiations to ensure that their previous agreements with Afghanistan would be carried on under the new Amir.

Habibulla declined a pressing invitation to come to India, but agreed to accept at his court a special, and temporary, Mission, led by Louis Dane of the Indian Foreign Department. When Dane arrived, at the end of 1904, he found that the Amir, like many others in Asia, had been very impressed by the defeat of the Russians by the Japanese earlier that year. Habibulla said that he was an independent ruler, just like the Emperor of Japan, and should be treated as such. Eventually, by a treaty made on 21 March, 1905, both sides agreed on the British continuing to conduct Afghan foreign policy, the continued exclusion of all foreign missions and an annual British subsidy to Afghanistan of eighteen lakhs of rupees. The Amir was also given the right to import arms through India. In 1907 he did visit the

155

Governor-General in India, and expressed himself as wishing to remain on friendly terms with the British.

Meanwhile, the hostility between Britain and Russia, which had lasted for nearly a century, seemed at last to be coming to an end. The rise of Germany, the discovery by the British during the South African War that they had not a single ally in Europe, the humiliation of the Czar's regime by defeat abroad and revolution at home, all combined to bring London and St Petersburg closer and to encourage statesmen on both sides to settle their differences in Asia. By the St Petersburg Convention of 1907, it was agreed that neither side would enter Tibet (which was agreed to be under Chinese suzerainty), that Iran should be divided into separate Russian and British spheres of influence, that the British would not occupy any part of Afghanistan while the Amir observed the treaty of 1905 and that the Russians would continue to deal with the Amir solely through the British.

But the time was passing when European states could arrange the affairs of Asian ones without opposition. Habibulla, responding to the spirit of nationalism spreading throughout Asia, refused to recognize the convention, as he had not been consulted during the negotiations and because he considered its terms detracted from his dignity and independence.

Despite this, the Amir maintained a peaceful co-existence with the British, even during the worst days of the First World War, when the Sultan of Turkey, the spiritual leader of the Muslim world, fought alongside Germany and called on all believers to wage holy war against the Entente powers. In September 1915 a Turco-German Mission, having crossed Iran, reached Kabul. Habibulla, under strong pressure from the anti-British party and from religious activists, felt obliged to accept the Mission, just as Amir Sher Ali had perforce accepted General Stolietov's party. But he sent a message to the Government of India saying, 'I am not a double-dealer. I mean to stand by the British if I can, but do not judge me by individual acts.' The Mission, led by the Turkish General Kasim Bey and the German Captain Niedermayer, remained at Kabul until May 1916, frustrated for months by the Amir's prevarications, and at last having to be content with a treaty in which the Amir agreed to attack India, but only on condition that a large Turkish army was first sent to Kabul to assist him in the enterprise. He also demanded 50,000 rifles, artillery, and £20 million in gold, which he said were essential to enable him to prosecute the war with any hope of success.

Even so, the Mission had not wasted all its time at Kabul. It had established contact with a number of revolutionaries within India, and had encouraged the wild Pathan border tribes to raid into British territory. The Amir, not wishing to provoke British reprisals, called an assembly of tribal leaders and warned them that *jihad* could only be waged lawfully with the consent of the king of their country. Behind the scenes, he bought off some of the leaders and managed to turn the rest against each other.

Several reasons may be advanced for Habibulla's decision to remain neutral. His noted personal indolence had increased as he had grown older, though he was still only in his fifties. He correctly appreciated British strength, even when weakened by the demands of other battle fronts, compared with that of his own forces. He could not be sure that the Central powers would win, and their defeat would leave him open to attack by the British from the south and their Russian allies from the north. He hoped for some reward from the British, in the shape immediately of an increase in his subsidy and ultimately of the achievement of full independence in foreign affairs.

On the British side of the frontier, a series of important changes in the administration of the border districts was carried out by Lord Curzon of Kedleston, Governor-General between 1899 and 1905. The most important of all was that he forced through a proposal that had been under consideration for more than forty years, but which had always hitherto been successfully resisted by the government of the Punjab province. This was, that the trans-Indus districts should be severed from the Punjab and formed into a separate province under a Chief Commissioner directly answerable to the Government of India. Thus, with the establishment of the North-West Frontier Province in 1901, Peshawar once more became the seat of a provincial capital. The Pathans there were freed from the domination of the Lahore government under which they had been since 1834, when Ranjit Singh annexed Peshawar to his own kingdom. Curzon also withdrew the regular troops from the tribal territory which lay between the Afghan and British-administered areas, and replaced them by paramilitary levies, dignified by the title of militia. These in fact consisted of Pathan tribesmen recruited from the independent tribes, under British officers and organized as battalions of lightly armed infantry. Thus the regular army was freed from the unpopular, expensive and inefficient duty of maintaining small garrisons to try to combat tribal raiders and plunderers, while the militia, cheap and with the advantage of local knowledge, acted as border security forces, offering regularly paid full-time employment to many bold spirits who might otherwise with equal readiness have become plunderers and raiders themselves.

The first Chief Commissioner of the North-West Frontier Province, Sir Harold Deane, governed until 1908, when he was succeeded by Sir George Roos-Keppel. Roos-Keppel was a man of powerful character, formidable in appearance and manner, dominating in his behaviour and confident in his own ability to govern, in the traditional paternalistic way, the tribes and people of his province. He established a strong personal rapport with the leaders of the frontier tribes and succeeded, during the First World War, in keeping most of them on terms of peace with the British. At the end of his period of office he prepared to hand over to Hamilton Grant, Secretary of the Indian Foreign Department and a former Chief Secretary of the North West Frontier Province. Grant was at this time in London, discussing with the Secretary of State for India, Edwin Montagu, what should be asked for on behalf of India at the forthcoming international peace conference at Versailles. On 10 January, 1919 Roos-Keppel wrote to the Governor-General, Lord Chelmsford, asking for permission to leave for England without waiting for Grant to return to India. 'Everything on the frontier is so extra-ordinarily peaceful that it is safe to prophecy a quiet summer,' he wrote, forgetting what he of all people should have remembered, that it was never safe to prophesy anything of that nature.

At the beginning of February, Amir Habibulla re-opened the question of British control over his foreign policy. Afghanistan, he wrote to Chelmsford, considered itself independent in every way, and desired to send a representative to the Versailles Conference. If the British would obtain from the conference some document recognizing 'the absolute liberty, freedom of action, and perpetual independence of the Sublime Government of Afghanistan', then an Afghan representative need not be sent. But if not, he would be. Chelmsford, for his part, was not unsympathetic. As he pointed out to Montagu, the restriction on Afghanistan having relations with foreign powers was in practice unenforceable, as had been shown by the reception at Kabul of the emissaries of two nations then actually at war with the British. It was, Chelmsford said, unimaginable that the British would in future ever go to war with Afghanistan to enforce this restriction, so why cling to an out-of-date provision that was of no value to the British and only an irritant to the Afghans?

On the night of 20 February, 1919, someone entered the tent of the Amir Habibulla and murdered him. The motive for the assassination defied explanation. One suggestion was that those responsible were nationalists, incensed at his failure to secure full independence from the British either by force during the First World War when the British were weak, or as a reward for his neutrality now that they had won. Another suggestion was that the Bolsheviks were to blame, because Habibulla had agreed to join with the Amir of Bokhara in a league to free the Muslims of Central Asia from the Russian yoke, the Czarist Empire having collapsed at the end of 1917. Yet another suggestion was that it could be blamed on internal discontent with the apathy and indolence into which Habibulla had lapsed, and which caused him to neglect affairs of state at this critical time. It might simply have been a murder committed on behalf of a potential successor to the throne. The one thing on which all agreed was that the Afghan colonel tried and executed for the crime was, even if he were guilty at all, which was generally doubted, not acting on his own impulse.

The title of Amir was assumed by Habibulla's brother, Nasrulla Khan, who obtained the recognition of Habibulla's eldest son and heir-apparent, Inayatulla Khan. These were both in Jalalabad, the winter capital, at the time, but another claimant, Habibulla's third son, Amanulla,

'The outskirts of Kabul, 1919'. An aerial reconnaissance photograph taken by the Royal Air Force during the Third Afghan War.

was at Kabul, where as Governor he had access to the treasury and the arsenal. The Government of India was anxious to see the government of Afghanistan change from one ruler to the next as smoothly as possible. Hoping to avoid a war of succession on its frontiers such as had occurred when Amir Dost Muhammad had died, it proposed to offer immediate recognition of Nasrulla Khan. The India Office in London demurred, on the grounds that it would be wiser to wait and see who succeeded in establishing himself, and on this occasion this view proved the better one. Nasrulla and Inayatulla, lacking reliable troops and ready money, were forced to recognize Amanulla and went to Kabul to offer him their allegiance. On 3 March, 1919, Amanulla wrote to the Governor-General of India, announcing his accession to the 'free and independent Government of Afghanistan' and offering to enter into a commercial treaty with 'the mighty Government of England' for the mutual benefit of their subjects.

All these references to freedom and independence were not lost upon the British. Chelmsford asked for, and received from the Commander-in-Chief India, an assurance that the military situation would be satisfactory in the event of trouble. Montagu suggested that Roos-Keppel might be retained on the frontier for a further period. Chelmsford decided against this, telling Montagu that Roos-Keppel was 'seedy and very anxious to go home' and that the new Amir would first have to establish himself firmly in power before he could give the British any trouble. 'I touch wood,' he wrote on March, 'but that is the opinion of those whom I have consulted. ... We have little knowledge of Amunulla as a man, but what we have is to the good, and he is reported to be friendly and well-disposed towards us.'

Montagu was inclined to accept this view of the new Amir. Writing from Versailles on 26 March, he told Chelmsford that Amanulla seemed to be acting with firmness and decision, and that if he succeeded in establishing himself, we may, I hope, find him as staunch a friend as his father'.

But, unfortunately from the British point of view, Amanulla's firmness and decision were not confined to his internal affairs. The new Amir, young (then aged twenty-six), energetic and progressive, was determined to lead his country into the modern world and to begin by freeing it from any subjection to its powerful southern neighbour. Hamilton Grant, at the India Office, noted on 28 March that Amanulla had included in the list of his new officials a Commissary for Foreign Affairs. What made this even more ominous was that the new Commissary was none other than the new Amir's father-in-law, Muhammad Tarzi. He was the founder and proprietor of the country's first, and up to this time, only, newspaper, the *Siraj-al-Akhbar*, which had throughout the war both moulded and reflected national, anti-British, anti-Russian and pro-Turkish opinion. Grant said that the new Commissary had been educated in Constantinople, was married to a Turkish lady and was to all intents virtually a Turk himself. 'His influence on the foreign policy of Afghanistan can only be anti-Christian, anti-British, and directed towards a close union with Turkey.' He urged caution in extending formal recognition to Amanulla before it was really necessary.

The Amir's proceedings did nothing to detract from Grant's forecast. He included among his closest advisers men who had consistently urged a pro-German policy during the war, and appointed as his new Commander-in-Chief General Salah Muhammad, another well-known member of the nationalist party. He was also influenced by his mother, Habibulla's senior Queen. This lady, who was known and feared for her temper, was the daughter of a leading Barakzai chief and a strong supporter of the anti-British cause.

On 13 April, 1919, in his Durbar at Kabul, Amanulla declared Afghanistan independent in both internal and external affairs, appointed an ambassador to Bokhara (itself then trying to regain its independence from Russia), and said he would send an envoy to Iran.

The British decided to ignore this, and prepared to send to the Amir a message of condolence from the King-Emperor on the death of his father Habibulla, an act which was, in effect, the recognition of Amanulla's own regime. George V had to have it explained to him why he was being asked, at the end of April, to send condolences for an event which had taken place at the end of February, but finally signed the draft on 1 May, 1919. His private secretary, Lord Stamfordham, told Montagu that the King had added a note, the exact words of which were, 'I hope we shall never have to refer to the present Amir as *His Majesty*'.

During March and April 1919 there was an outbreak of very serious disorders inside India. These sprang from a variety of sources: pressure for political reform from the Indian nationalist movement; economic hardship caused by the effects of the world war; the apparent determination of some Europeans, following their victory in the war, to try to disregard all its social consequences and return to the pre-war arrangements; and agitation against the provisions of the Indian Criminal Law Amendment Acts, known as the Rowlatt Acts from the name of the judge who presided over the committee which recommended their adoption. The Rowlatt Acts, originally intended as a response to anarchists and terrorists, provided for internment without trial and for trial without jury in certain circumstances. Indian nationalists mounted a virulent campaign against these acts, stirring up popular opinion with reports that their provisions included the compulsory medical examination of all couples before marriage, the prohibition of religious processions and the confiscation of plough oxen. Riots occurred in several cities in the north and west of India. Government buildings and railway installations were attacked. On 11 April, 1919, at Amritsar in the Punjab, a small military force under the personal command of Brigadier-General Dyer opened fire on a prohibited assembly, killing 379 persons. This act, though it cowed resistance, and was believed by Dyer himself to have prevented the outbreak of a revolution similar in scale to the Indian Mutiny, was one which profoundly shocked Indian public opinion.

It was to such disturbances that Amir Amanulla referred in a proclamation at the beginning of May. Hindus and Muslims alike, he said, had remained faithful to the British Government during the war, but had been rewarded by cruelties and injustices of all kinds, but especially in connection with their religion, their honour and their modesty. He declared that, in accordance with international law, he had no right to interfere, but that, in the name of Islam and of humanity, he considered the peoples of India were justified in rising up and causing disturbances. It was a pity, he added, that the British considered no-one but themselves to be human beings. To prevent these disturbances spreading from India to Afghanistan, he declared that he had ordered his Commander-in-Chief to move troops to the frontier.

On 3 May a detachment of Afghan troops crossed the border at the top of the Khyber Pass. They occupied the village of Bagh, and the springs on its outskirts at Tangi. From here they were able to control the pumping station in the pass below, and with it the water supply to Landi Kotal, a post held by two companies of Indian infantry. A number of labourers were killed by Afghan irregulars and the first blood had been spilt of the Third Afghan War.

The extent to which the Afghans meant to start a war is unclear. Amanulla certainly stood to gain from a successful war, if only as a way of securing his own position by uniting his people against a foreign foe and distracting internal opposition to his rule. He would certainly not have been the first ruler in history, European or Asian, to frame his policy on that assumption. His own position as Amir was by no means firm at this time, for he had alienated the conservative religious party by arresting their leader, his uncle Nasrulla, on suspicion of complicity in the assassination of Amir Habibulla, and by removing another prominent conservative, General Nadir Khan, from the post of Commander-in-Chief. But now, by making war on the old enemy, the British, he would simultaneously appeal to religious and historical sentiment among the conservatives, and to nationalist and progressive views among the radicals. But there were no large-scale troop movements or mobilization such as would have indicated a carefully planned invasion. Amanulla may have intended only to be ready to benefit from any disturbances inside India, and meanwhile to encourage the ever-present hope among the wild border tribes of being able to emulate their ancestors by sweeping down upon the defenceless rich plains of India, there to burn, rape, loot and murder all the way to the gates of Delhi.

But India, though by no means anxious to fight another Afghan war, was not as defenceless as all that. There were, indeed, weaknesses. Many troops were committed to the internal security role, and the prospect of a large-scale rising inside India to coincide with the Afghan invasion was one which played a significant part in the appreciation of the generals on both sides. In the event, this did not happen, partly because potential rioters could not be sure that Brigadier-General Dyer's example at Amritsar would not be followed elsewhere if the British became really threatened, partly because few Indian politicians, with their aspirations for Western-style secular democracy, cared for the prospect of being 'liberated' by an invading army of Afghan hillmen and partly because conservative Indian opinion too, led by the chiefs and princes of India, rallied to the British side. Even the ancient ex-Amir Yakub placed the services of himself and his sons at the disposal of the Governor-General, just in case the new war might result in a change of dynasty as had the previous ones.

The British forces in India in 1919 consisted of eight infantry divisions, five independent brigades, three cavalry brigades and a mounted brigade, this last composed of newly raised cavalry regiments on inferior horses. Despite this impressive list, few units were in a state to take the field immediately on the outbreak of war. Many of the British units were actually in the process of moving into the hill stations for the hot weather, and had become split up and separated from their transport and equipment

'Ali Masjid and the Khyber Pass'. This aerial view, taken in 1919, shows both the strength of this position on the ground and its vulnerability to attack from the air.

while the move was taking place. Many Indian units had reverted, for the first time since 1914, to the old practice of allowing block leave to large numbers of their men during the hot weather. These were now all widely dispersed to their home villages, far away from trains and telegraphs.

Even when the regiments re-assembled, they were not the same as those regular long-service professional troops with which India had been guarded in 1914. The old Indian Army, with its carefully selected small cadre of British officers and its rank and file chosen almost by patronage from the various communities deemed most suitable for military service, had suffered casualties unimaginable before the war, on battlefields in France, Flanders, Egypt, Gallipoli, East Africa, Persia and Russia. There were still 124 infantry battalions and over twenty cavalry regiments of the Indian Army serving outside India when the Third Afghan War broke out. Their replacements serving in India included many raw recruits, youths impelled by pressure from local landlords to join the army to make up the quota allotted by the British to each recruiting area. While it is true that the Indian Army, which expanded to a million men strong during the First World War, was always made up of volunteers as opposed to conscripts, it cannot be denied that the ranks of the Indian regiments at this time included many young men who, if left to themselves, would not have chosen to bear arms as a profession.

But of this vast mass of men, not all were in combat, or even support-ing, units. All of the units overseas had left behind a depot, each of which,

'Officers of the Afghan Regular Army 1919'. The ceremonial uniform of the Afghan Army consisted of a dark blue tunic and trousers with a waist sash for officers. The head-dress was a round, black, lambskin cap, with a metal badge representing a mosque upon a crescent, the national crest of Afghanistan. The general appearance of the uniform was not unlike that worn by the Iranian and Turkish armies at this period.

swollen by recruits, by men returning from the theatres of war sick or wounded, by men rejoining from detachment or leave and by all the training and administrative support needed to deal with them, had grown to battalion size itself. 'Thus,' says the official history of the Third Afghan War, 'whilst India was full of soldiers, they were chiefly to be found in the depots.' Demobilization had already started, and most units were below strength as a result. When the news came of the outbreak of another Afghan War, demobilization was halted and frantic efforts were made to bring units up to strength again.

Many of the same difficulties applied to the British element of the army in India. The pre-war garrison, all regulars, had included nine British regiments of cavalry, and fifty-two battalions of infantry. Some of these had gone to France in 1914 as constituent parts of the Indian Army formations. Nearly all the rest had been put together to form the 29th Division, the last division of pre-war regular soldiers, formed only to be wasted at Gallipoli. By 1919 the Indian taxpayer had for his money only eight British regular battalions, which had been left in India throughout the war, and two regular cavalry regiments.

The balance was made up by units of the Territorial Force. These, composed of patriotic citizens who in peace-time had trained at weekends and in the evenings to protect the shores of the United Kingdom against invasion, had been mobilized in 1914, and in due course sent to India to relieve the Regulars for service elsewhere. This was acceptable as long as the German war lasted, but now these citizen-soldiers, having little quarrel with the Amir of Afghanistan (whose war aims, whatever they were, did not include a descent upon the United Kingdom), wished only to return to the homes and families and civil occupations they had left at the call of duty four and a half years previously. Nevertheless, after these years of embodied service, the Territorials were as valuable as any regular soldiers and could not be released.

Their disappointment was intense, especially as they had been promised, when first sent to India, that they would be returned to theatres of war in Europe after a year. There was talk of a refusal to march, countered by the authorities with threats of courts martial. But no-one wanted to proceed to extremes and, in a conciliatory gesture, the Commander-in-Chief India, Sir Charles Monro, received a deputation of Territorial non-commissioned officers. He met them with a combination of sympathy and firmness which had the effect of easing the situation. The indefinable Territorial spirit reasserted itself, a combination of local pride, of the *esprit de corps* of units self-consciously different in origins and tradition from their regular counterparts, of moral ascendancy at serving neither from compulsion nor for a livelihood and the feeling of identity built up throughout the peace-time years of association in their drill-halls. But some unfortunate units, waiting for their troopship at Bombay, were broken up and distributed among the Special Service Battalions. These were formed from the large numbers of British officers and men on their way home from the Mesopotamian campaign to England for demobilization, but who had been obliged to kick their heels in India because of the shortage of passenger ships. They included conscripts and 'war-service only' volunteers of the New Armies, as well as individual Territorials and time-expired regulars. All told, eight battalions were raised from these men, while technicians and specialists were posted as individual reinforcements to existing units.

But whatever deficiencies the British had in manpower, their superiority in material was now unquestioned. Even before 1914 their possession of machine guns and magazine rifles gave the Indian Army a firepower vastly superior to the Afghans and tribal forces. But by 1919 they had added to these all the modern weapons taken into service during the First World War. The proportion of machine guns had been increased. The Lewis gun was readily available. There were trench mortars and hand

'A Bazaar Scene, Peshawar, 1919'. This city, the capital of the North-West Frontier Province, has been ruled in turn by Mughals, Iranians, Afghans, Sikhs, British and now Pakistanis. Its annexation by Ranjit Singh in 1834 led to an implacable quarrel with the Amir of Kabul, which was one of the events leading up to the outbreak of the First Afghan War. During the Third Afghan War only prompt action by the British authorities prevented a major rising in the city timed to coincide with the Afghan offensive on the frontier.

grenades, although some of the latter tended to explode prematurely or not at all. There were as yet no tanks in India, but there were armoured cars, unreliable and uncomfortable for their crews, but still a powerful addition to the order of battle. There were motor lorries and wireless sets. And above all, quite literally, there were the aeroplanes of the newly fledged Royal Air Force, ready to take part in their first Indian campaign.

Against these forces the Amir could muster a total of 50,000 regulars, dressed in khaki uniforms, and raised on a system of conscription by quota for lifetime service. The army was organized into twenty-one cavalry regiments, seventy-five infantry battalions, and three pioneer battalions, supported by 280 modern guns and some obsolete crank-operated Gardner machine guns. The Amir Habibulla had made full use of the provision of the 1907 agreement enabling him to import arms, and about half his infantry had been rearmed with modern rifles. The cavalry carried

166

*'A BE.2C Biplane of No. 31 Squadron, Royal Air Force, India, February 1918',
with the observer's seat (front) occupied by the Governor-General's daughter, the
Hon. Bridget Thesiger. This aircraft had a maximum speed of 72 mph at 6,500 ft,
and an operational ceiling of 10,000 ft. It could remain aloft for about three and a
quarter hours. Long obsolete in Europe, the BE.2C was the standard machine of the
RAF in India during the Third Afghan War.*

swords, but were dismissed by the British as little better than mounted
infantry, as they mostly rode ponies unsuitable for shock action though
capable of great endurance. But one of the lessons of the First World
War had been that the days of the horse soldier were numbered, so the
despised Afghan cavalry were theoretically more useful than their well-
mounted opponents.

But as in previous wars it was the irregular element that was relied on to
make up the weight. The tribal levies, each man carrying his own weapon
and with a few days' supplies in a bag, could assemble with incredible
rapidity to repel an invasion or harass a retreating enemy, but could dis-
perse with equal speed once their stock of food, ammunition, or personal
morale had been exhausted. The Amir maintained about 10,000 *Khassadar*,
who though armed wore no uniforms and were employed as local security
forces. To this total, in theory, the tribes along the border could add another
80,000 fighting men. The frontier tribes too had modern rifles, smuggled in
by the thousand. They soon learned, from local experience and from their
men who served with the Indian Army and frontier paramilitary militia,
the new tactics to go with them. Except for an occasional, *Ghazi*-led rush,

the Pathan tribesman no longer collected to fight in a mass, but, like his British enemy, lay down to conceal himself behind rocks, or in the earth, and engaged his opponent from a distance.

On 5 May Chelmsford telegraphed to London that it looked as though a war had started. 'On strong recommendation of Roos-Keppel I have authorised expulsion of Afghans from Bagh springs if they refuse to retire. I have ordered overwhelming force up so that an excuse may be found for peaceful retirement.' He asked Roos-Keppel, who was within thirty-six hours of his departure, to stay on and use his influence, together with lavish bribes, to keep the frontier tribes quiet. He also ordered the Afghan Vakil at Simla to return to Kabul bearing a letter urging the Amir to reconsider his course of action and to return to a state of peace and friendship with the British. 'You may ask why we have not had better information,' wrote Chelmsford to Montagu on 7 May. 'I can only answer that I do not believe that Amanulla himself knew until the last moment that he was going to embark on this enterprise. ... If the military here have not been living in a fool's paradise we ought to hit the enemy very hard in a day or two. I have laid stress on overwhelming force as we cannot afford to have an initial reverse.'

The somewhat exposed position of the small garrison at Landi Kotal, lying within a mile of Afghan battalions, with artillery, at Bagh, was eased on 7 May by the arrival of the first of the 'overwhelming' reinforcements ordered by Lord Chelmsford. These consisted of the 2nd Battalion of the Somerset Light Infantry (the same regiment which, as the 13th Foot, had formed part of the 'illustrious garrison' at Jalalabad, seventy-seven years before) and a mountain battery. They had driven up the Khyber from Peshawar in a convoy of sixty-seven motor lorries, the first evidence of the advantage which the new technology had given to British arms in this war, for they had travelled in a matter of hours a distance which on foot would have taken several exhausting days.

Chelmsford lamented the irony of fate that he, who had always opposed the idea of military adventures and the revival of the Forward Policy, should be faced with an Afghan War. 'Troops were sent up the moment the Afghans occupied the springs,' he told Montagu, 'but we asked Roos-Keppel not to turn them out as it did not appear absolutely certain that Amanullah was behind the move and I was anxious not to precipitate a collision. However Roos-Keppel at once deprecated holding our hand, and I immediately ordered the expulsion of the Afghans but laid stress on an overwhelming force being used both to impress the tribes and the Afghans and in the hope of forcing a retirement without collision. ... This has all come as a bolt from the blue.'

In fact, the letter from the Government of India ordering the Afghans to withdraw from Bagh never reached them. It was actually on its way from Landi Kotal when Roos-Keppel telephoned to stop it, on the grounds that it would either provoke the Afghans to attack before the British were ready, or else lose the element of surprise for the attack planned to take place at dawn on the 9th (the First Battle of Bagh).

There is no doubt that Roos-Keppel wanted a battle, and a quick victory over the Afghans. He had written to Maffey, Chelmsford's private secretary, on May, urging that they should be expelled from Bagh before they could incite the frontier tribes to rally to them. The British, he said, should show they were ready to fight if provoked. 'There will shortly be a big collection of troops and tribesmen at Dakka,' he wrote. If the British captured Bagh, the Afghans would be bound to counter-attack, and their forces in Dacca would be faced with a hot, waterless march of nine miles to reach Bagh.

> We can use aeroplanes to smash up their encampment at Dakka. We have twenty-four aeroplanes here, and an attack on Dakka and possibly on Jalalabad from the air would not only take the heart out of the Afghans but would give all those who are at present half-hearted a very good excuse for pulling out.

His main worry was for the security of his own province. In Peshawar the Afghan postmaster, Ghulam Hayder, spent the last days of peace preparing to distribute the Amir's proclamation that Hindus and Muslims alike were justified in rising up against their British oppressors in the name of religion and decency. On the outbreak of war he took refuge in a house inside a maze of streets where it was impossible for troops or police to reach him without becoming embroiled with the city mob. He confided to a trusted member of his staff that the Amir's master plan was for an attack on three fronts – down the Khyber, led by the new Commander-in-Chief, General Salah Muhammad; down the Kurram, under the old Commander-in-Chief, General Nadir Khan; and against Quetta under General Abdul Qudus Khan. They would attack simultaneously within ten days, while within India riots would be fomented to immobilize reinforcements. In Peshawar he had, in conjunction with Indian revolutionaries, got together 7,000 or more Pathans ready to join in attacks on the railway, the treasury, the wireless station and government installations. The tribal elders might be disinclined for war, but the young men were enthusiastic and would join the city mob.

All this interesting information was passed on to the British, as the recipient was an agent on Roos-Keppel's pay-roll. He added that the rising was timed to occur on 8 May. The successful co-ordination of all these movements, even if planned as they were reported, proved beyond Afghan capabilities, but the British could not afford to take chances.

At 2 p.m. on 7 May, while most of Peshawar took its siesta, four British columns began to march round the city walls. At their head were cavalry and mounted police. At each gate a detachment of horsemen wheeled out of line and prevented anyone from passing through. As the infantry and foot police came up they in turn, without stopping, left behind a detachment that closed and held the gate, while the horsemen trotted on to rejoin the column's head. Within eleven minutes there were cavalry vedettes at each of the sixteen gates. Within forty-four minutes the infantry were in position and every gate was securely in the hands of the authorities. Roos-Keppel then announced to the awakened populace that until the Afghan postmaster, the members of the Indian Revolutionary Committee, and various other named Bolsheviks and agitators were given up, no-one should pass the gates. He also threatened to cut off the water supply. This, in the fierce hot weather, proved to be the ultimate sanction.

No-one believed that Roos-Keppel would not be as good as his word, and by sunset the postmaster and the revolutionary leaders surrendered to the police. They arrived surrounded by an ugly crowd, but the presence of British armoured cars proved a sufficient deterrent against disorders. Reinforcements, asked for by Roos Keppel earlier, arrived the same night and by dawn the danger of a rising within Peshawar had receded.

At Landi Kotal the lorries continued to deliver further reinforcements of men and supplies. By 8 May there were five battalions of infantry, two batteries of guns, a machine-gun company, a company of sappers and two troops of lancers. This force, though impressive, was by no means overwhelming, especially as the Afghans too had been reinforced. Nevertheless, urged on by Roos-Keppel, who said that to remain inactive with so large a force would create an unfavourable impression on the tribes, the local commander, Brigadier-General G. F. Crocker, ordered an attack at dawn on the 9th. His intention was to secure control of the water supply to Landi Kotal, where the supplies were becoming inadequate for the number of men already there, and to drive the Afghans out of their position at Bagh.

But, disturbed by reports of Afghan regulars and tribal gatherings to his north, he detached nearly half his force to protect himself from any attack from this direction. This fatally weakened his attack westwards, against Bagh, and although the water supply was recaptured, the Afghans, summoning up reinforcements from the rear, easily held on to Bagh and the adjacent crags. The attackers (the 1/15th Sikhs and the 1/11th Gurkha Rifles) had to dig in to hold what ground they had gained at the foot of the Afghan position. This action, called the First Battle of Bagh, did little to convince the wavering tribes of the overwhelming might of the British.

The British position was retrieved by the Royal Air Force. At first, air activity had been confined to reconnaissance over Landi Kotal. There the airmen, flying in BE.2C biplanes, machines already obsolete by European standards, suffered the unusual experience of being shot at by rifle fire *from above*, as their slow rate of climb kept them below the summits of

British Aeroplanes
Bombing an Afghan
Mountain Position

How the Aeroplane   Checkmates the Mountaineer

'How the Aeroplane Checkmates the Mountaineer'. An artist's impression from
the Sphere Magazine, 14 June 1919. A flight of British light bombers are depicted
attacking an Afghan position. Lacking any form of air-defence artillery, the Afghans
had no answer to this form of warfare, and angrily compared the British raids on
Afghanistan with German raids on England, widely regarded by the British public
as evidence of German frightfulness.

the Khyber crags. But they flew well enough to reach Dacca, where they
arrived just as the Amir's officials were issuing rifles, blankets and supplies to a large body of tribesmen. All rushed for cover as the British
bombs fell. Then, as the aircraft departed, the Afghan officials emerged
and discovered that during the raid the tribesmen had seized the rifles and
other stores and made off with them to the hills.

About twenty-five people were killed by the bombing, the government offices were hit and the Naib Salar, the Governor of Jalalabad, lost

'Pathan tribesmen taking cover from the airman 1919'. The difficulty of picking off men from the air is clearly shown by this artist's impression. As long as the men on the ground remain still, their grey or drab-coloured clothing blends perfectly with the surrounding countryside. But in this scene the aircraft is a strategic bomber, the Handley Page V/1500, which would not be likely to be seeking opportunity targets among the rocks.

a foot. Other bombs damaged General Salah Muhammad's headquarters, though he was not in it himself at the time.

This gave the soldiers below Bagh a breathing space to organize their next attack. Major-General Fowler, General Officer Commanding 1st Division, took over command of the troops at Landi Kotal after the reverse of 9 May. Reinforcements arrived from Peshawar, which was by now quiet, and at dawn on 11 May Fowler attacked Bagh with six battalions, covered by the fire of eighteen pieces of artillery and twenty-two machine guns. He had another battalion covering his northern flank and three more in reserve. Careful preparation gave everyone confidence in the plan, and as the assault units filed out under cover of darkness, they were surreptitiously joined by men who had been detailed to stay behind as camp guards, being medically unfit, but who were determined not to be left out of the battle. Despite the heat of the day and the steep, rocky ground up which they had to climb, the infantry toiled upwards, stopping from time to time only to recover their breath. The first unit to reach the Afghan position was the 2nd Battalion of the North Staffordshire Regiment, the covering fire lifting only when they were seen to be within yards of their objective. A bayonet attack drove the Afghans from their first line and hand grenades were used to kill those who took cover in a series of rocky redoubts or *sangars* in the rear.

While the Staffords took the Afghan right the 2/11th Gurkha Rifles charged through the centre, capturing the Afghan artillery and cutting down the gunners. On the left, the 1/11th Gurkhas captured Bagh village, a field gun and a Gardner gun. As the Afghans, who had fought bravely and well, retreated, they were bombed and machine-gunned by the Royal Air Force. The British side lost eight killed and thirty-two wounded. The Afghans lost their camp, transport animals and five guns captured. Sixty-five Afghan soldiers were buried by the victors and their total casualties were estimated at 100 killed, 300 wounded.

But the airmen did not have it all their own way. 'We had a terrible misfortune last night,' Roos-Keppel lamented to Chelmsford on 13 May, 'when the great Handley-Page aeroplane which could have bombed Kabul was wrecked.' But he cheered up at the thought that the unexpected British offensive had disrupted the Afghan plan of campaign.

The Amir, for his part, represented himself as the injured party. Writing to Chelmsford on 10 May, he expressed regret that the British had seen fit to arrest his postmaster. He pointed out that although the manifesto complained of by the British indeed contained criticism of their tyrannical laws which had united Hindu and Muslim against the Raj, it also expressly mentioned his unwillingness to interfere in the internal affairs of other states. The mobilization of his troops and tribal levies along the frontier was purely to prevent disturbances spreading over into his own territory. It was to be regretted a thousand times, he wrote, that the British were still unprepared to recognize Afghanistan's complete independence, but 'the doors of calamity may not be opened upon the world because a demand for justice is right'.

None of this impressed the Government of India, which formed a Propaganda Committee to counter Amanulla's own efforts. Leaflets were scattered by the Royal Air Force, beginning: 'O brave and honest people of Afghanistan,' and going on to inform them that the army of Amanulla had been put to flight in front of Dacca and his guns captured by the vanguard of the vast army being assembled by Great Britain.

Will the peoples of Afghanistan allow this inexperienced youth, false to the memory of his martyred father, false to the interests of his country, false to the dictates of the Holy Koran, to bring calamity upon the brave people and fair country of Afghanistan? God forbid.

173

'A scene in the British camp at Dacca', on the Afghan side of the Khyber Pass, prior to the unexpected Afghan attack 16 May 1919. The horse lines were exposed to Afghan gun-fire, and many animals broke looses and stampeded into the hills.

The fighting at Dacca began on 13 May. In response to Roos-Keppel's continued insistence that to remain stationary would unsettle the tribes, units of the 1st Infantry Brigade crossed the Afghan frontier and established pickets all along the Khyber until it opened out into the Dacca plain. The 1st Cavalry Brigade, under Brigadier-General G. Baldwin, rode through the pass and established a camp at Dacca during the afternoon without opposition from Afghan forces. Having been held up on his march for lack of water, he gave the water supply first priority in his choice of a camping ground, at the expense of tactical considerations. Two battalions of infantry joined him on the next day, and on 16 May he rode back with his headquarters to rejoin his own brigade, the 10th Cavalry, at Peshawar, handing over Dacca and the troops there to General Fowler and HQ 1st Division.

Fowler was by no means happy with the camp site, which lacked natural cover and was open to long-range fire from the surrounding hills. These in turn were too far away for the garrison to establish a secure picket line in them. He ordered a move to a new site on the next day and returned to Landi Kotal. His lack of confidence in Baldwin's judgement was soon justified by the sudden return of the King's Dragoon Guards and the 1/15th Sikhs from a reconnaissance to the west, which had run into a large force of Afghans advancing to recapture Dacca. A successful mounted charge

'The British Camp at Dacca, 17 May 1919, after the Afghan attack'. The camp site had been selected for logistic convenience rather than tactical reasons. It was completely unprotected against Afghan artillery and long-range snipers, and for a time the British were in a precarious position.

by a squadron of the Dragoon Guards, one of the last cavalry charges in British military history, allowed the two horse artillery guns with the force to limber up and gallop back to camp, closely followed by the rest of the force and, hard on their heels, the Afghans.

With Afghan shells bursting inside his camp and Afghan riflemen approaching under the cover of broken ground and pouring in a heavy fire, the position of Brigadier-General Crocker, commanding the Dacca force, was a difficult one. The cavalry horses and transport beasts were hurried to the protection of the village and the bed of a dried-up stream. Two newly arrived battalions, the 2nd Somerset Light Infantry and the 1/35 Sikhs, were ordered out and succeeded in holding back the Afghans until nightfall, when both sides withdrew to their defences. The British losses had been ten killed, eighty-nine wounded, with eighty-eight casualties among the animal lines. During the night many more horses were lost as snipers caused a stampede in the artillery and cavalry lines.

Crocker decided to launch an attack at first light on the two hills to his west, from which the Afghan artillery were able to shoot down into his camp.

The northernmost of these, code-named Stonehenge, was attacked by the 1/35th Sikhs, supported by the 1/9th Gurkha Rifles. They reached the foot of the hill under cover of darkness and at dawn on 17 May began the long climb upwards. The Sikhs were within 100 yards of the summit when the Afghans, silently waiting for them, suddenly opened a rapid and accurate fire. Three Indian officers were killed, the colonel and two captains fell wounded. The men, caught by surprise in the open, suffered numerous casualties and finally ran for shelter back down the hill. One company rallied and joined the Gurkhas in a second attack covered by the artillery, but this too failed, leaving two platoons pinned down within twenty yards of the Afghan position.

On the southernmost hill, the attack by 1/15th Sikhs was equally unsuccessful, being halted by heavy rifle fire about 300 yards short of their objective. Any hope of being able to advance farther disappeared when the British artillery, consisting only of the six 15-pdrs belonging to the cavalry brigade, firing up at the hills from their position in the camp, ran out of ammunition at about 10 a.m.

The British were saved by the arrival of three lorry-loads of ammunition from Landi Kotal, followed at about 11.30 a.m. by Major-General A. Skeen with part of the 3 Infantry Brigade. These, consisting of the 1st Battalion the Yorkshire Regiment (The Green Howards), the 2nd Battalion of the 1st Gurkha Rifles, four howitzers and sixteen machine guns, enabled the British to resume the offensive. This got away to a bad start when the Yorkshiremen instead of going to the position allotted to them as a reserve, marched off to attack the southernmost hill. There they engaged what they took to be an Afghan concentration, but what turned out to be the battalion HQ of the 15th Sikhs, where two British officers and eight Sikhs became casualties before the firing could be stopped.

While this mistaken combat was taking place, the Somerset Light Infantry, with covering fire from the howitzers and machine guns and joined by the 1/9th Gurkhas, captured Stonehenge with little difficulty. The Afghans abandoned their positions, leaving behind five of the seven Krupp 75-mm mountain guns which they had used so successfully the previous day. The butcher's bill on the British side, twenty-eight killed and 157 wounded, with eleven British officers among the casualties, though negligible in terms of the recent fighting in France or Gallipoli was heavy enough by frontier standards, and arrangements for evacuating the wounded proved totally inadequate. Baldwin, who had wrongly sited the camp, was blamed for the losses.

Still, the Afghans had been defeated and their guns taken, just as the British propagandists claimed, and the main problem on this front for the British was now the protection of their communications and rear areas. Roos-Keppel had been disturbed by the decreasing reliability of the local paramilitary force, the Khyber Rifles. British columns had complained of being shot at from areas theoretically held by the Khyber Rifles. Desertions from this corps had increased to alarming proportions. On 17 May, all those who wished to take their discharge were invited to do so. Six hundred out of 700 accepted at Landi Kotal alone, but Roos-Keppel felt it better that they should leave without their rifles than desert with them.

'"M" Battery Royal Horse Artillery in action at Dacca, 17 May 1919'. A contemporary photograph published in the Illustrated London News, *9 August 1919.*

'British Army lorries in the Khyber Pass, May 1919'. The motor-lorry was among the most valuable pieces of equipment in the British armoury during 1919. Without it the British columns would have taken weeks rather than days to push into Afghan territory, and the campaign would have been prolonged to an unacceptable extent. Throughout the campaign the cry from the front was 'Motor Transport, more Motor Transport'.

Of the 250 or so who volunteered to stay, a large number were suspected of only doing so hoping that they could desert with their rifles. The whole corps believed that the British, in order to destroy the fighting power of the Afridi Pathans, from whom the Khyber Rifles were recruited, planned to use the Afghan War as an excuse to put them in the forefront of the battle and wipe them out with British artillery fire, a proceeding which would have been entirely in accordance with the Pathan concept of honour.

A general deterioration of the local security situation followed. Several large *lashkars*, or tribal gatherings, assembled in the foot-hills north of Peshawar and scarce resources of men and transport had to be committed to deal with them. Inside the city itself there were sporadic outbreaks of firing. In the Khyber Pass, despite the deployment of nearly an entire infantry division as pickets, telegraph wires were cut, convoys ambushed and road blocks thrown up, adding to the existing traffic congestion. The gorge at Ali Masjid was a noted site of traffic jams in temperatures of up to 125°F in the shade.

This tribal activity, encouraged by the Amir's agents, caused Chelmsford to advocate a renewed advance into Afghanistan. He did not share Roos-Keppel's war aims, which were no less than the annexation of Jalalabad province, thus surrounding the frontier tribes with British-administered territory and cutting them off from Afghanistan. Indeed, in Chelmsford's view such an idea stood condemned by the lessons of history, and he recommended that at the conclusion of hostilities the British should behave generously to the Afghans. But meanwhile he told Montagu on 21 May, 'the only sound policy is to advance on Jalalabad. ... We shall by so doing threaten Kabul and force the withdrawal of enemy force from our frontier'.

In accordance with this plan, arrangements were made for an advance. The 1st Division and the 1st Cavalry Brigade were concentrated at Dacca. Thirty days' supplies were stockpiled there and at Landi Kotal. But because of the transport problems it was not until the end of May that the force was ready to advance.

Then news came of startling developments on the central front. The British had abandoned the whole of Waziristan. On the banks of the Kurram River the British garrison of Thal lay under the guns of General Nadir Khan.

XI

End Game

The Conclusion of the Third Afghan War

On the southern front, Lieutenant-General S.R. Wapshare, with the 12th Mounted Brigade and the 4th Division at Quetta, was well placed to block any attempt by Afghan forces to reach the Bolan, though lack of transport prevented him from undertaking any major offensive operations. At the beginning of the war the Afghans had a cavalry regiment and five infantry battalions, with twenty-five guns, at Kandahar, and another two battalions at Kalat-i-Ghilzai. The Amir's chief minister, Abdul Qudus, was reported to be on his way to Kandahar with another 1,500 men, though in fact he did not arrive there until 31 May.

Wapshare decided that to forestall any Afghan attempt to stir up trouble among the tribes in Baluchistan lie would launch an attack over the border against the Afghan fort of Spin Baldak. This lay six miles away from the British frontier railhead of New Chaman, around which Wapshare concentrated units of the 11th and 57th Infantry Brigades. Spin Baldak was an impressive work, constructed during the reign of Abdur Rahman and, in its day, one of the strongest forts in the country. But by 1919 it was out of date and its strong walls, though still formidable against infantry, were otherwise little more than shell traps.

During the early hours of 27 May, 1919, the British troops crossed the Afghan border and made for Spin Kotal. By dawn, the 25th and 42nd Cavalry, supported by No. 22 Squadron of the Machine Gun Corps, were in position on the far side of the fort, severing its communications with Kandahar. The infantry, an impressive array consisting of two British battalions (one Regular, one Territorial), two Indian and two Gurkha battalions, was deployed on either side of the fort supported by No. 270 Company, Machine Gun Corps and twelve pieces of artillery. The gunners laid down a creeping barrage, in the way that had become usual in the First World War, but the Territorials (the 1/4th Royal West Kent Regiment) were not in the right place when it lifted, and it had to be repeated.

'The assault on Spin Baldak, 26 May 1919'. The guns depicted here seem to be an Indian Mountain Battery, although in fact the artillery attacking Spin Baldak consisted of six 18-pdr guns and six howitzers of the Royal Field Artillery.

The Sun-helmeted infantry rushing forward on the right may represent the 1st Battalion, Duke of Wellington's Regiment, one of the six British regular battalions left in India after the First World War.

'The Afghan fortress at Spin Baldak, after its occupation by the British, May 1919'. A photograph from the Illustrated London News 23 August 1919, showing the scene of hand-to-hand fighting between British and Afghan soldiers before the fort was eventually captured.

'The outer wall of Spin Baldak', showing the damage caused by British artillery and aerial bombardment. Spin Baldak was a relatively modern fortress built in the late nineteenth century by Amir Abdur Rahman to defend the road from the Bolan Pass to Kandahar. But by 1919 its much-vaunted defences were little more than shell or bomb traps, and it fell to British attack in a matter of hours.

They then advanced some distance, but after coming under fire from a few men behind a breastwork, went to ground. The Territorials, with no-one having any reason to seek a soldier's grave for the sake of a mud fort on the edge of Central Asia, remained there for the next two hours. Then the regulars of the 1st Battalion, the Duke of Wellington's Regiment, were brought up from the reserve to launch a flank attack. This succeeded without difficulty and the West Kents went forward once more, only to be stopped by another small party on the next obstacle. This was cleared by men from the Duke of Wellington's Regiment and the 1/129th Baluchis, who came up on the West Kents' flank. The British were now in a position to dominate the eastern side of the fort.

This heartened the 1/22nd Punjabis, who were attacking the western side. They had suffered the loss of three British lieutenants, a subahdar and eleven men earlier in the battle when hit by an ill-aimed bomb from a British aircraft, but now, in co-operation with the 1/4th Gurkha Rifles, they surged over the defences and into the fort. Some of the garrison had escaped earlier in the day, but the remainder fought on bravely against British bullets, hand grenades and gunfire until the early afternoon, when the last resistance ceased. The garrison had consisted of some 600 soldiers, of whom 170 were killed and 176 taken prisoner. The remainder escaped by passing between the two Indian cavalry regiments, each of which thought the other was responsible for the ground through which the fugitives passed, so that the only mounted pursuit came from the machine gunners of No. 22 Squadron. The fort was then occupied by units of the 57th Infantry Brigade, while Wapshare went back with the rest of his men to New Chaman.

On the central front, General Nadir Khan had under command a force of fourteen battalions and forty-eight guns based on Ghazni. He placed a strong detachment on the Peiwar Kotal, at the top of the Kurram valley, and concentrated the rest at Matun, an Afghan border town from which the Kaiku River flows eastwards to join the Kurram farther down its course. On 23 May he was reported to have left Matun, and his British opponent, Brigadier-General Eustace, had to guess his destination. Eustace decided to reinforce the British outpost at Parachinar, near the Peiwar Kotal, and to strengthen the force at Thal. This, just north of the Kaiku-Kurram confluence, was a small town from which a light railway ran about sixty miles eastwards, linking the Kurram valley with Kohat and, ultimately, Peshawar.

But there were not enough regular troops to hold the line of the Tochi river, some thirty miles south of Matun. Eustace, without informing the political authorities, ordered the evacuation of the posts held by the tribal militia and the destruction of whatever government stores could not be carried away.

This proved disastrous. As the garrisons withdrew, the local tribesmen rose in arms. A few of the local levies remained loyal to their salt, but the majority deserted or opened fire on their own officers. By the evening of 26 May the whole of Waziristan was in revolt and the North and South Waziristan Militias had ceased to exist. The system of frontier management by local paramilitary forces collapsed there just as it had in the Khyber.

On 27 May, General Nadir Khan, carrying his artillery on elephants over otherwise impassable tracks, emerged into the Kurram valley and sat down before Thal. There the British manned a hastily constructed series of trenches and field works giving a total defence perimeter of about five miles. The garrison, all Indian units under command of Brigadier-General Eustace himself, consisted of one squadron of cavalry, four battalions of infantry and a company of sappers and miners, supported by four mountain guns and two 3-inch mortars. But many of his troops were young and inexperienced and it was not known how they would stand up to the strains of an unequal combat. Nadir Khan had with him some 3,000 regular troops, with about the same number of tribal warriors, two 100-mm Krupp field howitzers and seven 75-mm mountain guns. The artillery, when brought into action on the heights above Thal, were able to bombard the British without fear of retaliation except for occasional sorties flown by the Royal Air Force. On 28 May the Afghan gunners succeeded in setting fire to the ration trucks in the railway yard, the petrol dump, the forage stacks for the transport animals and the wireless transmitting station. This proved too much for the men of the armed Frontier Constabulary, all of whom deserted during the night, allowing the vital water pumping station, which they had been guarding, to fall to the Afghans. A number of probing attacks by the besiegers were driven off without difficulty by British automatic weapons and rifle fire, but food, water and ammunition began to run short, and as casualties mounted (ninety men and 100 animals after six days) it was clear that the siege could not be withstood much longer.

The British Commander at Peshawar, General Sir Arthur Barratt, switched to the Kurram the reinforcements which he had been intending to send to Dacca. These were the men of the 16th Division then in the process of moving up from Lahore. The leading brigade, the 45th Infantry Brigade, had already arrived at Peshawar, commanded by the controversial figure of Brigadier-General Dyer, the hero, or villain (according to one's point of view) of the Amritsar incident. Major-General Beynon, with the rest of the 16th Division, was ordered to go direct to Kohat, which Eustace had left virtually undefended when he marched to Thal. Dyer and his brigade were ordered to go to Eustace's rescue. 'I want you to relieve Thal,' Barratt told him. 'I know you will do all that any man can do.'

Knowing that the situation of the besieged garrison was growing more critical daily, Dyer hurried his men to Kohat, using a convoy of sixty-two lorries and the overstretched resources of the North-Western Railway. At

Kohat, considering himself short of artillery, he took four of the six light field guns from the Frontier Garrison Artillery and towed them behind his lorries, carrying the gunners and their ammunition in the back. He loaded other lorries with tree trunks to look like guns and lashed the branches alongside to raise great clouds of dust and give the impression of formidable numbers.

On 30 May his men, by road and rail, had reached Togh, twenty-seven miles east of Thal. By this time, having collected various other units along his line of march, Dyer was in command of a cavalry squadron, twelve guns, an armoured car battery and nearly five battalions of infantry, among them the 300-strong 1/25th London Regiment, once a fashionable Territorial cyclist battalion. Dyer's biographer wrote,

> At Togh, the General addressed his troops, exhorting them to make a great effort to rescue their comrades at Thal. His words touched the hearts of that strangely assorted force of veterans and war levies, Punjabi peasants and London men of business so that they marched to the last of their strength; some of them dropped in their tracks. At four o'clock in the morning on 31 May they set out along a fairly open valley between steep hills. There was no wind and but little water, and as the day advanced the stony hillsides became a furnace, the naked rocks throwing back the sun so that it seemed to strike from the ground as from the sky.

The men of the 45th Infantry Brigade had had little food or sleep since leaving Peshawar, but they covered eighteen miles in twelve hours, Dyer marching at their head for most of the way before pushing on by car to select the camp site in person. The next morning they set out again on the last lap of their journey. Two miles short of Thal, Dyer was met by Eustace's senior staff officer with details of the Afghan positions.

Dyer decided to attack the tribal contingents which lay between him and the town. To the north were 2,000 tribesmen with some regulars and four guns, and to the south, under a local chieftain, Babrak, were another 4,000 tribesmen, part from the Khost area, part from Waziristan, neither part trusting the other. Dyer opened fire with his guns in both directions, to give the impression of attacking north and south simultaneously, but actually launched all his strength at Babrak's men. These scattered and fled, and by 4 p.m. their position had been taken by the 1/69th Punjabis for the loss of four men wounded. Dyer's field guns then silenced the Afghan battery to the north, and the road to Thal lay open.

The next morning Dyer took command at Thal and prepared to attack the Afghan main force in the hills west of the town. This had been reinforced and now totalled some 19,000 men and thirteen guns. He ordered out four battalions, the 1/25th Londons, the 2/41st Dogras, the 1/151st Sikh Infantry and the 3/9th Gurkha Rifles. Then came a dramatic turn of events. A messenger arrived from Nadir Khan saying that the Amir had ordered him to suspend hostilities pending negotiations with the British Government for an armistice. He asked for an acknowledgement of the message.

General Dyer, always a man for the grand gesture, acknowledged Nadir Khan's letter with an answer of uncompromising hostility. 'My guns will give an immediate reply,' he said, 'and a further reply will be sent by the Divisional Commander to whom the letter has been forwarded.' The reference to guns was particularly well made, for, as the British artillery, real and simulated, advanced towards him, Nadir Khan was watching through his field-glasses. 'In the name of God,' he protested, 'We have the whole artillery of India coming against us.' Bearing in mind his royal master's orders to discontinue hostilities, he decided to withdraw before the toiling British infantry could reach him. He retired three miles to the west, harassed by British aeroplanes, armoured cars and cavalry. The next morning, 3 June, a patrol of men from the 37th Lancers and 1/25th Londons found his camp abandoned, but as they had no transport they were unable to bring back the large quantities of abandoned stores they found there. Returning on 4 June with a string of 300 camels, they discovered that during their absence the local tribesmen had pillaged everything, including Nadir Khan's tent, with its carpet, stool and standard complete. Dyer prepared to follow up his retreating enemy, but before he could do so news came that an armistice (a word then currently in vogue) had been concluded with the Afghans on the previous day.

The first overtures for peace had come from the Afghan Commander-in-Chief as early as 14 May. He blamed the British for beginning hostilities without any declaration of war by either side, and accused them of inflicting heavy losses 'on the civil population and army of Afghanistan, by throwing bombs from aeroplanes'. But, he went on, as the Viceroy of India had sent the Afghan Vakil from his court to the Amir with a message saying that the British wanted peace, the Afghan troops had been ordered to suspend the fighting pending further diplomatic exchanges. This letter arrived just after the British occupation of Dacca, and Roos-Keppel's view then was, that as long as Amanulla was Amir, the British could treat only in Kabul. He proposed ignoring the letter, as in any case the advance to Jalalabad could not begin for another fortnight, except for letting the still wavering border tribes know that the Afghans had sued for peace.

It seems to have been the air offensive which decided Amanulla to seek an early end to the war, although the British airman were hampered by shortage of machines and spares. *The Times*, acting on information received from the motoring peer, Lord Montague of Beaulieu, published a leader wondering why the Royal Air Force in India was still flying obsolete aircraft, while new models were being burnt, or their engines sold for scrap, as part of the demobilization process in Europe.

'The arrival of an Afghan officer under flag of truce, Dacca 15 May 1919'. This envoy broght a letter from the Afghan C-in-C advising the British that the Afghans had been ordered by their Amir to observe a ceasefire so that peace talks could begin.

When a ship did arrive at Bombay with war supplies, it was found that the crates containing the reinforcement aircraft had been left behind on the quayside at Marseilles. Edwin Montagu, the Secretary of State for India, with an eye on the liberal conscience, demanded an assurance that no poison gas was to be used and gave instructions that only military targets were to be bombed. Chelmsford accepted the assurances of his bomber crews, who were now dropping over a ton of high explosives a day on Afghan cities, that this was the case. In fact they had succeeded in bombing not only the tomb of Amir Habibulla at Jalalabad but also that of Amir Abdur Rahman at Kabul, as well as various other public buildings and the only machine workshop in the country.

One of the aircrew in this campaign was Arthur Harris, a junior officer of the Royal Air Force, itself formed as the junior service only a year before. One result of his experience was to convince him that where the air force, as was the case in India at this time, was a mere appendage of the army, it would always be at the end of the queue for resources. In his autobiography, *Bomber Offensive*, Marshal of the Royal Air Force Sir Arthur Harris, as this officer eventually became, writes that ever afterwards he strove desperately to keep the air arm independent in every respect from the others. Moreover, having as a junior officer seen an enemy nation forced to sue for peace rather than have its cities reduced to rubble by British bombers, his belief in the power of a strategic bombing offensive must have been considerably strengthened. The young officer who flew over the hills of the North West

Frontier to Amanulla's Afghanistan became, as 'Bomber' Harris, the commander of the mighty bomber fleets which a generation later were to fly night after night across the North Sea to Hitler's Germany.

In 1919, and indeed for many years afterwards, the air marshals were greatly concerned to find a distinct role for their separate service to prevent it from being divided between its two senior sisters. The concept of strategic bombing was adopted as the Royal Air Force's special contribution to the making of war, and the results of the air raid on Kabul were seized upon as a vindication of this concept. Lord Trenchard, 'the father of the RAF', wrote to Robert Halley, who had piloted the Handley Page V 1500 aircraft which bombed Kabul, and congratulated him on winning the war single-handed!

The aeroplanes, Roos-Keppel reported on 27 May, had done wonderfully. Without them he thought that the British would be fighting with their backs to the wall instead of preparing to advance. But the machines were beginning to wear out from overwork. He asked Chelmsford for more planes, and more lorries. Maffey, whom Chelmsford had sent to be Chief Political Officer in Afghanistan, wrote from Dacca in the same vein. 'The burden of everybody's song here is – Motor Transport, more Motor Transport. Is it coming from England? Is there any reserve to be got at? Can we commandeer private firms' transport from Calcutta and Bombay?'

At this point, a letter was received from the Amir, dated 28 May. He told the British that he had sent his Commander-in-Chief to watch the border to guard against disturbances from India, and that this officer had dug in on ground marked on his maps as Afghan territory, after which the British had started hostilities. The Amir said he decided against declaring *jihad* in response to the Viceroy's letter brought by the Afghan Vakil, and instead sent the Vakil to the British with an offer to negotiate but,

> a day had hardly elapsed after the departure of our Envoy for your camp when one of your aeroplanes flew over Kabul and bombarded our Royal Palace, thereby causing great excitement and panic among our loyal people ... many other favourite buildings in our official quarter and unprotected town were bombed. It is a matter for great regret that the throwing of bombs by Zeppelins on London was denounced as a most savage act and the bombardment of places of worship and sacred spots was considered a most abominable operation, while now we see with our own eyes that such operations were a habit which is prevalent amongst all civilized people of the West.

Nevertheless, he said, he had ordered his troops to cease fire in order to allow peace talks to be opened.

The Government of India seized the chance of peace Amanulla offered. Its officials were weary of war. Its young soldiers were untrained for

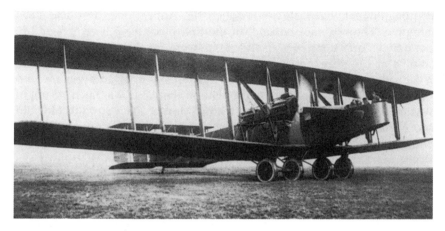

'The Handley Page V/1500'. A twin-engined aircraft with a maximum speed of 90 mph at 6,000 feet, an operational ceiling of 11,000 feet and an endurance time of six hours. Designed as a strategic bomber to bomb Berlin, it was used against the Afghan capital, Kabul. A single machine, No. J 1936, piloted by Captain Halley with Lieutenant Villiers as observer, took off from Risalpur airfield at 3.30 a.m. on 24 May 1919, and reached Kabul three hours later. It dropped eight 112 lb and twenty-six 20 lb bombs, destroying the tomb of the Amir Habibulla, the only machine workshop in the country, and a number of other buildings.

mountain fighting. Its old soldiers were looking for their long deferred furlough or demobilization. Its medical arrangements were beginning to break down under the strain of a cholera epidemic in the Khyber. Its logistic system was unable to provide all the supplies and comforts for the troops which, in the previous Afghan war, would have been luxuries, but which now were considered by public opinion to be necessities. Montagu had heard stories of 'another Messpot' in the making, and the Commander-in-Chief India, Sir Charles Monro, warned that if the war was long continued, his resources in these areas might well prove inadequate.

Chelmsford therefore wrote to Amanulla on 2 June, saying he was glad to hear of the proposal for an armistice. But he refused to accept the Amir's claim that the war was begun by the British. He promised to stop the bombing if the Amir withdrew his troops twenty miles from the British positions, ceased fire on all fronts, and informed the tribes he had asked for peace. Chelmsford urged the Amir to accept these proposals and the offer of friendship, and to consider, before rejecting them, that the British had just defeated the greatest military power in history.

Montagu had just returned from representing India at the Paris Peace Conference. For all his liberal tendencies, he was in no frame of mind to be gentle with a defeated enemy, and he wrote on 11 June to Chelmsford complaining of the haste with which the Amir's overtures had been accepted. They should, he said, in the first place have been referred to London, as questions of war and peace were for the Cabinet to decide. 'Whilst we were expecting to hear of your successful occupation of Jalalabad, we hear that an armistice has been asked for and you are willing to entertain the proposal.' The tone of the Amir's letter he thought was impudent, with no apology or admission of his war guilt. Nor did Montagu care for Chelmsford's silence, in his reply to the Amir, about the allegations concerning British terror bombing, and the attempt to liken the British air raids on Kabul to the German raids on London. Chelmsford was also rebuked for asking the Amir to exert his influence over tribes on the British side of the international frontier, and for generally appearing over-anxious to resume friendly relations not only with the Afghan people but with Amanulla. 'It seems to me,' wrote Montagu, 'you should have summoned him to appear to learn your terms and not to negotiate peace.'

Amanulla, for his part, remained defiant. He replied to Chelmsford's terms on 11 June, telling the British that the Afghan nation had repeatedly been a cause of destruction and ruination to any foreign power on its sacred soil, and declaring that this war against a non-Muslim power had resulted, despite all the losses and injuries suffered, in a national regeneration. Afghans, he said, would rather die than remain subject to a foreign government. Afghanistan was a nation in arms, the people were the army, and he could not pull back his army without evicting all the people in the area, which was impossible. Nor could he guarantee that British aircraft, whose provocative flying over Afghan territory was as pitch upon the faces of his subjects, would not be fired upon by indignant individuals. Still, he would accept the British desire for peace, and promised to name his delegation for a peace conference.

Negotiations dragged on throughout June and July, with charges and counter-charges on both sides. The British said that they would accept the withdrawal of the regulars only, but that any tribal partisans shooting at aircraft must expect instant retaliation. At least one aircraft was shot down by rifle fire, and the pilot and his observer rescued in the nick of time after a race between the troops and the tribesmen to reach them first. General Nadir Khan made not the slightest pretence of observing the armistice terms, and continued to encourage tribal warriors to shoot at British camps and pickets. On the southern front the British had to endure similar harassment from the irregulars, though Abdul Qudus himself hinted very broadly to the British Political Agent that he would not be averse to making a separate peace, if Amanulla proved obdurate, and that he could be a pro-British, anti-Soviet candidate for the throne himself, given a little support. On the Khyber front, where a water pipeline had been laid on the surface rather than underground, the water was too hot to drink, and the undisciplined followers drank out of polluted ditches. There were nearly 2,000 cases of cholera as a result. Monro announced his intentions of inspecting the men's welfare arrangements on

'A crashed aeroplane and tender, North-West Frontier, 1919'. The aeroplane and the motor lorry, the two indispensables of the British forces during the Third Afghan War. Here one is shown going to the rescue of the other.

the line of communications, and dummy 'soldiers' canteens' were hastily constructed all along his anticipated route. There was acrimonious correspondence between the Government of India, anxious for peace at virtually any price, and the India Office, which would have been happy to treat Amanulla and Afghanistan in the same way as the Kaiser and Germany.

Chelmsford had long made up his mind that Roos-Keppel was to be excluded from the peace negotiations. 'He is confessedly an Afghanophobe', Chelmsford told Montagu on 4 June. 'He hates the Afghans, and I think I may say with confidence, he would like to see Afghanistan thoroughly conquered.' This, in Chelmsford's view, would have been disastrous. Afghanistan must be left strong and friendly, or else the British might well find, at best, that there would be no-one to control the turbulent transborder tribes, and at worst, a Communist regime on their North-West Frontier. The chief British delegate was therefore to be Sir Hamilton Grant, the man already nominated to succeed Roos-Keppel as Chief Commissioner of the North-West Frontier Province. Roos-Keppel, once he became aware that no punitive terms were being imposed on the Afghans, seemed happy enough to have nothing to do with the proceedings, though he continued to insist that the Amir was only playing for time, perhaps waiting for

'A group of British officers sheltering from the sun at Dacca Camp'. While negotiations dragged on at the Rawalpindi peace conference, the soldiers at Dacca continued to suffer casualties from occasional snipers, disease and heat. The temperature at the time this photograph was taken was 125°F in the shade.

money and arms to arrive from the Soviets so that he could renew the war. As for his own position, he let it be known he wished to remain in post at Peshawar for the time being. According to Maffey this was partly in order to keep the rank and title of major-general which he had been granted during the emergency, and partly to spite Grant, for whose convenience he felt he had been repeatedly sacrificed.

The Afghan delegates eventually arrived for the peace conference at Rawalpindi on 26 July. They felt aggrieved at not being received by guards of honour, and at not being allowed to bring their own armed escorts. They spoke of declining to come to the conference table without them, until Grant called their bluff by offering to have their special train prepared to take them back to the Khyber. 'Still,' Maffey reported to Chelmsford, 'we had anxious moments.'

The conference began with each side blaming the other for starting the war, and each claiming that the other had been the first to sue for peace. The chief Afghan delegate, Sirdar Ali Ahmad, argued that it was in the best interests of the British for them to be on good terms with Afghanistan. For one thing, he said, just as England, though weaker than Germany in 1914, had eventually won a war by mobilizing all her resources and people, so now might Afghanistan, especially in view of the spirit of independence then awakening in small nations all over the world, and their claims for self-determination. For another, there was the Bolshevik threat. If Afghanistan fell to the Communists, then this would bring them to the borders of British India, and, if their influence spread across the frontier, they would destroy India just as they had destroyed Russia. Therefore, he argued, the British should seek the friendship of the Afghans, and make an ally of them in the common struggle against the Bolsheviks.

Grant replied by playing down the importance of the Communist threat. The old threat to Afghanistan and India, from Imperial Russia, had collapsed, he said, and the new one, from the Bolsheviks, did not keep the Government of India awake at nights. He dismissed Sirdar Ali Ahmad's veiled suggestion that the Afghans might be driven into the arms of the Bolsheviks by British intransigence.

'How can a State ruled by an autocratic King, and supported by an aristocracy of great and high-standing land-owning Sirdars like Your Excellency, amalgamate and work in sympathy with a violent rabble, who hold that Kings must be murdered, that monarchies must be abolished, that aristocracies must be swept away, and that all property must be common, even women,' said Grant, and went on, 'The Bolsheviks certainly have one doctrine, which many people – perhaps Afghanistan – share, and that is that the British Empire must be destroyed. But I do not think that the Bolsheviks will throw away the rest of their doctrine for this alone; and I believe that if Afghanistan trusts to this she will be making a great mistake.'

The Afghan delegates replied that Britain would do well to have some anxiety regarding Bolshevism, which they said had brought down so many mighty Western powers. Grant said that it had only succeeded in the defeated nations. The Afghans expressed the hope that it would not spread to the victorious ones. Grant said that anyway it was an ideology alien to India, and called on his two Indian delegates, one Hindu, one Muslim, to support this assertion.

All parties having agreed that they were equally opposed to the Communist doctrines of regicide, the redistribution of wealth and the nationalization of women, the conference moved on to the question of money. The chief Afghan delegate said that he understood that the British Government had sanctioned a grant to the late Amir of four crores of rupees in appreciation of his neutrality, but the Indian Government had paid only one. Grant answered that perhaps the chief Afghan delegate was thinking of the four crores mentioned in the proposed Afghan–German treaty, and that he had a copy in his drawer should the chief Afghan delegate wish to study it. Sirdar Ali Ahmad angrily replied that if that was the British attitude, he was sorry that the Afghans had not made the treaty with Germany. Grant said that the Sirdar should not speak in haste, and that the British were very grateful for the late Amir's friendship. Yes, was the reply, and they showed it by bombing his tomb.

At this point the conference was adjourned to allow tempers to cool, and when it resumed, Grant expressed regret at the bombing of the late Amir's tomb.

The Afghans then asked for any settlement to include the style 'His Majesty' being accorded to the Amir Amanulla. Grant, who had been in London when the King's pleasure on this subject had been made known, said cautiously that this was a personal matter between sovereigns. Ali Ahmad replied that this was merely a civilized form of address, and his own king did not stand in need of British recognition for its use. 'Perhaps not,' said Grant. 'Let him be called His Majesty by the Bolsheviks.'

After a few more meetings (during one of which the Afghans suggested that, as the British could not control Waziristan, it should be ceded to the Amir), Grant, on 1 August, issued an ultimatum. Either the Afghans made peace or the British would re-open hostilities in fourteen days. His terms were that the British would accept that Afghanistan's foreign policy could never again be conducted except by Afghans, but certain gestures of goodwill must be made in return. All hostile foreigners, especially Bolsheviks, should be dismissed from Afghanistan. All Indian seditionists should be expelled. There should be no intrigues with the British frontier tribes, but friendly co-operation between border officials. The Indian Vakil in Kabul should be allowed to move about freely. The existing frontier should be accepted. He wrote to Chelmsford that if the Afghans were treated generously the British might even end with a more complete control over their foreign policy, through friendship, than could be gained by any treaty obligations. 'Liberty is a new toy to the Afghan Government,' he wrote, 'and they are very excited and jealous about it. … Later on, if we handle them well, they will come to us to mend their toy when it gets chipped or broken.'

The Afghan delegation at first refused to consider these terms, but on 4 August accepted, subject to certain conditions. These included the demand that the treaty be made with the Afghan Government, not as hitherto with the Amir. The British disliked this, but eventually gave way in order to gain a speedy settlement. The next objection was to a phrase in the draft treaty referring to unprovoked aggression by the Amir. Grant accepted instead the phrase 'in view of the circumstances which gave rise to the war'. The Afghans asked for an amnesty for the tribes on the British side of the border. This was refused.

But above all, they wanted recognition in the treaty of their full external independence. Grant answered the final point by saying that the war cancelled all previous treaties. As British control over Afghan policy did not exist, there was no point in including a statement to this effect in a treaty. Instead he gave Sirdar Ali Ahmad a formal letter expressing this

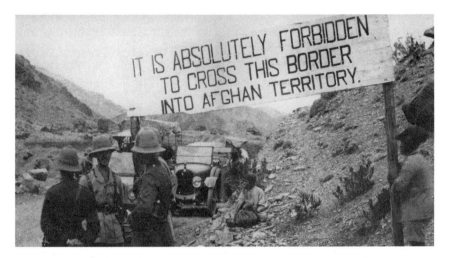

'The Afghan frontier 1919'. British officers beside a border sign-post. In the background, motor transport moves down the road in blithe disregard of its stern prohibition.

as the view of the British Government. By this act, he finally abandoned a feature of British Afghan policy that had always previously been considered essential, that the Afghans should have no relations with any foreign powers, except with British consent and advice.

Montagu, having been sent a draft of the letter, telegraphed to India that it should not be handed over to the Afghans, but in vain. Grant answered that they had already seen its contents, and for the British to hold back on this vital point at the last moment might lead the Afghans to break off negotiations after all. Montagu took the view that Grant's treaty was a most unsatisfactory one from the standpoint of the British. They had fought an expensive, unpopular and rather messy campaign, with nothing to show for it. Indeed, what had started as a pre-emptive lightning strike to push back the Afghans 200 yards into their own undisputed territory, had ended with the collapse of the border control system, talk of another 'Messpot' in respect of medical and welfare matters and the abandonment of British claims to control Afghan foreign policy. He refused to sanction the grant of honours and awards in connection with the war, arguing that hostilities might break out again. But it may well be that he had no wish to reward Grant and his team for concluding a unfavourable treaty, nor to give any more publicity than necessary to a war fought just after the conclusion of the war to end all wars.

The Treaty of Rawalpindi, signed at 11 a.m. on 8 August, ended the last of the wars between Afghanistan and British India, and the story of Britain's attempts to control the Afghans, begun eighty years before, came to an end.

Envoi
Afghanistan 1919–2003

British power in India had only another twenty-eight years to run. In 1947 the British withdrew from the sub-continent, and a new country was created on Afghanistan's south-east frontier, the Islamic state of Pakistan.

Russian power in Central Asia, on the other hand, revived, as the Soviet Union established itself there. The attempt by the Amir of Bokhara to regain his independence from Russia, just as the Amir of Afghanistan had gained his from Britain, ended in 1923, and Bokhara became the Soviet Socialist Republic of Uzbekistan.

Amanulla declared that Afghan independence dated from the signing of the Treaty of Rawalpindi. He was accorded the style of 'His Majesty' by the British immediately after the treaty, and took the title of King (Padshah) in June 1926. His zeal for the introduction of reforms along western lines offended many of his more conservative subjects, and a serious rebellion occurred in 1924, led by a son of the ex-Amir Yakub. This was put down, but the Amir reluctantly bowed to pressure from reactionary religious leaders, and cancelled some of the clauses in the new constitution which he had introduced. Among the most objectionable of these, in the eyes of his subjects, were those which guaranteed the rights of women, and deprived husbands and fathers of power over their female dependents.

Diplomatic relations were opened between Afghanistan and as many different nations as cared to accept them. Foreign legations appeared in Kabul, including one from the Soviet Union. A British Mission too arrived, with none of the problems which had previously been raised when the British had wished to be the sole power represented. King Amanulla toured Europe and the Middle East during the first half of 1928, and was received by the heads of state of each country in turn. During the tour he was received by King George V at Buckingham Palace, and dined with the Lord Mayor of London at the Guildhall.

196

On his return to his own country, Amanulla once more attempted to westernize his reluctant subjects. European styles of dress were introduced, and made compulsory for ministers and officials. Suriya, the Queen of Afghanistan, an ardent feminist, who had already shocked Afghan opinion by wearing modern evening dresses when in Europe, dramatically tore off her veil at a public gathering of notables. Amanulla proposed the introduction of monogamy, compulsory education for both sexes, the secularization of the law, and other radical reforms.

By the closing months of 1928, resentment against the King and his plans had spread throughout all classes and regions. An armed insurrection broke out in November. The next month the rebels reached Kabul. The British Mission came under fire, and the women and children of the British community were evacuated to Peshawar by special flights of the Royal Air Force.

On 14 January, 1929, King Amanulla abdicated in favour of his elder brother Inayatulla, and fled to Kandahar. The new king held out for three days and was then himself flown out to Peshawar by the Royal Air Force before the rebels closed in. Amanulla made an unsuccessful attempt to reclaim his throne but was defeated at Kalat-i-Ghilzai, and eventually went into exile in Italy.

In 1919, General Nadir Khan had returned from Thal a hero to his own people. A monument was put up at Kabul to his campaign, featuring at its base a chained lion to represent the British Army. He was re-appointed to the post of Commander-in-Chief, but later quarrelled with the Minister for War over frontier policy. In 1924 the Amir sent him to France as Afghan Minister in Paris. Nadir Khan was a conservative in his views, and in 1926 resigned from the Amir's service rather than be associated with the progressive measures then being introduced.

In March 1929, with Afghanistan in turmoil, he returned to his own country via British India, gathered an army, and, by October the same year, had succeeded in establishing himself at Kabul. The bandit forces which had held power since the previous king's flight were routed, and Nadir Khan, now Nadir Shah, was proclaimed King of Afghanistan.

Nadir Shah was the great-grandson of Sultan Muhammad Khan, the elder brother of Amir Dost Muhammad who had once ruled Peshawar. The new king ruled in the tradition of Dost Muhammad and Abdur Rahman, doing much to rebuild his shattered country after the disasters of war. Herat, which for a time had resumed its ancient independence, was re-united with the rest of the country in 1931. While resuming the traditional patterns of government, and so conciliating the orthodox (Nadir Shah was a conservative in religious as in political opinions), he continued the less controversial aspects of Amanulla's progressive measures.

But his own position was constantly challenged by those who regarded him as a usurper, or as too pro-British, or simply as too autocratic. In

November 1933 he was assassinated as the result of a personal blood-feud. The crown then passed to Nadir's son, the nineteen-year-old Zahir Shah. He, with the support of his uncles, came peacefully to the throne, and was accepted by all the provincial governors and tribal chieftains as the lawful heir.

In foreign policy, Afghanistan continued the policy of absolute non-alignment. During the Second World War, there were strong pro-Axis sympathies in the country, but the government was obliged to comply with Allied demands to expel all Germans and Italians except accredited diplomats. This, though unpopular, enabled Afghanistan to avoid the fate of Iran, where the Shah was deposed by the Allies and the country occupied by Anglo-Soviet forces.

After this war, Afghanistan continued to pursue her traditional policy of neutrality between two world powers, although now the two sides were the USA and USSR rather than the British and the Russian Empires. In 1964 a constitutional monarchy was established, and the royal family was excluded from political office. The 1969 parliamentary elections were followed by left-wing agitation, and in July 1973, during the absence of King Zahir Shah on a visit to Italy, he was deposed in a bloodless coup. His cousin and brother-in-law, Muhammad Daud Khan, then aged sixty-four, proclaimed a republic, with himself as President. Under his regime Afghanistan accepted aid from the Soviet Union, but also from the oil-rich, Islamic, but pro-Western, rulers of Iran and Kuwait. In 1977 a new constitution was introduced, providing for a number of economic and agrarian reforms, but also setting up a one-party state in which no laws contrary to the Islamic code would be allowed.

On 27 April, 1978, President Daud was overthrown in a coup led by the Armed Forces Revolutionary Council. Daud, together with his chief ministers, his Commander-in-Chief, and thirty members of his family, was killed. The Presidency was then assumed by Nur Muhammad Taraki, secretary-general of the previously banned *Khalk* or 'Masses' faction of the Communist party. The country, now called the Democratic Republic of Afghanistan, moved rapidly closer to the Communist bloc. In February 1979, the US Ambassador in Kabul was murdered by terrorists, and shortly afterwards American aid was substantially reduced. Discontent among the religious and tribal elements in the country erupted into serious disturbances at Herat in March 1979, and Government authority was restored only after much bloodshed. Despite a considerable influx of Soviet military equipment and 'advisers', outbreaks of rebellion continued throughout the country, and in September 1979 President Taraki himself was killed in an internal dispute among the leaders of his party. He was succeeded by President Hafizulla Amin, whose use of coercion to hasten the establishment of a socialist regime throughout the country only led to greater disorders.

At the end of December 1979, Afghanistan was invaded by large numbers of Soviet troops. President Amin was killed, and was succeeded by Babrak Karmal, the leader of a rival Afghan Communist group, the *Parcham* (Flag) party. The Soviets claimed that they had been invited into Afghanistan by Karmal to help protect the gains of socialism against counter-revolutionary forces stirred up by foreign agents. This claim was rejected by international opinion, and Soviet aggression was condemned by the United Nations. Muslim states were shocked at this invasion of a small Muslim country to establish a godless Communist system of government. Neutral countries were dismayed at the occupation of a country that had always tried to maintain a policy of non-alignment, and whose forces posed no threat to its powerful neighbour. Western nations were alarmed at Soviet expansion into an area within striking distance of the Indian Ocean, and of the Gulf oil fields, vital to the economies of the free world.

To show their disapproval of the Soviet move, the USA and other members of the Western Alliance reduced their commercial and cultural contact with the USSR. An embargo was placed on the sale of American grain, and of advanced technology, to the Soviet Union. Plans for participation in the Moscow Olympic Games were reduced or cancelled altogether.

Inside Afghanistan, the Soviet invasion provoked widespread resistance. The Soviet forces, and Afghan troops still loyal to the Communist regime, clashed with tribal guerrillas, who were joined by many former Afghan regular soldiers. In a country where most men are accustomed to the use of firearms, where the code of the people is that blood must be wiped out by blood, where the difficulty of the terrain allows insurgency to become in some areas almost a way of life, the arrival of an invading, unbelieving, foreign army only intensified existing resistance to the Communist regime.

The Russian invasion of Afghanistan stirred, in the minds of many people, folk memories of the British wars in that country. But some of these popular impressions, as this book's narrative of events has shown, are rather inexact. It is an oversimplification, for instance, to say that 'Britain has fought three wars to keep the Russians out of Afghanistan'. The First Afghan War was fought not so much to keep the Russians out as to let the British in, and to install a British puppet at Kabul. The parallel between Shah Shuja and Babrak Karmal is a very close one. The Second Afghan War was fought to establish a British presence in Afghanistan against the wishes of its people and government. The Third Afghan War was fought to keep the Indian frontier safe at a time of troubles inside India, and it ended with the Afghans achieving the right to allow nationals of any country into their territory, including Russians. In none of the three cases were the war aims of the British Indian Government actually achieved.

Another mistaken suggestion is that the invading army was defeated and driven out by the strength of Afghan patriotic resistance. In fact, although in each war the British suffered reverses, some of them extremely serious and dramatic, nevertheless the end of each war saw British armies and British generals supreme in the field. This supremacy was due to the superior weaponry, organization, and training of the invading forces. What sent the British back from Afghanistan, in the two major wars when they would have wished to stay, was a combination of economics, war weariness, and party politics. In both the First and Second Afghan Wars, the cost of maintaining garrisons necessary to quell insurgents placed an unacceptable burden on British Indian finances. The logistic effort required to keep troops in a barren country, where small armies are defeated, and large armies (unless fed from outside) starve, proved beyond the Indian Army's meagre resources. The soldiers grew dispirited at seemingly unending warfare in a harsh landscape with a vindictive savage behind every rock. British public opinion came to question the morality, or at least the expediency, of campaigns that demonstrably failed in their declared aim of establishing a friendly regime at Kabul. In Afghanistan as elsewhere, the one thing that could not be done with British bayonets was to sit on them. British ministers decided that, although their troops could occupy the country (or at least its roads and cities, which were the only places worth occupying), the strategic benefits were outweighed by the political and economic costs.

The 'Limited Contingent of Soviet Forces fulfilling its international obligation in defence of the gains of Socialism' in Afghanistan was, in the long run, no more successful in maintaining a client state in Afghanistan than had been the British Indian armies before them. Patriotic resistance turned into a holy war (*jihad*), with the 'freedom fighters' (or terrorists) aided by arms and money from the USA and Arab states. In May 1987 Babrak Karmal was arrested and exiled. His successor, Muhammad Najibullah, promised a policy of national reconciliation, so allowing the Soviets to withdraw in February 1989. In December 1991 the USSR ceased to exist, and its successor, the CIS, had no common border with Afghanistan. In April 1992, *mujehaddin* forces captured Kabul and the country then disintegrated into anarchy. In 1995 a fundamentalist group calling themselves the Taliban ('disciples' or students of religion) restored order but imposed a regime based on the most conservative interpretation of Islam. Najibullah, who had refused the chance to flee with a departing warlord, was put to death with the usual atrocities. Mostly Pathans (or Pushtuns, as Western writers now referred to them), the Taliban combined their tribal customs with the puritanical doctrines that had been taught in the religious schools in refugee camps in Pakistan. Women (many thousands of whom were war widows) were barred from employment. Men were forbidden to shave. Television sets were smashed. The great Buddhist figures at Bamiyan were destroyed. Criminals were subjected to public executions or amputations.

On 11 September 2001, Islamic extremists destroyed the World Trade Centre in New York, causing thousands of deaths among those working there. The United States government located the leader of those responsible, Osama bin Laden, in Afghanistan, and called upon the Taliban to hand him and his adherents over for justice. When the Taliban, influenced by the Pathan code of sheltering a guest, refused, the United States intervened to support the Northern Alliance, a group of warlords who still held out against the Taliban regime. An overwhelming American air offensive, supported by ground troops, drove out the Taliban early in 2002, and a national assembly, or Loya Jirga, was convened to set up a new government. King Zahir, in his eighties, returned from exile to act as a figurehead during the deliberations. A multi-national force was assembled to help the new regime maintain its authority. From 2003, British soldiers are once more serving in Afghanistan and at the time of writing the conflict still rages.

AFGHANISTAN REPUDIATES WESTERN IDEALS.

'Afghanistan Repudiates Western Ideals'. A Punch *cartoon of January 1929 referring to the rebellion which overthrew King Amanulla. This monarch's over-hasty introduction of political and social reforms, including the compulsory wearing of European dress, provoked a violent reaction resulting in his downfall.*

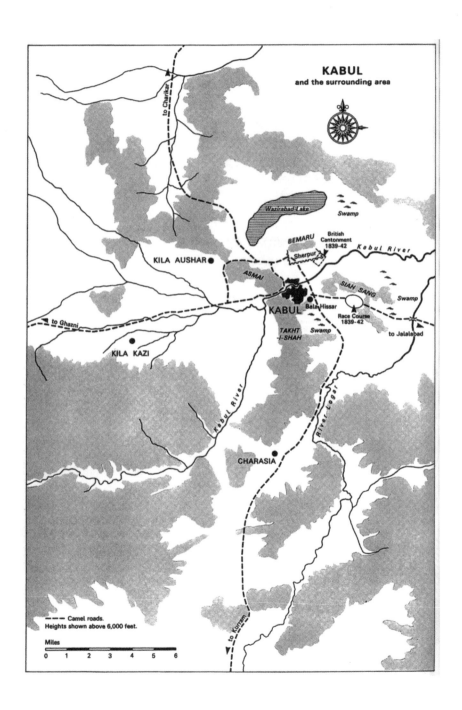

KABUL
and the surrounding area

Wazirabad Lake

Swamp

BEMARU

British
Cantonment
1839-42

Kabul River

KILA AUSHAR

Sherpur

ASMAI

SIAH SANG

Swamp

KABUL

Bala Hissar

to Ghazni

Race Course
1839-42

TAKHT
-I-SHAH

Swamp

to Jalalabad

KILA KAZI

Kabul River

River Logar

CHARASIA

to Kurram

Camel roads.
Heights shown above 6,000 feet.

Miles

0   1   2   3   4   5   6

to Charikar

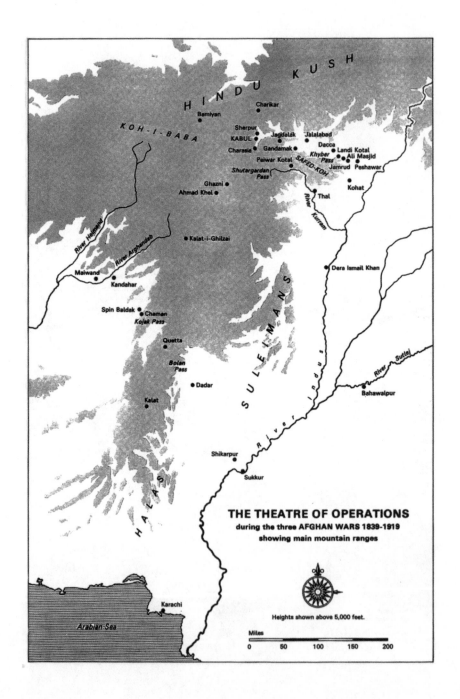

THE THEATRE OF OPERATIONS
during the three AFGHAN WARS 1839-1919
showing main mountain ranges

Heights shown above 5,000 feet.

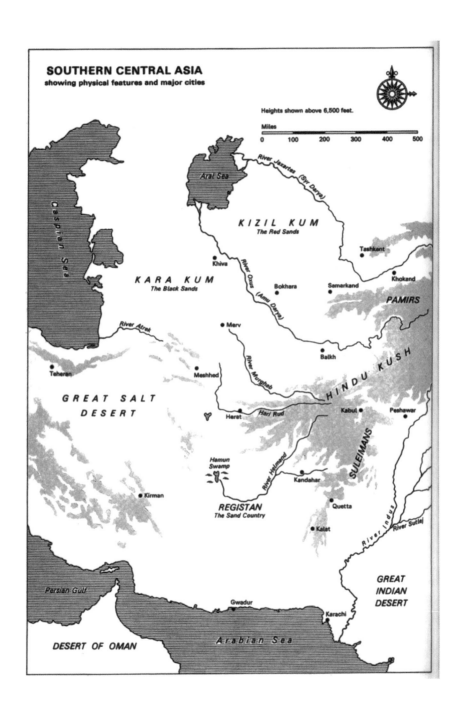

205

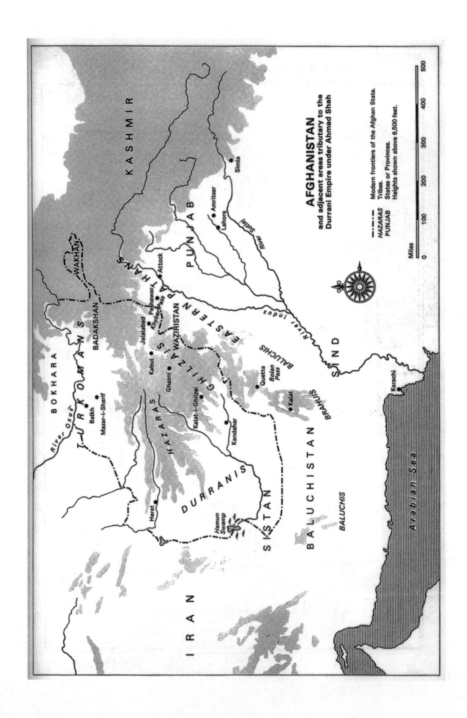

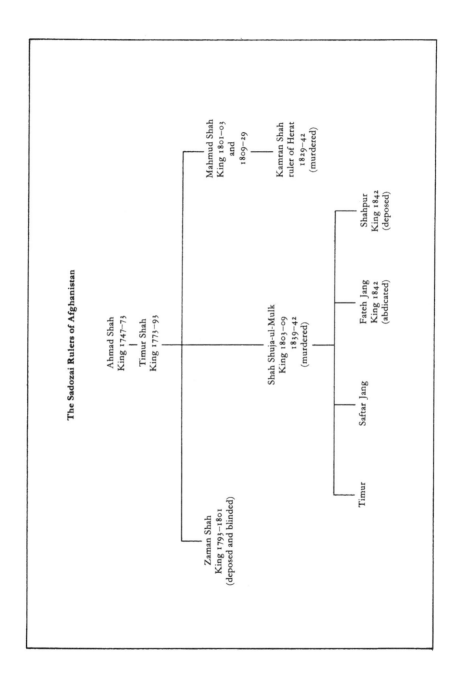

The Sadozai Rulers of Afghanistan

Ahmad Shah
King 1747–73

Timur Shah
King 1773–93

Zaman Shah
King 1793–1801
(deposed and blinded)

Mahmud Shah
King 1801–03
and
1809–29

Kamran Shah
ruler of Herat
1829–42
(murdered)

Shah Shuja-ul-Mulk
King 1803–09
1839–42
(murdered)

Timur

Saftar Jang

Fateh Jang
King 1842
(abdicated)

Shahpur
King 1842
(deposed)

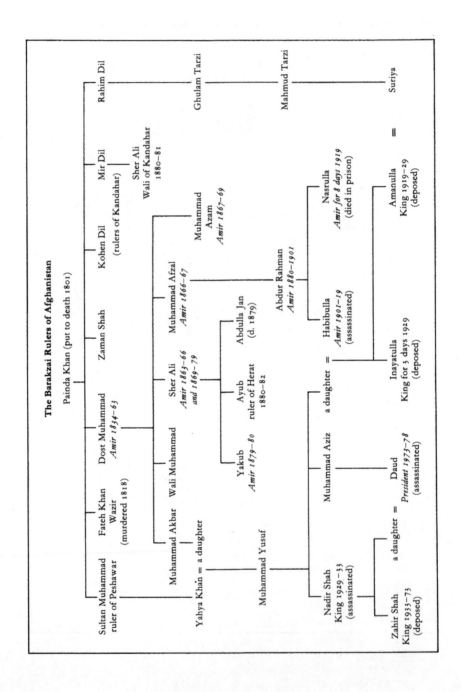

The Barakzai Rulers of Afghanistan

Painda Khan (put to death 1801)

Select Bibliography

Documents

India Office Library and Records (Foreign and Commonwealth Office)
a) Official.
    Political and Secret Department Records
      Letters from and Despatches to India 1876–80
      Third Afghan War Correspondence 1919
b) Private (European MSS)
    Papers of Edward, 1st Earl of Lytton
    Papers of Frederic, 1st Viscount Chelmsford

National Army Museum
Papers of Frederick, 1st Earl Roberts

Published Works

Allworth, E. (ed.) *Central Asia: A Century of Russian Rule* (1967)
Balfour, Lady Betty. *The History of Lord Lytton's Indian Administration 1876–1880* (1899)
Barrow, George. *The Life of General C. C. Monro* (1931)
Blake, R. *Disraeli* (1966)
Bruce, G. *Retreat from Kabul* (1969)
Butler, W.F. *Life of Sir George Pomeroy Colley* (1899)
Cadell, P. *History of the Bombay Army* (1938)
Cardew, F.G. *The Second Afghan War 1878–80* (abridged official account) (1908)
———— *A Sketch of the Services of the Bengal Native Army to the year 1895* (official history) (1903)
Caroe, O. *The Pathans 55 BC–AD 1957* (1958)
Carter, T. *Historical Record of the Forty-Fourth, or the East Essex Regiment of Foot* (1864)
Colvin, Ian. *The Life of General Dyer* (1929)
Davies, C.C. *The Problem of the North-West Frontier 1890–1908* (1932)

209

Dodwell, H.H. (ed.) *The Cambridge History of India Vols. 5 & 6* (1929–30)
Durand, H.M. *The First Afghan War* (1879)
Edwardes, M. *Playing the Great Game: A Victorian Cold War* (1975)
Elsmie, G.R. *Field-Marshal Sir Donald Stewart* (1903)
Encyclopedia of Islam (new ed. 1956–   )
Eyre, V. *The Military Operations at Kabul … with a journal of imprisonment in Afghanistan* (1843)
Everett, H.J. *The History of the Somerset Light Infantry (Prince Albert's Own)* (1934)
Fletcher, A. *Afghanistan, Highway of Conquest* (1965)
Forbes, A. *The Afghan Wars 1839–42 and 1878–80* (1892)
Forrest, G.W. *Life of Field-Marshal Sir Neville Chamberlain* (1909)
Fraser-Tytler, W.K. *Afghanistan, A Study of Political Developments in Central Asia* (1950)
GS Branch, AHQ India. *The Third Afghan War 1919* Official Account 1926
Gleig, G.R. *Sale's Brigade in Afghanistan* (1846)
Gopal, S. *The Viceroyal of Lord Ripon 1880–1884* (1953)
Hanna, H.B. *The Second Afghan War 1878–79–8o: Its Causes, its Conduct and its Consequences*, 3 vols. (1904)
Harris, A. *Bomber Offensive* (1947)
Heathcote, T.A. *British Policy and Baluchistan 1814–1876* (unpublished University of London PhD History thesis – 1970)
The Indian Army 1822–1922: The Garrison of British Imperial India (1974)
Hensman, H. *The Afghan War of 1879–80* (1882)
Hughes, B.P. *The Bengal Horse Artillery* (1977)
James, D. *Lord Roberts* (1954)
Kaye, J.W. *History of the War in Afghanistan*, 3 vols, 3rd edn. (1874)
Mactory, P. *Signal Catastrophe, The Story of the disastrous Retreat from Kabul 1842* (1966)
Norris, J.A. *The First Afghan War 1838–42* (1967)
Petre, F.L. *The Royal Berk Regiment (Princess Charlotte of Wales's)* (1925)
Roberts, F.S. *Forty-One Years in India: from Subaltern to Commander-in-Chief* (1897)
Sale, F. *A Journal of the Disasters in Afghanistan 1841–2* (1843)
Shadbolt, S.H. *The Afghan Campaign of 1878–80*, 2 vols (1882)
Spear, P. *The Oxford History of India Vol. 3* (1958)
Stephen, L. and Lea, L. (eds.) *The Dictionary of National Biography*, 22 vols. (1885–1937)
Thompson, E. and Garratt, C.T. *The Rise and Fulfilment of British Rule in India* (1934)
Yapp, M.E. *British Strategies in India* (1980)

Acknowledgements

I should like to express my gratitude to all those who have helped me in the preparation of this work; to John Hunt, Esq, BA, FLA, and his staff in the Central Library, Royal Military Academy Sandhurst; to the Keeper of the India Office Records, Foreign and Commonwealth Office; to the Deputy Director and head of the Records Department, National Army Museum, Chelsea; to Dr Malcolm Yapp, who supervised my research at the School of Oriental and African Studies in the University of London; to Mrs Maureen Broomfield and Miss Marilyn Weeks, who typed the manuscript; to Captain Catherine Dent, RAMC, for her explanation of the characteristics of cholera; to Miss Anne Bedford, who read through the typescript to see if it told a story; and most of all to my wife, for her constant encouragement and for preparing the index.

T.A. Heathcote, Camberley, Surrey

Picture Acknowledgements

Every effort has been made to contact the owners of the copyrights for the illustrations used in this book, and we apologise for any omissions caused through difficulty in tracing such sources. Acknowledgement is made for kind permission to use illustrations from the following sources:

Illustrated London News Picture Library, pp. 172, 174, 175, 177 (both), 180–1, 182 (both), 187, 191, 192
India Office Library and Records, pp. 19, 78–9, 82, 98, 107, 113, 137, 152, 163
Mary Evans Picture Library, p. 43
National Army Museum, pp. 8, 11, 23, 28, 30–1, 33, 44, 48, 52–3, 56, 60–1, 65, 69, 71, 73, 85, 92, 100, 101, 105, 115, 120–1, 127, 131, 141, 146–7, 150–1
Punch Publications Ltd., frontispiece, p. 202
Radio Times Hulton Picture Library, pp. 11, 88, 109, 153, 164, 195
Robert Hunt Library, pp. 166, 171
Royal Air Force Museum, pp. 159, 167, 189

Index

INDEX